Sarah Cook
307 752 6965

THE SPIRIT OF CATHOLICISM

BY

Dr. KARL ADAM

Professor of Catholic Theology in the University of Tübingen

TRANSLATED BY

DOM JUSTIN McCANN, O.S.B.

Master of St. Benet's Hall, Oxford

NEW YORK

THE MACMILLAN COMPANY

1930

SET UP BY BROWN BROTHERS LINOTYPERS
PRINTED IN THE UNITED STATES OF AMERICA
BY THE FERRIS PRINTING COMPANY

TRANSLATOR'S NOTE

THE chapters of this book, with the exception of the two chapters on the Communion of Saints, were delivered as lectures in the University of Tübingen, in the summer term of 1923, to an audience of several hundred persons of mixed religious beliefs. The University of Tübingen possesses two faculties of theology, a Catholic faculty and a Protestant, both alike supported by the state. The author is a priest and professor of dogmatic theology in the Catholic faculty. The lectures were published in book form, under the title of *Das Wesen des Katholizismus* [i.e., the essential nature of Catholicism], in the year 1924, and each year since then has seen a new edition. The essay on the Communion of Saints, here divided into two chapters, was added in the third edition (1926). In the fourth edition (1927) the author submitted his book to a thorough revision, and issued it in a cheaper form. The present translation is made from this fourth edition, which is unaltered in the fifth and last German edition (1928). Some references to German literature have been omitted and a few explanatory notes added, for the assistance of the English reader.

The translator would like to express his gratitude to the author for his permission to translate the book, and to his publishers (Messrs. L. Schwann, Düsseldorf) for their generous consent.

ST. BENET'S HALL,
OXFORD.

January, 1929.

ANALYTICAL CONTENTS

attained by faith in Christ. How is faith in Christ
attained? The apostles attained it preparatorily by His
personal teaching, fulfillingly by the pentecostal gift
of the Holy Spirit. So we also: preparatorily by the
teaching of His living, apostolic Church, fulfillingly
by the operation of His grace. Not from lifeless records, but from the living witness of a living organism
sustained and animated by Him, from immediate contact with Christ living in His Church. Christianity
more than a system of thought: a living stream of
divine life flowing out from Christ and bearing His
truth and His life, pure and uncontaminated, down the
centuries.

Was the Church founded by Christ Himself, or is it
the creation of His disciples? The objection, that our
Lord's attitude towards Jewish religion and ecclesiastical authority is inconsistent with His foundation of
a Church, scientifically untenable. The objections of
the eschatological school. Examination of our Lord's
teaching concerning the coming of the Kingdom and
concerning the end of the world. Chronological mis-
conceptions of some of His disciples. The plain teaching of His parables. The foundation of the Church in
the direct line of His thought: a Church in gradual
process towards perfection and ever ordinated towards a
supernatural and other-worldly goal.

Special position of St. Peter among the twelve
attested not only by the history of the primitive community, but by the witness of St. Paul. Unsatisfactory theories advanced in explanation of this pre-
eminence. The all-sufficient explanation to be found in
Matthew XVI, 13-19. This passage no Roman forgery
or anti-Pauline interpolation. Significance of its
details, especially of Simon's new name with its immediate and universal success. Certain that he was given
a special authority by Christ Himself. But does this
appertain to his successors? The divine intentions
of our Lord, the witness of history. The Church based
on Peter the only guardian of genuine faith in Christ
and the only hope for our civilisation.

The meaning of the doctrine. The three-fold Church :—
the Church Militant, the Church Suffering and the
doctrine of Purgatory, the Church Triumphant.
The life of the saints in heaven one of infinite variety
and fruitfulness. They co-operate effectively with the
Head in the organic life of the Body of Christ. Variety

ST. FRANCIS PREPARATORY SEMINARY
BETHANY, OKLA.

THE SPIRIT OF CATHOLICISM

CHAPTER I

INTRODUCTORY

"The truth shall make you free" (John viii, 32).

WHAT is Catholicism? By that question we do not merely ask what is that characteristic quality which distinguishes Catholicism from other forms of Christianity; we go deeper than that, and seek to discover what is its governing idea and what are the forces set in motion by this idea. We ask what is the single basic thought, what is the essential form that gives life to the great structure which we call Catholicism? Regarded from the outside Catholicism has the appearance of a confused mass of conflicting forces, of an unnatural synthesis, of a mixture of foreign, nay contradictory, elements. And for that reason there have been those who have called it a complex of opposites. The religious historian, Heiler, believes that he can discern as many as seven essentially different strata in a cross-section of this vast structure.[1] So enormously rich and manifold and conflicting do the particular elements of Catholicism seem to

[1] In *Der Katholizismus, seine Idee und seine Erscheinung* (1923, p. 12), a new and much enlarged edition of his *Das Wesen des Katholizismus* (1920), six lectures delivered in Sweden in the autumn of 1919. Friedrich Heiler is Professor of the Comparative History of Religion in the University of Marburg and a distinguished non-Catholic religious writer in present-day Germany. His theological position is a highly individual one, but he may be said to have affinities with Archbishop Söderblom on the one hand, and on the other with that "High Church" party (possessing an organ with the title *Una Sancta*) which is one of the most interesting phenomena of post-war German Protestantism. Heiler's book above cited, though containing much severe criticism of alleged defects in Catholic teaching and practice, is yet characterised by a profound sympathy with Catholicism.

the student of comparative religion, that he supposes that he must at the outset discard the notion of an organic development of a primitive Christianity which was planted by Christ Himself, and must regard Catholicism as the coalescence of evangelical and non-evangelical elements, of Jewish and heathen and primitive constituents, as a vast syncretism which has simply taken up into itself all those religious forms in which men have ever expressed their religious striving and hope, and has fused them together into a unity. And so, for the religious historian, Catholicism becomes a microcosm of the world of religion.[*]

We Catholics do not quarrel with the methods of the religious historian, so long as he keeps within his proper limits, within the limits of historical data and proved historical fact, and so long as he does not claim in his classification of religious types to pass decisive judgment upon the essential nature of the religious structure which he has under examination. We Catholics acknowledge readily, without any shame, nay with pride, that Catholicism cannot be identified simply and wholly with primitive Christianity, nor even with the Gospel of Christ, in the same way that the great oak cannot be identified with the tiny acorn. There is no mechanical identity, but an organic identity. And we go further and say that thousands of years hence Catholicism will probably be even richer, more luxuriant, more manifold in dogma, morals, law and worship than the Catholicism of the present day. A religious historian of the fifth millennium A. D. will without difficulty discover in Catholicism conceptions and forms and practices which derive from India, China and Japan, and he will have to recognise a far more obvious "complex of opposites." It is quite true, Catholicism *is* a union of contraries. But contraries are not contradictories. Wherever there is life, there you must have conflict and contrary. Even in purely biblical Christianity, and especially in Old Testament religion, these conflicts and contraries may be observed. For only so is there growth and the continual emergence of

[*] Harnack, *Reden und Aufsätze* (1904), Vol. II, p. 170.

new forms. The Gospel of Christ would have been no living gospel, and the seed which He scattered no living seed, if it had remained ever the tiny seed of A. D. 33, and had not struck root, and had not assimilated foreign matter, and had not by the help of this foreign matter grown up into a tree, so that the birds of the air dwell in its branches.

So we are far from begrudging the religious historian the pleasure of reading off the inner growth of Catholicism by means of the annual rings of its trunk, and of specifying all those elements which its living force has appropriated from foreign sources. But we refuse to see in these elements thus enumerated the essence of Catholicism, or even to grant that they are "structural elements of Catholicism" in the sense that Catholicism did not achieve historical importance save through them. For the Catholic is intimately conscious that Catholicism is ever the same, yesterday and to-day, that its essential nature was already present and manifest when it began its journey through the world, that Christ Himself breathed into it the breath of life, and that He Himself at the same time gave the young organism those germinal aptitudes which have unfolded themselves in the course of the centuries in regular adaptation to the needs and requirements of its environment. Catholicism recognises in itself no element that is inwardly foreign to it, that is not itself, that does not derive from its original nature.

And so, with this consciousness, Catholicism finds inadequate all those descriptions of its essential nature which are based merely on the study of comparative religion. For such descriptions are superficial, they touch only the hem of its garment. They are in some sort like the naïve, childish, not to say silly conceptions of certain heated controversialists, for whom Catholicism is lust of power, saint-worship and "jesuitry." Such people have not discerned that deep source whence its life in all its manifestations flows forth, and which gives the whole an organic unity. "He has the parts within his hand, but not. alack! the

spirit band." [3]   The attempt of the religious historian is
at its best like an attempt to explain the life of a living
cell by mere enumeration of all the material that forms it.
To describe a thing is not to explain it fully.   And so this
purely descriptive research calls for something beyond itself,
for a scientific investigation into the essential nature of
Catholicism.

The Catholic of a living faith, and he alone, can make
this investigation.   Our investigation goes only so deep as
our love goes.   An attitude of mere neutrality, or a cold
realism are of no use here.   Or, rather, only the man who
himself lives in the Catholic life-stream, who in his own
life daily feels the forces which pulsate through the vast
body of Catholicism and which make it what it is: only
he can know the full meaning and complete reality of it.
Just as the loving child alone can truly know the character
of its beloved mother, and just as the deepest elements of
that character, the tenderness and intimacies of her maternal
love, cannot be demonstrated by argument but only learnt
by experience, just so only the believing and loving Catholic
can see into the heart of Catholicism, and feeling, living,
experiencing, discover with that "esprit de finesse" of
which Pascal speaks, that is with the comprehensive intuition of his innermost soul, the secret forces and fundamental motive powers of its being.   And so an investigation
into the nature of Catholicism inevitably becomes a confession of faith, an expression of the Catholic consciousness.   It is nothing else, and seeks to be nothing else, than
the simple analysis of this consciousness.   It is the answer
to the question: How does the Catholic experience his
Church, how does it work on him, where lie for him the
creative forces of Catholicism, the intimate centre of its
creative being?

It is no mere accident that this question has become at
this very hour so much alive, and that the answer to it is
occupying the attention of others besides those who belong
to the household of the faith.   Friedrich Heiler points in

* Goethe, *Faust*, Pt. II.

emphatic terms to this growing interest in, and under-standing of, Catholicism. "The Roman Church," he writes, "is exercising to-day a very strong attraction on the non-Catholic world. The German Benedictine monas-teries, especially Beuron and Maria Laach, have become places of pilgrimage for non-Catholics, who find inspiration in the Catholic liturgy there practised. The rising high-church movement in German Protestantism is drawing nearer and nearer to the Roman Church, and one of its leaders has already returned to her bosom. More con-siderable still is the conversion movement in England. Whole Anglican convents and monasteries are going over to the Church of Rome. A vigorous Catholic propaganda is promoting and intensifying the existing trend towards Catholicism. The Roman Church is to-day making power-ful efforts to win back all Christians separated from her, in the East and in the West. There has been founded over the tomb of St. Boniface a society for the re-union of the Christian churches. . . . Catholic voices are already pro-claiming with assurance of victory the imminent collapse of Protestantism."[4] Heiler is correct in discerning a revival of the Catholic Church even in the souls of non-Catholics. But he is wrong in speaking of that "assurance of victory" with which Catholics are alleged to be pro-claiming the imminent collapse of Protestantism. The phrase is a profane and unholy one. It degrades religion and makes it a party affair. When we are treating of reli-gion we should have humility, reverence, thankfulness and joy, but no dogmatical assurance of victory. The future of Protestantism: that is God's business. And it rests with Him whether the West is to return from its diaspora, from its dispersion and disintegration, home to the mother Church, in whose bosom all were once united as one family. All that we can do is to give testimony to the truth, to pray God to open all hearts to this truth, and to make it ever more manifest to the best minds among us, that the great and urgent task of the West is to close at long last the

[4] Op. cit., p. 8.

unwholesome breach that has divided us for centuries, to create a new spiritual unity, a religious centre, and so to prepare the only possible foundation for a rebuilding and rebirth of Western civilisation. We thankfully recognise that there is a daily increasing appreciation of the urgency of this task, and that the times are past in which men regarded Catholicism as a compound of stupidity, superstition and lust of power.

Two reasons may be given for this revival of the Catholic ideal in the Western soul, the one external the other internal. The first reason lies in the direct impact on our minds of the appalling consequences of the Great War. We have witnessed the collapse of great states and traditions of culture. On the battlefields of the Great War lie strewn the ruins of former political and economic greatness. The eye turns inevitably from this sight to that world-embracing society which in the midst of this ruin stands out like some unshaken rocky peak, serene and untouched by the catastrophe, and which alone of all the political, economic and religious structures of the world has suffered no collapse, but is as young to-day as on the day of its birth. We are experiencing to-day before our very eyes, we are seeing realised before us, that irresistible, unconquerable, living might of the Catholic Church, which the great English historian, Macaulay, once described in the eloquent words: "There is not, and there never was on this earth, a work of human policy so well deserving of examination as the Roman Catholic Church. The history of that Church joins together the two great ages of human civilisation. No other institution is left standing which carries the mind back to the times when the smoke of sacrifice rose from the Pantheon, and when camelopards and tigers bounded in the Flavian amphitheatre. The proudest royal houses are but of yesterday, when compared with the line of the Supreme Pontiffs. That line we trace back in an unbroken series, from the Pope who crowned Napoleon in the nineteenth century to the Pope who crowned Pepin in the eighth; and far beyond the time of

Pepin the august dynasty extends, till it is lost in the twilight of fable. The republic of Venice came next in antiquity. But the republic of Venice was modern when compared with the Papacy; and the republic of Venice is gone, and the Papacy remains. The Papacy remains, not in decay, not a mere antique, but full of life and youthful vigour. The Catholic Church is still sending forth to the farthest ends of the world missionaries as zealous as those who landed in Kent with Augustine, and still confronting hostile kings with the same spirit with which she confronted Attila. . . . Nor do we see any sign which indicates that the term of her long dominion is approaching. She saw the commencement of all the governments and of all the ecclesiastical establishments that now exist in the world; and we feel no assurance that she is not destined to see the end of them all. She was great and respected before the Saxon had set foot on Britain, before the Frank had passed the Rhine, when Grecian eloquence still flourished at Antioch, when idols were still worshipped in the temple of Mecca. And she may still exist in undiminished vigour when some traveller from New Zealand shall, in the midst of a vast solitude, take his stand on a broken arch of London Bridge to sketch the ruins of St. Paul's?" *
That is the vision that amid the desolation of the present holds our gaze spell-bound. We discern the immortality, the vigorous life, the eternal youth of the old, original Church. And the question rises to many lips, and to the lips of the best among us: What is the source of this strong life? And can the Church impart it, and will she impart it, to the dying western world?

The second reason which especially moves the modern man, the man of the Great War and the revolution, to take note of the Catholic Church is a more inward one, derived from reflection and intimate self-examination. It is the mark of the modern man that he is torn from his roots. The historian of civilisation must tell us how he come to that state. The sixteenth century revolt from the

---

* Essay on L. von Ranke's *History of the Popes*.

Church led inevitably to the revolt from Christ of the eighteenth century, and thence to the revolt from God of the nineteenth. And thus the modern spirit has been torn loose from the deepest and strongest supports of its life, from its foundation in the Absolute, in the self-existent Being, in the Value of all values. Life has lost its great meaning, its vital strength and high purpose, its strong, pervading love, that can be enkindled only by the divine. Instead of the man who is rooted in the Absolute, hidden in God, strong and rich, we have the man who rests upon himself, the autonomous man. Moreover, this man, because he has renounced the fellowship of the Church, the *communio fidelium,* the interrelation and correlation of the faithful, has severed the second root of his life, that is to say, his fellowship with other men. He has lost that closely-knitted union of self and others, that communion with the supra-personal whole, which proves itself in joy and in sorrow, in prayer and in love, and by means of which the individual can ever renew and regulate his strength, and without which he becomes dry and sterile. Nowhere else, in no other society, is the idea of community, of fellowship in doing and suffering, in prayer and love, and of growth and formation in and through such fellowship, so strongly embedded in doctrine, morals and worship, as in the Catholic Church. And so the rupture of Church unity has of itself loosened the bonds of social fellowship and thereby destroyed the deep source and basis of a healthy, strong humanity, of a complete humanity. The autonomous man has become a solitary man, an individual.

But the process of uprooting went further still. After the age of "enlightenment" had dethroned reason and dispossessed that power of thought which grasps the whole in one comprehensive view, to replace it by the power which pursues detail and difference, the interior economy of man, his spiritual unity, broke up into a mere juxtaposition of powers and functions. Men spoke now not of their souls, but of psychic processes. The consciousness of being a personal agent, the creative organ of living powers, became increasingly foreign to the educated. And after Kant and his school had made the transcendental subject the autonomous lawgiver of the objective world and even of the empirical consciousness itself, after man instead of holding to the objectivity of the thing and of his own self began to speak of an objectivity which possessed none but a purely logical validity, and of a purely logical subject, then the whole consciousness of reality became afflicted with an unhealthy paralysis. The "As If" philosophy here, and solipsism there, like vampires, suck all the blood out of resolution and action.* The autonomous man, cut off from God, and the solitary man cut off from the society of his fellow-men, isolated from the community, is now severed also from his own empirical self. He becomes a merely provisional creature, and therefore sterile and unfruitful, corroded by the spirit of "criticism," estranged from reality, a man of mere negation.

This bloodless, sterile man of mere negation cannot ultimately live. For man cannot live by mere negation. The impulse to live is strong within him; and that impulse is stronger than any unnatural, gray philosophy. Man cries for life, for full, whole, personal life. He is sated with negation and desires to affirm. For only in decisive affirmation and strong resolution lie action and life.

Is it wonderful, then, that this very state of mind should have aroused an interest in Catholicism that is no mere academic interest? We shall have to show in detail that Catholicism—regarded in its special character and as contrasted with non-Catholic Christianity—is essentially decision and affirmation, an affirmation of all values wheresoever they may be, in heaven or on earth. All non-Catholic bodies originate, not in unconditional affirmation, but in denial and negation, in subtraction and in subjective

* The "As If Philosophy," or "Fictionalism," regards our intellectual conceptions as nothing better than fictions. It admits that they are useful; but, unlike Pragmatism, regards this usefulness as no criterion of truth. The founder of this thorough-going scepticism is Hans Vaihinger. His book, "Die philosophie des Als Ob" (Berlin, 1911), has been translated into English as "The Philosophy of 'As If'" (London, 1924).

selection. The history of Catholicism is the history of a bold, consistent, comprehensive affirmation of the whole full reality of revelation, of the fulness of the divinity revealed in Christ according to all the dimensions of its unfolding. It is the absolute, unconditional and comprehensive affirmation of the whole full life of man, of the totality of his life-relations and life-sources. And it is the unconditional affirmation, before all else, of the deepest ground of our being, that is to say of the living God. And Catholicism insists on the whole God, on the God of creation and judgment, and is not content with any mere Father-God of children of sinners, still less with the miracle-shy God of the Enlightenment and of Deism, a sort of parliamentary deity. And it would have the whole Christ, in whom this God was revealed to us, the Christ of the two natures, the God-man, in whom heaven and earth possess their eternal unity, and not the mere romantic Christ of the dilettante or the ecstatic Christ of the critic. And it would have the complete community, the *orbis terrarum,* as the medium wherein we grasp this Christ. For the fellowship of men is a fundamental fact, and through it alone comes the growth of personality. And Catholicism calls for the whole personality, not merely pious feeling, but also cool reason, and not reason only, but also the practical will, and not only the inner man of the intelligence, but also the outer man of sensibility. Catholicism is according to its whole being the full and strong affirmation of the whole man, in the complete sum of all his life relations. Catholicism is the positive religion *par excellence,* essentially affirmation without subtraction, and in the full sense essentially thesis. All non-Catholic creeds are essentially antithesis, conflict, contradiction and negation.' And since negation is of its very nature sterile, therefore they cannot be creative, productive and original, or at least not in the

' Cf. Tertullian's judgment on the heretics of his time: *Nihil enim interest illis, licet diversa tractantibus, dum ad unius veritatis expugnationem conspirent. . . . Schisma est enim unitas ipsa* (*De Praescriptione,* c. 41, 42). Similarly St. Augustine: *Dissentiunt inter se, contra unitatem omnes consentiunt* (Sermo XLVII, 15. 27).

measure in which Catholicism has displayed these qualities
throughout the centuries. The modern man feels this positive character to be something that he needs, and therefore
his gaze is turning towards Catholicism, if perchance it may
do something for him.

Influential writers of our time encourage this attitude,
or at least recommend a more sympathetic appreciation
of Catholicism. Söderblom, the distinguished religious
philosopher and Protestant Archbishop of Upsala, would
have his co-religionists recognise "that Roman Christianity
is essentially something other than lust of power, saint-
worship and jesuitry. In its deepest essence it connotes a
type of piety, which is not Protestant piety, and yet is
perfect in its kind. Nay, it is more perfect than Protestant
piety. . . . We have too little developed Schleiermacher's
great plan of an apologetic devoted to the study of the
essential nature of the various religions and sects known
to history, and of a polemic which, utterly devoid of
all sectarianism, should in the name of that essential
nature fight against those degenerations which everywhere
assail it." [1] And Heiler has recently lamented the insufficient understanding of the nature of Catholicism by
non-Catholic theologians. "Generally speaking, Protestant
polemic sees only the outer walls of the Catholic cathedral, with their cracks and crevices and their weather-
beaten masonry; but the wondrous artistry of the interior
is hidden from it. The most vital and the purest aspects
of Catholicism remain still, even in this our day, practically unknown to Protestant theology; and for that reason
it is denied any complete or intimate appreciation of
Catholicism." [2]

And if the learned theologian fails to comprehend the
essence of Catholicism, can we wonder that among the

[1] Quoted by Heiler and set in the forefront of his work. Archbishop
Söderblom is the apostle of a reunion of Christendom on a Protestant
basis. The nearest approach to his conception of a Protestant Catholicism is perhaps to be found in that "Free Catholicism" which has some
advocates in this country.

[2] Op. cit., p. 5.

Protestant masses who are not theologians, whatever their degree of education or lack of it, there is an ignorance of Catholicism which is deeply deplored by the more far-seeing minds on their own side, and which as the cause of the worst kind of prejudice produces indifference and dislike, nay, even contempt of Catholic piety, and intensifies continually the lamentable cleavage between the Catholic and Protestant sections of our people? That great Protestant scholar and historian of dogma, Adolf Harnack, remarks of this ignorance: "I am convinced from constant experience of the fact that the students who leave our schools have the most disconnected and absurd ideas about ecclesiastical history. Some of them know something about Gnosticism, or about other curious and for them worthless details. But of the Catholic Church, the greatest religious and political creation known to history, they know absolutely nothing, and they indulge in its regard in wholly trivial, vague, and often directly nonsensical notions. How her greatest institutions originated, what they mean in the life of the Church, how easily they may be misconceived, and why they function so surely and so impressively: all this, according to my experience, is for them, apart from a few exceptions, a *terra incognita.*" [10]

It shall be our task to lead into this unknown land those students also who have not been familiar with it from their youth, who have not lived in its sunlight and eaten of its bread. It is unnecessary to say that all controversy and any sort of disparagement of the religious feelings of others shall be scrupulously avoided. On the other hand you should not forget that it is the highest and noblest privilege of a German scholar to be a "professor" and to proclaim the faith that is in him. A scholar cannot but profess that truth which he has discovered in the depths of his own soul by using all the scientific means at his disposal and by practising an absolute honesty. He must profess the truth which he recognises as the decisive truth and reality. And so he may not put us off with vague hypotheses or with

[10] *Aus Wissenschaft und Leben* (Giessen, 1911), Vol. I, p. 97.

undecided alternatives; he must define and he must decide. Such is the spirit in which these lectures were written, and it is in that spirit that I would have you accept them. There is light and guidance for us all in the words of St. John: the truth will make us free.

CHAPTER II

CHRIST IN THE CHURCH

"Behold, I am with you all days even unto the consummation of the world" (Mt. xxviii, 20)

IF we ask the Catholic Church herself to tell us, according to her own notion of herself, what constitutes her essential nature and what is the substance of her self-consciousness, she answers us through the mouth of the greatest of her teachers, that the Church is the realisation on earth of the Kingdom of God. "The Church of to-day, of the present, is the Kingdom of Christ and the Kingdom of Heaven": such is the emphatic assertion of St. Augustine (*De civ. Dei* xx, 9, 1). The "Kingdom of Heaven" and "Kingdom of God," taken up from the prophecy of Daniel (vii, 9-28) and proclaimed by Christ, that Kingdom which grows great like the mustard seed, and like leaven permeates the world, and which like a field of corn shelters both wheat and cockle until the harvest, this "Kingdom of Heaven" is, so the Church believes, implanted in her own being and there manifested. The Church believes that she is the manifestation of that newness, that supernature and that divinity which come in with the Kingdom of God, the manifestation of holiness. She is the new supernatural reality brought by Christ into the world and arrayed in the garment of the transitory; she is the divine attesting itself under earthly veils.

And inasmuch as the fulness of this divine power was creatively revealed in the Person of Christ, Paul, the Apostle of the Gentiles, expresses its deepest mystery when he borrows Hellenistic forms and calls the Church the Body of Christ (I Cor. xii, 27; Col. i, 18, 24; Eph. i, 22; iv, 12): "For in one Spirit were we all baptized into

14

one body, whether Jews or Gentiles, whether bond or free; and in one Spirit we have all been made to drink" (I Cor. xii, 13).

Christ the Lord is the real self of the Church. The Church is the body permeated through and through by the redemptive might of Jesus. So intimate is this union of Christ with the Church, so inseparable, natural and essential, that St. Paul in his Epistles to the Colossians and Ephesians explicitly calls Christ the Head of the body. As the Head of the body Christ makes the organism of the Church whole and complete. And Christ and the Church can no more be regarded separately than can a head and its body (Col. i, 18; ii, 19; Eph. iv, 15 ff).

This conviction that the Church is permeated by Christ, and of necessity organically united with Him, is a fundamental point of Christian teaching. From Origen to Augustine and Pseudo-Dionysius and thence to Thomas Aquinas, and thence on to our own unforgettable Möhler,[1] this conviction stands in the centre of the Church's doctrine. Her teachers delight to express in ever new forms that sentence of Augustine wherein he celebrated the mystical oneness of Christ and the Church: the two are one, one body, one flesh, one and the same person, one Christ, the whole Christ.[2] Nor could this intimate connexion of Christ and the Church, this their intimate oneness, receive profounder or plainer expression than in the figure of a marriage of Christ and the Church which St. Paul, inspired by the language of several of the prophets (Osee i-iii; Jer. ii, 2; Is. liv, 5) is the first to employ (II Cor. xi, 2). According to St. Paul the Church is the Bride of Christ, for whom He gave Himself. And with a like train of

[1] John Adam Möhler (1796-1838), Professor of Catholic Theology in the University of Tübingen, a distinguished theologian and attractive personality, author of several remarkable books. The best known of these, *Symbolik*, was translated into English in the last century by J. B. Robertson under the title *Symbolism, or Exposition of the doctrinal differences between Catholics and Protestants as evidenced by their symbolical writings* (London, 1843).

[2] *Unum, unum corpus, una eademque persona, unus Christus, totus Christus.*

thought the Seer of the Apocalypse celebrates the "marriage of the Lamb," and sings of His "bride" that hath prepared herself (xix, 7-8). Later mystical theology wove out of these scriptural thoughts its wondrously sweet bridal mysticism, in which Christ is the lord, the Church His bride, and the two in closest union generate the children of life.

This supernatural being of the Church expresses itself chiefly in her most primary creations, in dogma, morals and worship.

Her dogma aims at being nought else than the exact formulisation and description of all that precious reality, and all that abounding life which have entered this our actual world along with the Uncreated Word. The dogmas of Christology, in the narrower sense, delineate the Person of the God-man and describe the radiation of the glory of God in the face of Christ Jesus. The dogmas of Soteriology set forth His redemptive activity in His life, passion and death, and at the right hand of the Father. The dogmas that concern the Trinity lead us to the fundamental source of this divine life, to the bosom of the Father, and join the actual manifestation of Jesus to the eternal processions of the inner life of the Trinity. The dogmas of Mariology describe the bodily and natural relations of the Humanity of Jesus and His redemptive work to His own blessed Mother. The dogmas of Grace secure the character of the redemption as unmerited and due wholly to God, and fix the new basic mood of the redeemed, namely, love, peace and joy in the Holy Ghost. The dogmas that deal with the Church, the sacraments and the sacramentals, show how the new life that welled up in Christ is communicated to the men of all times and places. The dogmas of the Last Things set forth Jesus as the Judge and Fulfiller, and show how, when His redemptive work is complete, He gives back His lordship to the Father, that "God may be all in all."

Thus all the dogmas of the Catholic Church are stamped with the name of Christ; they would express each and

I want to be Christ-like.

every aspect of His teaching, they would bring the living, redeeming, ruling, judging Christ before our eyes according to all the dimensions of His historical manifestation.

And not otherwise is it with the Church's morality and with her worship. The fundamental object of all her educative work, of all her instruction, preaching and discipline, is to make the Christian a second Christ, an *alter Christus,* to make him, as the Fathers express it, "Christ-like." This one highest aim of its endeavour gives Christian morality its inner unity. There is no two-fold morality in the Church, since there is but one Christ to be formed. But the ways and manners in which men strive towards this goal are infinitely various, as various as the human personalities which have to mature and grow up to the stature of Christ. Very many of the faithful will be able to form the image of Christ in themselves only in very vague and general outline. Yet, just as nature at time sees fit to give of her best and to manifest her super-abundant power in some perfect types, even so the fulness of Christ which works in the Church breaks out ever and again in this or that saintly figure into brilliant radiance, in marvels of self-surrender, love, purity, humility and devotion. Professor Merkle's book * may provide even outsiders with some insight into the deep earnestness and heroic strength with which the Church in every century of her existence has striven after the realisation of the image of Christ, after the translation of His spirit into terms of flesh and blood, after the incarnation of Jesus in the individual man.

And the worship of the Church breathes the same spirit, and is as much interwoven with Christ and full of Christ as is her morality. Just as every particular prayer of the liturgy ends with the ancient Christian formula: *Per Christum Dominum nostrum,* so is every single act of

* *Religiose Erzieher der katholischen Kirche aus den letzten vier Jahr-hunderten* (Leipzig, n.d.), a series of chapters on prominent Catholic "educators" (in a wide sense), beginning with St. Teresa of Avila and ending with Cardinal Newman.

worship, from the Mass down to the least prayer, a memorial of Christ, an ἀνάμνησις Χριστοῦ. Nay, more, the worship of the Church is not merely a filial remembrance of Christ, but a continual participation by visible mysterious signs in Jesus and His redemptive might, a refreshing touching of the hem of His garment, a liberating handling of His sacred Wounds. That is the deepest purpose of the liturgy, namely, to make the redeeming grace of Christ present, visible and fruitful as a sacred and potent reality that fills the whole life of the Christian. In the sacrament of Baptism—so the believer holds—the sacrificial blood of Christ flows into the soul, purifies it from all the infirmity of original sin and permeates it with its own sacred strength, in order that a new man may be born thereof, the re-born man, the man who is an adopted son of God. In the sacrament of Confirmation, Jesus sends His "Comforter," the Spirit of constancy and divine faith, to the awakening religious consciousness, in order to form the child of God into a soldier of God. In the sacrament of Penance Jesus as the merciful Saviour consoles the afflicted soul with the word of peace: Go thy way, thy sins are forgiven thee. In the sacrament of the Last Anointing the compassionate Samaritan approaches the sick-bed and pours new courage and resignation into the sore heart. In the sacrament of Marriage He engrafts the love of man and wife on His own profound love for His people, for the community, for the Church, on His own faithfulness unto death. And in the priestly consecration by the imposition of hands, He transmits His messianic might, the power of His mission, to the disciples whom He calls, in order that He may by their means pursue without interruption His work of raising the new men, the children of God, out of the kingdom of death.

The sacraments are nought else than a visible guarantee, authenticated by the word of Jesus and the usage of the apostles, that Jesus is working in the midst of us. At all the important stages of our little life, in its heights and in its depths, at the marriage-altar and the cradle, at the

sick-bed, in all the crises and shocks that may befall us,
Jesus stands by us under the veils of the grace-giving sacrament as our Friend and Consoler, as the Physician of
soul and body, as our Saviour. St. Thomas Aquinas has
described this intimate permeation of the Christian's whole
life by faith in the sacraments and in his Saviour with
luminous power.[*] And Goethe, too, in the seventh book
of the second part of his *Dichtung und Wahrheit* speaks
warmly of it, and he closes his remarks with the significant
words: "How is this truly spiritual whole broken into pieces
in Protestantism, a part of these symbols being declared
apocryphal and only a few admitted as canonical. How
shall we be prepared to value some highly when we are
taught to be indifferent to the rest?"

But the sacraments which we have enumerated are not
the deepest and holiest fact of all. For so completely does
Jesus disclose Himself to His disciples, so profound is the
action of His grace, that He gives Himself to them and
enters into them as a personal source of grace. Jesus shares
with His disciples His most intimate possession, the most
precious thing that He has, His own self, His personality
as the God-man. We eat His Flesh and drink His Blood.
So greatly does Jesus love His community, that He permeates it, not merely with His blessing and His might, but
with his real Self, God and Man; He enters into a real
union of flesh and blood with it, and binds it to His being
even as the branch is bound to the vine. We are not left
orphans in this world. Under the forms of bread and wine
the Master lives amid His disciples, the Bridegroom with
His bride, the Lord in the midst of His community, until
that day when He shall return in visible majesty on the
clouds of heaven. The Sacrament of the Altar is the strongest, profoundest, most intimate memorial of the Lord, until
He come again. And therefore we can never forget Jesus,
though centuries and millennia pass, and though nations
and civilisations are ever perishing and rising anew. And
therefore there is no heart in the world, not even the heart

[*] *Summa Theologica, Pars tertia,* Q. LXV, Art 1.

of father or mother, that is so loved by millions and millions, so truly and loyally, so practically and devotedly, as is the Heart of Jesus.

Thus we see that in the sacraments, and especially in the Sacrament of the Altar, the fundamental idea of the Church is most plainly represented, the idea, that is, of the incarnation of Christ in the faithful. And therefore the Catholic can only regard that criticism of the sacraments as superficial, which derives them, not merely in this or that external detail, but in their proper content and dominant meaning, from non-Christian conceptions and cults, as for instance from the pagan mysteries. On the contrary the sacraments breathe the very spirit of primitive Christianity. They are the truest expression and result of that original and central Christian belief that the Christian should be inseparably united with Christ and should live in Christ. In Catholic sacramental devotion Christ is immediately conceived and experienced as the Lord of the community, as its invisible strength and principle of activity. In the sacraments is expressed the fundamental nature of the Church, the fact that Christ lives on in her and that the divine is incarnated in human form.

Therefore dogma, morality and worship are primary witnesses to the consciousness of the Church that she is of supernatural stock, that she is the Body of Christ. But more than this, the same consciousness determines the spirit of her ordinances and laws, the special manner and method in which she would have her supernatural life realised, and especially her conception of authority and of sacrament. We have spoken of the supernatural life in the Church; let us now throw light on the special forms in which this life is presented.

Since the Church would be nought else but the Body of Christ, the realisation in history of His divine and human Being, therefore the glorified Christ is the proper source of her power and authority, so much so that this authority is exercised only in His name and in the true and deepest sense belongs only to Him. The whole constitution of the

Church is completely aristocratic and not democratic, her authority coming from above, from Christ, and not from below, from the community. The new powers come from Christ, the Incarnate God, and from Him flow through the apostles to the Church. The government of the Church is, so to say, in the vertical and not in the horizontal line. That ancient African writer, Tertullian, defined this vertical system as early as the second century in the pregnant sentence: "The Church is from the apostles, the apostles from Christ, Christ from God." [*] The apostles did not act in their own right, but as "sent" and as representatives of Christ: "He that heareth you, heareth me, and he that despiseth you, despiseth me; and he that despiseth me, despiseth Him that sent me" (Luke x, 16; cf. Mt. x, 40). And the apostles on their part, as the New Testament in general and the pastoral epistles in particular show us, appointed by imposition of hands, wherever they founded new communities, the "firstlings," i.e., the first converts, to be leaders (προεστῶτες) who should, as St. Peter so strikingly and beautifully says (I Peter v, 2): "shepherd the flocks of God" in their stead. So the apostolic authority did not reside in the communities, but in the elders, leaders, overseers, who were chosen by the apostles in the name of Christ to take their place. And after the death of the apostles it was these elders who transmitted the authority which had been committed to them, by the imposition of hands, and organised the new communities round men empowered with this authority. Certainly the communities played their part in the matter, and helped by their advice to determine who should be entrusted with the commission. But in itself the power was exclusively an apostolic power, a thing reserved to the bishops who derived from the apostles. We may assert that the whole literature of early Christianity attests this conception. It is developed with classic lucidity in one of the earliest of Christian writings, the First Epistle of St. Clement (Ad Cor. xliv, 3).

[*] *Ecclesia ab apostolis, apostoli a Christo, Christus a Deo (De praescriptione, 37).*

Therefore ecclesiastical authority rests upon the apostolic succession (*successio apostolica*), upon the uninterrupted communication by imposition of hands of that commission which the apostles received from Christ. This apostolic commission, as passed on from bishop to bishop right down to our own day, is, if we regard its inmost nature, nothing else than the messianic authority of Jesus. By means of the apostolic succession, this authority is perpetuated and imparts the truth and grace of Jesus to humanity. And, therefore, behind ecclesiastical authority stands Jesus Himself. As the scholastics put it, Jesus is the "principal cause" (*causa principalis*) of all functions exercised by the Church, their ultimate source and the basis of their efficacy. Man is only an instrument, the *causa instrumentalis,* through whom Christ Himself acting in the Church teaches and sanctifies and governs. And so in the functioning of the Church, the human self, the human personality, the individual as such, falls wholly into the background. Not any human personality, but the redemptive might of Jesus controls the Church. The expression and resultant of this force is Church authority. The official authority of the Church is essentially a service of Christ (*ministerium Christi*), that is to say, a service which is fulfilled only in the name and by the commission of Christ, and derives its importance exclusively from the authority of Christ. It is true that the personality of the official may considerably affect the manner and method in which he carries out the will of Christ. Nevertheless the substance of his function, the core of his activity, is wholly independent of personal traits and weaknesses. For it is not the particular man and his personality that preaches, baptizes, and governs in the Church, but Christ alone. Therefore, Church authority, as thus conceived, derives immediately from the fundamental conviction that the Church is inwardly permeated by her "Lord." This is no unevangelical borrowing from pagan sources, or from Jewish or Roman law, but an expression of that primitive Christian thought: "It is Christ who evangelizes, Christ who baptizes." (*Christus est, qui evangelizat, Christus est, qui baptizat.*) So the aim of the Church in her official system is simply to secure that great and primary Christian idea that there is properly only one authority, only one teacher, only one sanctifier, only one pastor: Christ, the Lord.

Consequently such a conception of authority does not paralyse and petrify the believer, but enfranchises him, directing his gaze to Christ and Christ alone. No human authority, no extraneous personality, may stand between Christ and the believing subject. Divine truth, grace and life must flow into the soul directly from Christ Himself. Therefore—however paradoxical it may seem—the authority of the Church secures the liberty of the individual Christian, by its impersonal and extra-personal character. It protects that liberty from the spiritual domination and claims to mediatorship of alleged leading personalities, and sets Christ and the believer in direct contact with each other. Therefore the effect of such authority is not to separate, but to unite; or rather, it protects and secures that mysterious magnetic field and those wondrous magnetic forms which originate in the polarity of Christ and the soul. It protects and secures the direct contact and interplay of life between the Head and its members.

That is as true of the Church's teaching office as of her priestly and pastoral authority. The basis of her teaching authority is that sentence of the Lord: "One only shall be your teacher, Christ" (Mt. xxiii, 10). When the Catholic priest proclaims the word of God, he that preaches is not a mere man, but Christ Himself. For the Catholic consciousness, therefore, a sermon by the pope in the Sistine Chapel has no more weight than the words of a simple parish priest in a remote village church. For it is not Peter, or Paul, or Pius that preaches, but Christ: *Christus est, qui evangelizat.* All the doctrinal controversies of Christianity are dominated by this Christo-centric conception of the Church's teaching authority. It is because Christ is the sole canon of her preaching, that the Church adheres so obstinately and so rigidly to His traditional message. It is for this reason that she can endure no modernism, no fraternising with the spirit of the age. Her teaching is, and aims at being, nothing else but a handing on of that message of Christ which was proclaimed by the apostles. St. Paul enjoined his disciple, Timothy, to guard that which had been committed to him (*Timothee, custodi depositum!* II Tim. i, 14; cf. I Tim. iv, 16; vi, 14). That is exactly the doctrinal programme of the Church. Her conservatism and her traditionalism derive directly from her fundamentally Christo-centric attitude.

Rooted in this fundamental attitude the Church has always resisted the domination of leading personalities, of schools or movements. When any school of thought seemed to be obscuring or menacing the traditional faith, she has not hesitated to override even her greatest sons, an Origen, an Augustine, yes, in some points even a Thomas Aquinas. And whenever men have sought to interpret Christ's message, not by tradition, by firm adherence to history to the original faith and to the uninterrupted fellowship, but by means of private speculation, from out of the limited experience of their little individual selves, then the Church has proclaimed her emphatic anathema. And she would utter this same anathema, even if an angel came down from heaven teaching aught else than what she has received from the apostles. The doctrinal history of the Church is simply an obstinate adherence to Christ, a constant carrying out of the command of Jesus: "One only shall be your teacher, Christ." *

Just as Christ stands behind the teaching office of the Church, so also He stands, as "Lord" of the community, behind her sacramental activity. Only one who overlooks this decisive fact can allege that "the scholastic conception of the efficacy of the sacraments reveals the primitive idea of the automatic effect, of the 'manna' of the sacred

* Cf. St. Augustine: *Christus est, qui docet. Cathedram in caelo habet . . . schola ipsius in terra est, et schola ipsius corpus ipsius est. Caput docet membra sua, lingua loquitur pedibus suis. Christus est, qui docet: audiamus, timeamus, faciamus* (*De disciplina christiana,* XIV, 15).

action." [7] According to Catholic theology the sacraments
work *ex opere operato*, and not *ex opere operantis;* that
is to say that the sacramental grace is not produced and
effected through the personal, moral and religious efforts
of the recipient, but rather through the objective accomplishment of the sacramental sign itself. In every sacrament
there is something objectively given (*opus operatum*),
namely, the special conjunction according to the institution
of Christ of a material element (the "matter") and certain
words (the "form"). When this conjunction is effected
in the recipient according to the intentions of the Church,
then the sacrament is a "work of Christ" (*opus Christi*),
which independently of the subjective share of the recipient
(*opus operantis*) by force of its valid accomplishment causes
the sacramental grace. Thus, in the case of baptism, when
the water is poured upon the forehead of a child in the
name of the Trinity, the child by the very performance of
this act is admitted into the family of God. The heavens
at once open and the Father's voice proclaims: "Thou art
my beloved child."

Therefore the sacramental action does in fact transmit
the Saviour's grace "without any subjective factor," at
least so far as regards the sanctification of an infant child.
When it is a question of the sanctification of an adult,
who has attained religious and moral consciousness, the
recipient must prepare himself subjectively for the grace
which is objectively imparted in the sacramental act, by
acts of faith, contrition and repentance. Therefore, according to the teaching of the Church, this ethico-religious
effort of the adult is not the effective cause of his sanctification, its *causa efficiens,* but only its preparatory cause,
causa dispositiva. The effective cause of grace is exclusively Christ Himself, who proclaims and effects His
gracious will through signs determined by Himself. Primarily, therefore, and *in actu primo,* grace is a free gift and
favour, a thing already guaranteed by the sacramental act

[7] Heiler, op. cit., p. 221.

apart from all personal effort. But whether I shall effectively grasp this grace which is thus provided and profit by it, that depends upon my subjective dispositions. Therefore practically (*in actu secundo*) my subjective sanctification is not the work of grace alone, but the resultant of two factors, the grace of Christ and my good will. Can it then be alleged that this sacramentalism is akin to primitive magic, to the belief in a "manna" or something of the sort which makes certain special objects the conveyors of supernatural forces?

In fact, the criticism which thinks it right to speak of the sacraments as having a "magical character" divorces them from their proper and sole source, namely from Christ, the true and only giver of grace, and gives them an indedependent status. So that they become, not signs of grace, but independent sources of it, instruments endued with their own power, sacred charms. In reality, however, no sacrament stands thus in its own right, or can so stand for a single moment. It has its whole meaning and its whole power in and through Christ alone. As St. Thomas teaches, it is no more than the instrument (*causa instrumentalis*) of Christ the Giver of grace, the visible sign whose physical being He employs in order to effect in the soul of the believer the supernatural results which are indicated in the symbolical form of the sign. Nay, more, according to that Scotist view which is now advocated by many theologians, the sacrament itself possesses no strictly "physical" causality in any way immanent in its sign. On the contrary, the sacramental grace flows directly from Jesus into the soul of the believer. The sacrament is no more than an appointed sign of Christ, an objectivisation of the gracious will of Jesus, a visible and perceptible "I will, be thou made clean!"

Certainly it is true that even according to this view there remains something objective and impersonal in the notion of a sacrament. It remains true that the grace of Christ is not causally connected with the ethico-religious activity of the believer or the priest, but with the objective accomplishment of the sign. But why is that so? The very impersonal and objective character of the sacrament, like the impersonality of the Church's teaching activity, expresses that profoundest claim of the Church, her most intimate union with Christ, her working purely out of the fulness of Christ, her sanctifying through the might of Christ alone. Precisely because it is not the human element in her which sanctifies men, but the power of Christ alone, therefore the blessing of Christ is not tied to human activity, not to the faith and repentance of the sinner, not even to the prayers and sacrifices of saintly, magnanimous souls and specially gifted personalities, whether saintly prophets, bishops, or priests, but to a wholly impersonal thing, a dead sign, which has no other merit save that of being a sign of Christ, a valid expression of His gracious will. The purpose, therefore, of the formula *ex opere operato*, is to secure the deepest essence of Christianity, that thing for which St. Paul suffered and fought, the absolute unmeritedness of grace, and the thought that Christ is "all in all." And since this idea of the impersonality of the sacraments springs directly from the heart of Christianity, it is consequently as old as Christianity itself, and as old as the Body of Christ, the Church. Students of biblical theology emphasise the fact that the sacramental doctrine of St. John and St. Paul has already got this impersonal conception, that it recognises an efficacy *ex opere operato*, at least in effect, and is therefore completely Catholic in its character. And how could it be otherwise? When Christ is placed in the centre, when we are told emphatically that of His fulness we have all received, then all human intermediaries must stand aside. There can be no human mediators, as Augustine remarked against the Donatists. Christ is the sole worker. When individual Christians in the Corinthian church attached themselves to various gifted personalities and formed a Peter party and a Paul party and an Apollo party, as though they would found their salvation upon these personalities, then St. Paul with the burning zeal of his witness for Christ cried out against this humanisation of the Gospel. "What is Apollo and what is Paul? . . . His servants, through whom ye were made believers. . . . other foundation can no man lay but that which has been laid, which is Christ Jesus" (1 Cor. iii, 4-5, 11). The sacramental idea is nothing but the realisation and maintenance of this basis of Christianity. In her age-long conflicts with Montanists, Novatians, Donatists, and again later on with Waldenses, Albigenses and Hussites, the Church reiterated the sentence of St. Augustine: "The sacraments sanctify through themselves, and not through men" (*sacramenta per se sancta, non per homines*). For man does not baptize, and man does not absolve, but Christ alone. When the Christian sacrament by this its impersonal character eliminates all human intermediaries, it secures an immediate and free exchange of life between the Head and the members. And so the freedom of the personal religious life is nowhere so perfectly safeguarded as in Catholic piety. And the forms of piety, in which the Catholic's sacramental experience of Christ achieves self-expression, are as manifold as the innumerable leaves of the trees.

There is yet something to be said about the relation of the pastoral office of the Church to the Head of the Church. St. John tells us (xxi, 15 ff.) that the risen Christ enjoined the apostle Peter: "Feed my lambs, feed my sheep." Peter is not to feed his own sheep, but Christ's sheep. So that the pastoral authority is plainly a delegated authority, and the pastor a deputy of Christ. That is the sort of authority which St. Paul exercises against the incestuous Corinthian; he gives him over "to Satan for the destruction of the flesh, that the spirit may be saved in the day of our Lord Jesus Christ," and he does this "in the name of our Lord Jesus Christ" and "with the power of our Lord Jesus." Every disciplinary measure of the Church is inspired by her conviction that she is acting in the name and in the power of Jesus. It is true that the pastoral authority of the Church does not, like her teaching or priestly authority, point directly to certain supernatural realities which have been determined once for all by Christ's revelation, to the realities that is of doctrine and sacrament. Its object is rather to introduce these supernatural realities into practical life, to apply Christian rules and principles to the progressive and constantly changing life of nations and individuals. And in consequence there is no absolute certainty that all the particular measures of the pastoral authority are according to the mind and spirit of Christ.

So it is possible, as St. Augustine often insists, that the human element may obtrude itself and colour the administration of Church discipline, and that there may be errors and mistakes. Yet, even though there be mistakes of detail, the luminous goal, the directive principles and the decisive means of Church discipline are—so the Catholic is convinced—determined by Christ, and pertain to His truth, love and power. The Catholic knows that the rule of the Church incarnates absolute truth, justice and love, and so he has solved the problem of Dostoievski[*]: Is not all human exercise of authority tantamount to a usurpation? Yes, if it be merely human, it is. For every merely human governance necessarily rests on might, whether it be the tyranny of an individual or the despotism of a community. Only in theocracy is a man free from men, for he serves not men but God. Therein lies the secret of that child-like obedience, so incomprehensible to the outsider, which the Catholic gives to his Church, an obedience whereby he freely and cheerfully submits his own little notions and wishes to the will of Christ expressed in the action of authority; an obedience whereby his own small and limited self is enlarged to the measure of the great self of the Church. That is no corpse-like obedience or slave mentality, but a profoundly religious act, an absolute devotion to the Will of Christ which rules the Church, a service of God. And so this obedience is not cowardly and weak, but strong and ready for sacrifice, manly and brave even in the presence of kings. It is faithful even to the surrender of earthly possessions, yes, even to the sacrifice of life itself, offering itself to the Christ who lives in

[*] cf. *The Brothers Karamazoff*.

the Church. This fidelity is instinct with the noble spirit of the faith. If a storm were to burst to-morrow over the Christian churches and their members were called upon to testify even unto death, I know not if all these communities would stand firm, strong and faithful, ranged round the one Christ; I know not if the bonds that in times of peace hold their members together would not be broken and utterly shattered, and those Christians blown like chaff before the wind. But one thing I know, that the bond which binds the Church and her members together will be broken by no devil and no demon. For it is not of this world. It is woven by the Church's "Lord," by the God-man, Christ Jesus.

CHAPTER III

THE CHURCH THE BODY OF CHRIST

The Church is his body, the fulness of him that filleth all in all
(Eph. i, 23).

WHEN we define the Church as essentially the Kingdom of God and the Body of Christ, it follows as her first particular attribute that she is supernatural and heavenly. The Church is ordinated towards the invisible, spiritual and eternal. Of this we have spoken already. But the Church is not only invisible. Because she is the Kingdom of God, she is no haphazard collection of individuals, but an ordered system of regularly subordinated parts. And because the Church is the Body of Christ, she is essentially an organism, with its members purposively interrelated, and a visible organism. That is her second particular attribute. The advocates of a purely spiritual religion, both in ancient and in modern Christianity, have maintained that the divine is in the Church as a sort of freely suspended force, as a saving power that invisibly penetrates into this or that person. But that is not so. On the contrary the divine is objectivised, is incarnated in the community, and precisely and only in so far as it is a community.

That is to say that the supernatural redemptive might of Jesus, as it operates in the Church, is not tied to a single person, so far as he is a person, and is not manifested in a single person, but essentially only in the totality, in the community of individuals. The Spirit of Jesus is objectivised and introduced into our earthly life, not through the medium of specially gifted personalities, but exclusively in and through the community, in and through the union of the many in one. So the Church possesses the Spirit of Christ, not as a many of single individuals, nor as a sum of spiritual personalities, but as the compact unity of the faithful, as a community that transcends the individual personalities. This union, this community, is a fundamental datum of Christianity, not a thing created by the voluntary or forced association of the faithful, not a mere secondary and derivative thing depending on the good pleasure of Christians, but a thing which is antecedent to any Christian personality, a supra-personal thing, which does not presuppose Christian personalities, but itself creates and produces them. The Christian community is not created by the faithful; on the contrary the community creates them. The Christian community, the Church as a fellowship, comes first, and the Christian personality, the Church as a sum of such personalities, is second. The Church did not spring into being when Peter and Paul, James and John, grasped the mystery of Jesus, His God-man being, and on the basis of their common faith formed a fellowship which was called after Him. No, the Church was already in existence—fundamentally, germinally, virtually —before Peter and John became believers. The Church as a whole, as a community, as an organic unity is a divine creation. In the last resort she is nothing else than the unity of fallen humanity accomplished by the Sacred Humanity of Jesus, the Kosmos of men, mankind as a whole, the many as one.

This is a thought which does not lie on the surface, but we must grasp it if we would understand the visible nature of the Church, her external manifestation. If Christ is what the Church confesses Him to be, the Incarnate God and Saviour of men—as indeed He is—then it must be His mission to reunite to God mankind as a unity, as a whole, and not this or that individual man. The wretchedness of fallen humanity, the essence of the original sin, consisted in this, that the supernatural union with God, in which man was originally created, and through which alone he could attain his perfection, his wholeness, his completion, was by Adam's fall broken and dissolved. When Adam fell away from God, all humanity in him and through him fell away likewise. That is a basic conviction of Christianity, which was adumbrated in certain post-canonical Jewish writings, and received formulation as a Christian doctrine especially at the hands of St. Paul. At the basis of this Christian dogma of an original and inherited sin, and of our redemption through the new man Christ, lies the great and striking thought that mankind must not be regarded as a mass of homogeneous beings successively emerging and passing away, nor merely as a sum of men bound together by unity of generation, as being descendants of one original parent, but as one single man. So closely are men assimilated to one another in their natural being, in body and in mind, so profoundly are they interlocked in thinking, willing, feeling, and acting, so solidary is their life, their virtue and their sin, that they are considered in the divine plan of redemption only as a whole, only as a unity, only as one man. This one man is not the individual man, but the whole man, the totality of the innumerable expressions of that humanity which is reproduced in countless individuals. This one man includes all men who were thousands of years ago and all who shall be thousands of years hence. Such is the one man, the whole man. And the guilt and destiny of every single man are not merely his own guilt and his own destiny; they concern the whole of humanity in proportion to the importance which Providence has assigned him in the organism of humanity.

These are thoughts that may seem strange to the modern man, or which at least would have seemed so a short time ago. The individualism of the Renaissance, the dismemberment of man and his relations in the age of Enlightenment, and finally the subjective idealism of Kant, whereby our minds were taught to relinquish the objective thing, the trans-subjective reality, and to indulge in boundless subjectivism: these influences tore us from the moorings of our being, and especially from our true and essential basis, that humanity which produces, supports and enfolds us. We became imprisoned within the walls of our own selves, unable any more to attain to humanity, to the full, whole man. The category "humanity" became foreign to our thought, and we thought and lived only in the category of self. Humanity as wholeness and as fulness had to be rediscovered.

But there is now beginning, under the influence of early Christian ideas, of socialism and of the great war—quite apart from purely philosophical, epistemological reactions —a gradual revolution of our whole mental attitude. We are beginning to feel uncomfortable in the narrow hermitage of our own selves and are seeking a way out. And we are discovering that we are not alone, but that by us, with us, round us, in us, is all humanity. We are realising with astonishment that we belong profoundly to this humanity, that a community of being and destiny, and a joint liability bind us to it. We are learning that we come to our whole self only by its means, that our individual being broadens out into the whole man only in it and through it. With this new mental attitude we are able to appreciate the fundamental Christian conceptions of the first man and the new man, of Adam and Christ, in their profound significance. Adam, the first man, called to share by grace in the divine life, represented in God's eyes the whole of mankind. Adam's fall was the fall of mankind. Detached from its original supernatural goal, mankind then, like some planet detached from its sun, revolved only in crazy gyration round itself. Its own self became the centre of its striving and yearning. Man came to feel God, the very source of his spiritual life, as a burden. The first "autonomous" man in the ethico-religious sense was Adam, when he took the fruit of the tree of life. And so man no longer had any source whence he might renew his strength, except his own small self. He had abandoned the eternal source of living water, and dug himself a poor cistern in his own self. And the waters of this cistern were

soon exhausted. Man fell sick and died. His self was his
sickness and his self was his death. And all mankind died
with him. Then, according to the eternal decision of God's
love, the New Man came, the man of the new, permanent
and indissoluble union with God, Christ the Lord. In Him
erring mankind, man radically cut off from the divine
source of his life, was finally reunited to God, to the Life
of all lives, to the Fount of all power, truth and love.
Mankind—not merely this man and that, not you and I
only, but the whole of mankind, the unity of all men—
was brought home again from its terrible diaspora, from
its dispersion, back to the living God. The whole man
came once more into being, permanently united with God,
and so effectively united that he could never more, as the
unity of mankind, be for any fault cut off from the divine
source of his life. Therefore Christ, as the God-man, is
the new humanity, the new beginning, the whole man in
the full meaning of the phrase.[1]

Whence it follows clearly that the Church was already,
in the mystery of the Incarnation, established as an organic
community. The "many," the sum total of all who need
redemption, are in their inner relationship to one another,
in their interrelation and correlation, in their organic communion, objectively and finally the Body of Christ, never
more separable from Him for all eternity.

It is clear therefore, in the light of the redemption,
that the Church did not come into being only when Peter
and John and Paul became believers. It became objectively existent when the divine Word united humanity,

---

[1] None of the Fathers sets forth the mystical unity of Christ and the
faithful so clearly and impressively as does St. Augustine. He would
have the nature of the Church conceived in terms of this unity: *Cum ille
caput, nos membra, unus est Filius Dei* (*In ep. Joan.* Tr. X, 3). *Aliter
enim est in nobis tamquam in templo suo, aliter autem, quia et nos ipse
sumus, cum secundum id, quod ut caput nostrum esset, homo factus est,
corpus eius sumus* (*In ev. Joann.* Tr. CXI, 5). *Et nos Ipse est* (*Sermo*
CXXXIII, 8). *Ille caput cum ceteris membris unus homo est. Et cum
ascendere nemo potest, nisi qui in eius corpore membrum ipsius factus
fuerit, impletur: quia nemo ascendit, nisi qui descendit . . . igitur jam
non duo, sed una caro* (*Sermo XCI, 6, 7*).

the unity of all men who needed redemption, with Himself in His divine and human being. The Incarnation is for Christians the foundation and planting of that new communion which we call the Church. The Body of Christ and the Kingdom of God came into being as objective reality at the moment when the Word was made flesh.[*]

We must take these fundamental dogmatic thoughts to heart if we would appreciate the Catholic conception of the Church in all its profundity. Only so shall we understand why the idea of community is its dominant idea, and why the community cannot be the product of the faithful, a creation of these or those persons, but must be a supra-personal unity, a unity which permeates and embraces the whole of redeemed humanity. As such a unity the Church is nothing vague or undefined, but the actual inner unity of redeemed humanity united with Christ. In the Catholic conception of the Church the decisive element is not this or that person, but all mankind.

Two important consequences follow from this. One of these has already been developed, the fact, namely, that the organ of the redeeming spirit of our divine Saviour, its incarnation and manifestation, is not the individual personality, but the community as community. The purpose of Christ is realised in the community. Therefore the visibility of the Church does not consist merely in the visibility of its individual members, but in the visibility of its compact unity, of its community. But where there is a community, a comprehensive unity, there is distribution and co-ordination of functions. That is the second consequence that follows from the mystery of the Incarnation. The Christian unity is no mere mechanical unity, but a unity with inner differentiation, an organic unity. The Body of Christ, if it be a true body,

[*] St. Augustine: *Dominus autem securus moriens dedit sanguinem suum pro ea, quam resurgens haberet, quam sibi jam conjunxerat in utero virginis. Verbum enim sponsus et sponsa caro humana; et utrumque unus Filius Dei et idem filius hominis: ubi factus est caput ecclesiae, ille uterus virginis Mariae thalamus ejus, inde processit tamquam sponsus de thalamo suo* (*In ev. Joann.* Tr. VIII, 4).

must have members and organs with their special tasks
and functions, which each in its measure serves the development of the essential form of the body and which therefore serve one another.   When St. Paul, the first apostle
to formulate the expression "Body of Christ," develops
this conception in the twelfth chapter of his First Epistle
to the Corinthians, he already stresses this point and
speaks of the organic functioning of this body: "Now
there are diversities of graces, but the same Spirit.   And
there are diversities of ministries, but the same Lord.   And
there are diversities of operations, but the same God, who
worketh all in all. . . . For as the body is one and hath
many members; and all the members of the body, whereas
they are many, yet are one body: so also is Christ. . . .
God indeed hath set some in the Church, first apostles,
secondly prophets, thirdly doctors; after that miracle-
workers, then the graces of healings, helps, governments,
kinds of tongues, interpretations of speeches." It is therefore the view of the apostle that the community is of its
nature differentiated, that the body works as a unity through
a diversity of organic functions, that the unity of the whole
attests the unity of the spirit of Jesus.   It is true that St.
Paul does not distinguish the various functions of the one
organism with theological precision.   Such precision came
with later developments and with the speculation that
sprang from them.   Time made it clear that some of the
gifts, such as those of the apostolate, of teaching, and of
government belong to the nature of the Church and could
not be discarded; whereas others, such as the gifts of
prophecy, miracles and tongues, were the manifestation of
a superabundant Christian life, and to be regarded not
as structurally necessary to that life, but rather as signs and
expressions of it.

But the fundamental thought, that the Body of Christ
is and must be an organic body, that it works by its very
nature in a manifold of functions, and that this manifold
is bound together by the one Spirit of Christ into an inner
unity: this thought is native to St. Paul, and it is the heri-

tage and fundamental principle of the whole Christian
Gospel.

Let us now consider more nearly the organisation of the
Body of Christ, its unity in fulness, and fulness in unity.
The first point to be insisted on is this, that since the community and not the individual is the bearer of the Spirit
of Jesus, and since its visibility consists especially in the
manifestation of this essential unity, therefore the visible
organism of the Church postulates for its visibility a real
principle of unity in which the supra-personal unity of all
the faithful obtains perceptible expression and which supports, maintains and protects this unity. The pope is the
visible expression and the abiding guarantee of this unity.
So, if we regard the matter thus, it becomes plain that the
original nature of the Church, her fundamental determination as a unitary organism, achieves its purest expression
in the papacy. Were the Gospels silent regarding Peter's
call to be the rock, and the key-bearer, and the pastor of
the Church, the very nature of the Church itself, with that
necessity and force whereby every essential form implanted
in an organism presses to its full realisation, would have
produced the papacy out of its own bosom. In the papacy
the community strives after and achieves the consciousness
of its essential and necessary unity. In the papacy it
grasps and realises itself as the one Kingdom of God, as
the one Body of Christ on the earth. And so the Catholic
never regards the pope as separated from this unity, as an
independent factor, as a charismatical personality, as a
personality possessed of supernatural powers like a Moses
or an Elias. The pope is to him the visible embodiment
of the unity of the Church, that real principle whereby
redemption-needing mankind achieves its form as complete and perfect unity. In the pope, his unity with his
brethren becomes visible to the Catholic. His view broadens
and his eye passes beyond all the limitations of personalities,
beyond all bounds of nations and civilisations, beyond all
seas and deserts. And the whole massive Christendom,
with all the organic interrelation of its parts, its great and

sacred communion of love, becomes manifest for him in the
pope, and stands out before him as a sublime and glorious
reality.   Therefore no misuse of papal authority and no
human failings in the wearers of the tiara can rob him
of his veneration and his love for the papacy.   When he
kisses the pope's hand, he kisses all his brethren, who are
joined together into one in the person of the pope.   His
heart broadens out into the heart of all Christendom, of
the unity in fulness.

Moreover the pope himself teaches, acts, strives, suffers
only from out of this unity.   It is true, that, inasmuch as
he is by the wise disposition of Providence at the same time
bishop of Rome, he can make regulations and give decisions which are valid only for his immediate Roman
flock and which therefore possess only a local significance.
But when he speaks as pope, as successor of St. Peter, then
he speaks as the visible basis and pledge of unity, out of
the compact fulness of the Body of Christ, as that principle
in which the supra-personal unity of the Body of Christ
has achieved visible reality for the world of space and time.
Therefore he does not speak as a despot in his own right,
as some absolute monarch, but as the head of the Church,
in intimate vital relationship to the complete organism of
the Church.   So he cannot, like a Delphic Oracle, give
dogmatic decisions purely at his own discretion and according to his own subjective notions.   On the contrary, he
is bound, as the Vatican Council emphatically declares,
bound strongly in conscience, to proclaim and interpret that
revelation which is contained in the written and unwritten
mind of the Church, in the twin sources of our faith, sacred
Scripture and Tradition.

On the other hand, it is of the nature of the Church as a
supra-personal unity, and thereby also of the nature of the
papacy, that the pope should not be regarded as a mere
representative of the Church, as a sort of mouthpiece of
the general mind.   For the very reason that the community
is not exhaustively represented by the members of the
Church nor owes its original existence to them, but is a

supra-personal unity established in the Incarnate God, a principle of organisation which is effective in and of itself, a power in its own right: for that reason the pope, in whom this community by Christ's will obtains visible form, rules absolutely *ex sese,* that is to say that in his activity he is in no respect dependent on any member of the Body of Christ, neither on the whole episcopate, nor on individual bishops, nor on the rest of the faithful. He is not merely one "pastor" alongside others; he is the pastor to whom alone the sheep of the Divine Pastor are committed (cf. Jn. xxi, 15 ff.). And he is not merely one stone in the holy building, nor only the first stone, but the rock (cf. Mt. xvi, 18), to whom all other stones have no other relation than that they are supported by it, and are in their whole being and activity dependent upon it. The new Code of Canon Law (canon 218 §1, 2) formulates with truly monumental power this papal plenipotency (*suprema et plena potestas jurisdictionis in universam ecclesiam*), which is "independent of every human authority" and immediately embraces not only all and single "churches," but also all and single "pastors and faithful."

What the pope is for the whole Church, that in an analogous sense the bishop is for the particular community, for the diocese. He is the representative and objective form of its inner unity, he is the mutual love of its members made visible, the organic interrelation of the faithful made perceptible (Möhler). That explains why the Catholic knows no more venerable names on earth than those of pope and bishop, and why in the centuries when the western world was impregnated with the Catholic consciousness, no honour was too great, no ornament too precious to be bestowed upon pope and bishop. This did not, and does not, hold good of the person of pope or bishop—no one makes so sharp a distinction between the person and his office as does the Catholic—but it did and does hold good exclusively of their sublime function, that namely of representing and assuring the unity of the Body of Christ in the world. When a man is present at a pontifical High

Mass, and sees with amazement the vast circumstance of pomp and splendour, the rich ceremonial with which the person and the actions of the pontifex are surrounded, if he sees in all this nothing but a consequence and survival of the court ceremonial of Rome and Constantinople, he has grasped only half the truth. The motive force, the dominant idea of this magnificence, is the joy of the Catholic in his Church, in her overpowering unity, in that affirmation of the communion of the brethren, of the one Body of Christ, which is so to say personified in the bishop. One God, one faith, one love, one single man: that is the stirring thought which inspires all the Church's pageantry and gives it artistic form. It is a seeking and finding of love, of love for Christ and for the brethren who in Him are bound together into one.

This fundamental conception of papacy and episcopacy of itself answers the objections raised against the primitiveness of Church authority on the ground that Christ preached humility and brotherly love. This criticism sees in our Lord's words, when He settled the dispute among His disciples, "the strictest internal argument" against the hypothesis that He instituted the papacy.* The disciples were irritated by the request of the sons of Zebedee, that they should sit the one on the right and the other on the left of the Lord in His Kingdom. Jesus called them to Him and said: "You know that they who seem to rule over the Gentiles lord it over them: and their princes have power over them. But it is not so among you. But whosoever will be greater, shall be your minister. And whosoever will be first among you shall be the servant of all. For the Son of man also is not come to be ministered unto, but to minister, and to give his life a redemption for many" (Mk. x, 42-45).

In these words Jesus discards for His disciples that absolute power, that domination, which was exercised by contemporary rulers, especially by the Hellenistic princes. The mark of the disciple of Jesus is to be service, and not

* Heiler, op. cit., p. 40.

brutal domination. In God's Kingdom there is to be no "lording it over them" and no "letting them feel one's power," but loving ministry and ministering love. The words themselves make it plain enough that the Master is not excluding all authority and all power from His society, but only that power which is essentially brutal and domineering. This meaning of our Lord's words is brought out still more clearly by the evangelist Luke (xxii, 24 ff.) who gives Mark's logion in the form: "He that is the greater among you, let him become as the younger: and he that is the leader as he that serveth." By those words Jesus makes it perfectly clear that there shall be a "greater" among his disciples, and that there shall be those who are "leaders." So that his recommendation of brotherly humility and love is not directed against the principle of authority in itself, but against the egotistical misuse of this principle. How else could Jesus have set Himself up as a pattern of service and brotherly love, and yet in the same breath call Himself the "Son of Man," that is the Lord of the future and of the judgment, the holder of authority? Just as His brotherly service does not exclude His supreme dignity as Son of Man, so his recommendation of humility and love cannot be intended in an anti-hierarchical sense. Therefore it is a misinterpretation of the plain intention of Jesus to argue that the idea of a primacy is irreconcilably opposed to His teaching concerning humility and brotherly love. The contrary is true. The teaching of Jesus obtains its luminous fulfilment exactly in papacy and episcopacy, if they be correctly conceived. For the papacy, regarded in the light of the supernatural essence of the Church, is nought else but a personification of love, the manifestation of the unity of the Body of Christ on earth. It is therefore in its essential nature the exact opposite of domination; it is born not of brutality, but of love. Papacy and episcopacy are divine power put to the service of love. Certainly the pope has sometimes to speak out in sharp and peremptory admonition. It is as when Paul cried: "Shall I come to you with a rod?"

(1 Cor. iv, 21). And sometimes his anathema rings through the world "in the same tones and with the same language" (Heiler) as St. Paul used when he excluded the incestuous Corinthian from the Christian community. Nevertheless, even this angry and corrective love remains love, love for the community of brethren. The pope has in so far the primacy of love. Nor is there any hierarchy in the Church that may express itself otherwise than in ministering love. Woe to the pontiff who misuses his primacy of love for personal ends, to gratify his lust of power, his avarice, or other passions! He sins against the Body of Christ, he offers violence to Jesus. He has to render an account beyond that required of any other member of the Body of Christ. How terribly at the Judgment may the words sound in his ears, when the risen Lord shall ask him: "Peter, lovest thou me, lovest thou me more than these?" That is the great and sacred privilege of his office, to love Christ and His Body more than all other men, to realise that honourable title which Gregory the Great assumed: "Servant of the servants of God" (Servus servorum Dei). Pope Pius XI, in his first Encyclical, laid it down that those who preside are nothing but "servants of the general weal, servants of the servants of God, especially of the weak and needy, after the pattern of the Lord." [*]

The pope's office is essentially service of the community, love and devotion. And when we prescind from the office, when we consider only the personality of pope or bishop, then there is no distinction of rank in the Church, then the saying of Jesus is true: "Ye are all brethren" (Mt. xxiii, 8). In the same Encyclical Pope Pius lays stress on the point that "only in this kingdom is there a true equality of right, wherein all are endowed with the same greatness and the same nobility, being ennobled by the same precious Blood

[*] *Arcanum Dei* (1922). St. Augustine delights to describe this Church authority as a ministry of love. cf. *Praesunt non ut praesint, sed ut prosint* (*Contra Faustum* XXII, 56). *Sic praeest fratribus, ut eorum servum se esse meminerit* (*Contra ep. Parm.* III, 3, 16).

of Christ." In the Kingdom of Christ there is only one kind of nobility, namely nobility of soul. The wearer of the tiara is the rock of the Church and has the charisma of that office not for himself, but for his brethren. For himself he has no greater Christian rights and no lesser Christian duties than the poorest beggar in the streets. Indeed he is in especial need of the mercy of God and requires the intercessions of his brethren. And if his conscience be burdened with sin, then he also must kneel at the feet of his confessor, who may be the homeliest Capuchin friar. And were he to appeal to Jesus with the request of the Sons of Zebedee: "Lord, grant that I may sit at Thy right hand or Thy left in Thy glory," then would his director give him the same answer: "You know not what you ask. Can you drink the chalice which Jesus drank?"

Church history demonstrates, to every unbiassed student, how earnestly and austerely most wearers of the tiara have taken their personal obligations, and how their lofty office has not impaired their humility, love and devotion, but transformed and deepened them. It is true that there have been popes, especially in the tenth century and at the Renaissance, who have given sad evidence of the frailty of human nature. But their number fades into insignificance before the dazzling company of saints and martyrs which the See of Rome has already given to the world. The words of the Protestant theologian Walter Köhler about Pope Pius X are true *mutatis mutandis* of the overwhelming majority of the popes of Rome: "He recked nothing of the political power of the modern state. He was a priest, and his endeavour was to hold the Host aloft, to look neither to right nor left, and to bear his Saviour through the world." Such is the idea of the papacy and such its essential nature: to bear the Saviour through the world, to devote self to Christ in the service of the community.

So all egotism, all domination, all special privilege is fundamentally foreign to the Church. And therefore and in that measure the Church fulfils the noblest dreams of democratic equality.   Unity and brotherly love have here built themselves a house, a house in which, as St. Cyprian says and St. Augustine repeats (*De bapt. c. Don.* vii, 49), only those dwell who are of one heart and one mind.   The spirit of the Master pervades that dwelling, the spirit which enriched us with the luminous words: "One only is your Master, ye all are brethren."

CHAPTER IV

THROUGH THE CHURCH TO CHRIST

"Where two or three are gathered together in my name, there am I in the midst of them" (Mt. xviii, 20).

BEHIND our enquiry into the nature of Catholicism, there lie necessarily the question of the living God and the question of the mystery of Christ.

It is of course impossible to set forth even roughly, still less to solve, the whole mass of problems connected with these questions. Let it be sufficient to show clearly and simply the way by which the Catholic comes to the living God and to Christ. In this process we shall find that further light will be thrown on the nature of Catholicism, so as to illuminate its manner of seeing, thinking and feeling.

The structure of Catholic faith may be summarised in a single sentence: I find God, through Christ, in His Church. I experience the living God through Christ realising Himself in His Church.

So we see that the certitude of Catholic faith rests on the sacred triad: God, Christ, Church.

How does the Catholic attain certitude about God, and achieve his "I believe"? He comes thereto finally by the way of revelation and grace, but in the first instance and preparatorily by the way of natural reason. The Vatican Council lays it down that God, as the beginning and end of all things, can be certainly known from the visible world. This knowledge of God will be more easily attained, the more clearly we are conscious that the quest after God, the religious enquiry and investigation, is specifically different from any profane enquiry, as for instance an investigation into the habits of insects. The conditional, finite, imperfect character of our being gives the religious enquiry this specific character. If I consider my own nature I readily discover that I am not an absolute being, but utterly and entirely conditioned. Everywhere I find bounds and limits. Everywhere are lines which suddenly break off short. The fact that there is an Absolute is not the laborious product of speculative philosophy, but rather the mediate consequence of a dispassionate consideration of my being. For when I recognise that I am a conditioned being, by that very fact I affirm the existence of the Absolute. Thus I reach without more ado the practical judgment that my utterly conditioned being is ordinated to and postulates an Absolute. I do not stand on the same level with the Absolute. And so my mental attitude towards this Absolute must have a moral and religious character, that is to say that it must be characterised by humility, reverence, purity and love.

When the enquiry is not based upon this moral foundation, when a man enters upon it in full autonomy and with purely profane instincts, as though it were a purely indifferent question and one which did not concern man's vital interests, or even as though he were judge and God a suspected defendant, then he is sadly misconceiving the very basis of his being and in a wholly inadmissible fashion making himself absolute. We sometimes steal into the sphere of the Absolute, as though we stood on a level with It, or as though It were incarnate in us. At the bottom of all uninterested or autonomous thinking about God lies such a secret delusion. And this secret delusion is the real source of error which all too easily makes the enquiry unfruitful. If there is really a living, personal God, it does not rest with me, a relative and conditioned being, but it rests with God alone, whether I may know Him. The question is not, *Can* I know God? but *May* I know Him? Every purely profane enquiry is excluded. God

will not let His fire be stolen from Him. If my enquiry is
moral and religious, in the sense which has been described,
then only may my mental attitude be characterised as positive and no longer negative, no longer destructive and solvent, but constructive and creative. Only in this positive
mood can I surely interpret nature to its ultimate mystery
and find in it the footprints of God. I see clearly how
thousands of lines of the macrocosm and the microcosm
lead concurrently to a single point, by which alone their
unity and their ultimate meaning are intelligible. I attain
to the recognition of a primal First Cause, to the assump-
tion of an ultimate Idea and an ultimate Will dominating
the world; and I reach even further still, for I come to
believe in an absolute, supra-personal, intelligent Will
which realizes Itself in the world of reality.

But natural reason leads me only so far, only to God as
the principle and meaning of all things. It does not lead
me to a commerce of life and love with this God, nor can
it tell me whether such a living intercourse is possible.
It is true that creation gives testimony to God's omnipo-
tence, wisdom and goodness; but it does so only so far
as these attributes are mirrored in natural things. It does
not give testimony to the might of His creative love, it
does not let us see into the heart of God. It does not lead
us out beyond the bare data of nature. Is God only the
Creator and Supporter of my being? Or is He more than
that, and would He be more than that? The inner world
of God, who "dwelleth in light inaccessible" (I Tim. vi,
16), remains for us the "mystery kept secret from eternity" (Rom. xvi, 25), unless He reveals Himself to us by
His living word, in an act of the most generous personal
giving and by a manifestation that passes beyond the dead
witness of nature. Thus the inner God, the whole God, the
"mystery which had been hidden from ages and generations" (Col. i, 26) is revealed to us men only by the supernatural way, only by the fact that He Himelf speaks to us.
Such is the Christian's glad tidings: "God, who at sundry
times and in divers manners spoke in times past to the

fathers by the prophets, last of all in these days hath
spoken to us by His Son" (Hebr. i, 1-2).

In Christ the entrance of the Divine into our humanity
became a permanent and blessed reality. "And the Word
was made flesh." This faith in Jesus, in the *Deus Incar-
natus,* is the second pillar which supports the edifice of the
Catholic faith.

But how comes the Catholic to this faith in Jesus, in the
Son of God? When we answer this question there emerges
to view a characteristic element of the Catholic mind, the
overwhelming importance of the Church in the production
of the certitude of faith. The Catholic does not come to
Christ mediately and by literary channels, as by the Scriptural records, but immediately through personal contact
with Christ living in His community. How is this to be
understood?

Certainly he regards the Bible as a sacred book, written
by the hand of God and therefore infallible in its definite,
doctrinal statements. And certainly he accepts with joy
and gratitude the luminous portrait of Jesus that is drawn
by the Gospels. "Without the Scripture," says Möhler,
"the true form of the sayings of Jesus would have been
withheld from us. We should not have known how the
God-man spoke, and I think I should not be able to live
any more, if I ceased to hear Him speak." [1] Yet the
Catholic does not derive his faith in Jesus from the Scriptures. For he had this faith already, before the first
Epistle and before the first Gospel was written. His
faith dates back to St. Peter's confession at Cæsarea
Philippi: "Thou art the Christ, the Son of the living
God."

In loving converse with Jesus, under the influence of
His deep and moving words and His mighty works, but
especially through immediate intercourse with His living
Person, a new thing matured in the little band of His
disciples, the new realisation that the Christ was manifested

[1] *Die Einheit in der Kirche,* 1925, p. 42. The first edition of this remarkable book on the note of "unity" appeared in 1825.

in Jesus. Since men cannot grasp the glory of God in its
naked immediacy, but only in a mirror, only in *ænigmate*,
only in the broken forms of the human and finite, there
was needed a movement from God, a divine illumination, a
new and profounder vision, in order that man might pierce
the created veils and with absolute certainty recognise
the divine in Jesus. Hence the words of our Lord to
Peter: "Flesh and blood have not revealed it to thee, but
my Father who is in heaven." Therefore, at the very
beginning of the history of the Christian faith, there stands
the conviction that not mere reason, nor learning, not even
theological learning, conducts us to the mystery of Jesus,
but the grace of God alone; and that therefore humble,
reverent, and loving openness to the world of the supernatural is more effective than all learned reasoning. "No
one cometh to the Son, unless the Father draw him" (John
vi, 44). In the quest of the divine our attitude must be
one only of expectation and attention, for the adequate
answer comes only from on high. And so there is nothing
more preposterous than to seek to demonstrate the Divinity of Jesus with severe scientific exactitude, in the sense
that even the religiously and morally indifferent, yes even
the morally defective, the egoist and the man immersed in
the things of sense, should be able to lay hold of the Godhead of Jesus with their hands and should no longer
resist the faith. As though faith were a self-evident thing,
as that twice two is four. The infinite and holy God does
not allow Himself to be profaned. He gives Himself only
to those who seek Him with profound reverence. What
sort of a God would He be, who should suffer Himself
to be calculated by anyone, like the sum of the angles of a
triangle, and what sort of Christianity would that be,
whose principal and most zealous adherents—because of
the mathematical demonstrability of the Divinity of Jesus
—must necessarily be the wise and the clever of this world,
the selfish and the self-satisfied, and not the poor in spirit
and the pure of heart! Mystery and grace are of the
essence of the divine. Hence the vast significance of the

words of Jesus: "Flesh and blood have not revealed it to thee, but my Father who is in heaven."

The "mighty wind" of Pentecost kindled that pure glow which was in the breast of Peter into a blazing fire and the fire seized upon all those who surrounded Peter. They no longer merely guessed at their faith; it was an immediate experience and certainty, a certainty stronger than the certainty of Jewish persecution and Roman tyranny. They knew that "this Jesus hath God raised again . . . and He is exalted to the right hand of the Father" (Acts ii, 32, 33). That was the hour of the birth of the new faith and of the new Church. Why did the apostles believe? Because the Holy Spirit opened their eyes and they understood what had gone before: the manifestation of Jesus, His life, death and resurrection. The human form that veiled His Divinity became transparent to them, and now for the first time they all of them in a comprehensive and overwhelming intuition saw "the glory of God in the face of Christ Jesus." All that they had guessed, and hoped, ar l believed of His mystery during His earthly career: all th t was no more than human faith, human and therefore frail certitude. Only at times, as at Cæsarea Philippi (Mt. xvi, 16-17), had a deeper insight come to them. But it had not gripped the whole man, and under the influences of everyday circumstance, especially under the terrors of Good Friday, it soon fled into the remotest recesses of their consciousness. But now, in the fiery glow of their Pentecostal experience, there emerged divine and sanctifying faith. Then all those small and scattered rays combined to form one great radiance, the immediate realisation of the Divinity of Jesus and all that that fact implied. So clear was this intuition and so strong this certainty, that those disciples were utterly changed men. Before, they had been men of little faith, with their continual questioning and their childish egotism; but now they went out into the civilised world full of the spirit of self-sacrifice and strong in soul. And they carried the new fire to the hovels of slaves and into the palaces of emperors. Twelve simple,

uneducated fishermen revolutionised the world, and that
with no other instrument than their new faith and their
readiness to die for that faith.

So the new faith entered upon the stage of history, not
as a human work, but as an elemental experience of the
spirit, as the power of God. The historian will estimate
this experience differently, according to his fundamental
standpoint. But he cannot contest its actuality. And if
he should happen to interpret it otherwise, then the psychologist intervenes and points out that the experience of
Pentecost did not remain an isolated event, but has worked
on the history of the world with unexampled power, and
that a permanent religious union of minds has resulted
from it. Such a permanent union of minds would be
psychologically inexplicable, had not man's fundamental
aptitude for the divine found, and did it not continually
find, precisely in this experience its fulfilment and its satisfaction. So the experience of Pentecost corresponds to a
basic fact of the human spirit, to its aptitude for the
divine, and thereby has an importance that transcends the
particular experience, an importance as wide as humanity.
All other individual religious experiences, such as those of
Simon Magus, of Dositheus, of Elchasai, are lacking in this
distinctive quality of effecting a permanent union of minds.
They vanish from history as quickly as they come, and by
that very fact prove themselves false experiences, possessing no human and universal importance fundamentally
rooted in the spirit of man.

The experience of Pentecost was a torch which was never
again to be extinguished in humanity. That is the decisive fact which the historian may not ignore. On his
own principles the psychologist can conclude that this is no
case of mass-suggestion or hallucination, but a genuine,
pure and original experience, the practical emergence of a
new and higher reality in the consciousness of that Pentecostal community. And unbiassed philosophy can on this
basis establish the supernatural origin of the Pentecostal
experience and so even provide a rational basis for St.

Paul's testimony to the Gospel: "It is the power of God unto salvation for everyone that believeth therein" (Rom. i, 16).

The Pentecostal experience of the first disciples, because it was effected by God, has two characteristics: its comprehensive catholicity and its compact unity. Catholicity, universality, belongs essentially to the divine. Where the divine is, there can be no respect of persons. It cannot be that the reality manifested in Christ should be only for some men and not for others, only for the Jews and not also for the Greeks, only for the civilised world and not also for barbarians. The divine belongs to all, and it requires all. For only in the whole can the divine realise itself, only in the totality of men and not in the individual. One Christian, no Christian. The Pentecostal experience bears this distinctive mark of the divine in its miracle of tongues: "How have we heard every man our own tongue wherein we were born? Parthians and Medes and Elamites, and inhabitants of Mesopotamia, Judea and Cappodocia" (Acts ii, 7). In the same moment that the new faith entered the world it was a faith that embraced all mankind, a Catholic faith. The church that was to be, was proclaimed in all tongues.* And this catholicity was a catholicity of unity. They were all assembled around the apostolic college, around the one Peter. And they all understood one another. One God, one Christ, one faith, one language. Fulness in unity, unity in fulness—so did the new faith enter the world.

And how did it go through the world, how did it come to us, to me? Not otherwise than as it came to the apostles: through the living word and through the quickening Spirit.

We know that Jesus prepared His disciples for the miracle of Pentecost through His living word alone. And His disciples too wished to be nought else but "eye-witnesses and first ministers of the word" (Luke i, 2). We

---

* *Futura ecclesia in omnibus linguis praenuntiabatur* (S. Aug. Sermo CCLXVI, 2).

see them at once, after the miracle of Pentecost, proclaiming the Gospel and giving testimony to Christ "in Jerusalem and Judea and in Samaria and even unto the ends of the earth" (Acts i, 8). Certainly some of them composed historical records of the life of Jesus and of the acts of the chief apostles. And they wrote also letters to single persons and communities, wherein they set forth the Christian teaching and the Christian life according to the enquiries and the special circumstances of those to whom they wrote. Yet these written communications were only supplementary to their oral preaching, sometimes in confirmation of it or preparatory to it. Even the Epistles to the Romans, Ephesians and Hebrews, in spite of their more general range, are concerned particularly with the special needs of the people to whom they are addressed, and make no sort of claim to be an exhaustive exposition of the Christian faith. So little thought was given to any final literary expression of the Gospel, that some apostles left no writing whatever after them and that apostolical writings could even disappear (1 Cor. v, 9; Coloss. iv, 16).

Therefore above all it was the living word which was to bring the new faith to mankind. "The things which thou hast heard of me before many witnesses, the same commend to faithful men who shall be fit to teach others also" (2 Tim. ii, 2). Such was St. Paul's charge to his disciple Timothy. But even the living word did not achieve the work itself. That word effected only human faith, a purely human certitude. The supernatural, final, highest certitude came from the working of the Spirit. And since the Holy Spirit, since the divine of its nature communicates itself to all men, to the collective whole, and is of its very creative and enkindling life, therefore the Holy Spirit of its nature works only in and through a comprehensive, living community, through the unity of love, through the unity in fulness. The catholicity and unity of the Pentecostal miracle were permanently embodied in the spirit of love and fellowship of the Christian communities, animated by Christ and gathered round the apostles and Peter especially. These communities were "one heart and one soul," planted by one apostolical preaching, brought to interior growth by one Holy Spirit. This Spirit was sacramentally guaranteed to them in the visible signs of Baptism and Confirmation. Baptism gave admission into the new spiritual fellowship, and the sacrament of Confirmation sealed and perfected this admission. This Spirit deepened the natural effect of the apostolic preaching and led to the intuitive experience that "the Lord is a Spirit" (2 Cor. iii, 17).

Therefore it was not literary records, incontestable documents, which were the primary means of bringing the message of Jesus to men, but the broad stream of the uniform life of faith of the primitive Church, a life based on the preaching of the apostles and animated by the Holy Spirit. How could it have been otherwise? A living thing, in all its depth and in all its extent, cannot be comprised within a few written sentences. Only that which is dead can be adequately delineated in writing. The living thing is continually bursting the temporary form in which literature must perforce embody it. At the very moment that literature is endeavouring to arrest and fix it, the stream of life is escaping and moving swiftly on. Therefore all literature, and even the Bible itself, is stamped with the character of its time, and bears a form which, however vital its content remains, yet all too easily seems stiff and strange to later generations.

And so the writings of apostles and evangelists point beyond themselves to the supernatural life of faith of the primitive Church, whence they themselves grew. The New Testament does not stand outside this life of faith as a special and independent source; it stands within this life. It is supported and dominated by this life, for there were many Christian communities already in existence before any apostle took up his pen. Consequently the Bible possesses no independent authority apart from the faith of the Church. Through all the chinks and crevices of the New Testament we descry the gleam of the living waters of the broad stream of the primitive faith, which supports the Bible and from which alone the Bible gets its stability, as it does its final interpretation. The Gospels present us with only a fragmentary record of Jesus, from which it is impossible to construct an exhaustive picture. And so I learn the complete Christ, not from the Bible, but from the uniform life of faith of the whole Church, a life fertilized by the teaching of the apostles. Without the living, uniform tradition of the Church, essential elements in the picture of Christ would remain either enigmatical or hidden from me. And without it I could achieve neither an historical nor a religious sympathy with Jesus. Such is the meaning of that profound saying of St. Augustine: "I would not believe the Gospel, did not the authority of the Church move me." [*]

The new life, flowing out from the apostolic communities, spread ever wider and wider, and impregnated the world. The preaching authority was taken over from the dying apostles by disciples who had been commissioned by them and appointed as presidents and overseers of the Christian communities. This fact is plainly attested by history. And from these disciples right down to our own day there runs a continuous line of preachers holding this apostolical commission. And along with this authoritative line there arose the space-time fellowship of the faithful, that is the Church. The unity of the apostolic preaching was maintained by steady contact wtih the churches founded by the apostles, especially by contact with Rome, where Peter proclaimed this message and was buried in his martyr's grave. With the unity of the apostolic preaching was con-

---

[*] *Ego vero evangelio non crederem, nisi me catholicae ecclesiae commoveret auctoritas (Contra ep. Manichaei, c. V).*

He too teaches that Christ is to be grasped only through the Church, His body. cf. *De fide rerum quae non videntur,* III, 5: *Proinde, qui putatis nulla esse indicia, cur de Christo credere debeatis quae non vidistis, attendite quae videtis: ipsa vos ecclesia ore maternæ dilectionis alloquitur . . . me attendite, vobis dicit ecclesia, me attendite quam videtis, etiamsi videre nolitis.* Similarly in Sermo CXVI, 6: *Quomodo illi (sc. apostoli) illum (sc. Christum) videbant et de corpore credebant, sic nos corpus videmus, de capite credamus.*

joined the unity, the space-time community of the Holy Spirit. The Pentecostal community broadened out into the universal Church. Certainly, in the rude struggle for existence, its external forms became more rigid and it became more fully organized. But, for all that, it remained ever the same Spirit and the same Body. The same apostolic authority preaches the same Christ, and it is the same fellowship of love, the unity in fulness animated by the Spirit, by which this preaching gives to every individual the certitude of immediate experience.

And so I grasp the living Christ by means of the living Church. That is as true to-day as it was on the first day. My faith in Christ is given me antecedently and preparatorily by the living apostolic word, perfectly and fulfillingly by the living Pentecostal Spirit. Like the apostles, the Church in her living teaching sets before me the image of the Lord, as the Bible luminously portrays Him, and as she has borne Him still more lovingly and radiantly for centuries in her heart. In a full and true sense she can say that she herself has seen this Jesus, that she stood beneath His Cross, and that she heard His Easter greeting: Peace be to you. Therefore she brings me into the closest historical relation to Jesus. She eliminates time from His picture, and she puts me in religious contact with Him. She can point out that the message of Jesus is not only recorded in precious documents, but is sealed by the life-blood of thousands, is experienced as a living message by millions even in our own time, and has given thousands of her sons and daughters a new heart and a new conscience. She can assert further that no other religion has ever approached even distantly the moral and religious sublimity of Christianity. And she can maintain that the radiance of this divinity flashes forth and is externally manifested to-day also in noble saintly figures, that it attests itself in graces that appear ever and again with new brilliance, and in miraculous gifts.

Since her apostolic word proclaims and attests this and much else, the Church can make credible to me the super-

natural mystery of Jesus. Her preaching prepares the
way for my faith in Jesus. Her testimony becomes in that
measure a motive of credibility, as the School expresses it,
but is not yet a true motive of faith. It gives me human
faith, a certitude which is not as yet absolute, which is
still frail.

But to living word is added the Spirit, the inspiration of
the one divine Spirit in the communion of the faithful.
That Spirit, and that Spirit alone, deepens my moral certitude, my human faith, produced by the teaching of the
Church, and makes it absolute, strongest, divine faith, the
experience of Pentecost. The more closely the Catholic
gets into touch with his Church, not merely externally,
but internally, with her prayer and sacrifice, with her word
and sacrament, the more sensitive and attentive will he
be to the inspiration of the divine Spirit in the community,
the more vitally will he grasp the divine life that flows
through the organism of the Church. And when he thinks
and prays, suffers and strives with the living Church,
then he experiences a broadening, deepening and fulfilling
of his whole being. And so he acquires a personal and
direct certitude that it is the very Life of all life by which
he is sustained, that verily, as St. Paul expresses this
experience, "the Lord is a Spirit" (2 Cor. iii, 17). This
certitude is a personal experience, the most personal experience that he has. He may delineate and describe it in
rational language, though very crudely and imperfectly,
but he cannot impart it to any other. For it is derived
from that complete personal contact of his soul with the
Spirit of Jesus that inspires the Christian community.
But because it is a certitude that he has tested for himself,
no man, no doubt, no ridicule can deprive him of it.
Therefore, to be absolutely exact, I do not believe the
Church, but the living God, who attests Himself to me
in the Church. Nor is it I that believe, but the Holy
Spirit that is in me. The Catholic grasps and affirms
Jesus ultimately and decisively in the flowing life of His
Church, in the Church as the mystical Body of Christ.

Here certainly lies the sharpest line of demarcation separating the faith of a Catholic from that of a Protestant, or rather, separating the Catholic faith from that purely rationalistic apprehension of Christ which is establishing itself among the disciples of the so-called critical theology.

That critical theology, the child of the age of "enlightenment" and mistakenly committed to that scientific method which is prescribed for the profane sciences by their special subject matter, behaves as though Christianity is and must be a mere object of knowledge, a mere subject for scientific investigation, as though the living Christian faith could be resolved into a series of ideas and notions which might be examined, considered and classified according to their provenance. Christianity then becomes, not unitary, original and abounding life, but a juxtaposition of ideas and conceptions, which, deriving from the most various sources, have gradually by the power of collective faith gathered round the single person of Jesus of Nazareth and contributed to shape our image of Him. Such is the rationalistic foundation of the critical theology, and it rests on a bad misunderstanding of the nature of religion in general and of Christianity in particular. For the most important representatives of the latest religious psychology—I refer to James, Österreich, Scheler, Scholz—have established it as a fact accepted even by the non-religious that religion is something spontaneous and not a derivative thing, that it is a fundamental fact of the human spirit and therefore original, unitary life, and not mere thinking, a life that has its own legitimacy, its own inner unity and purpose. It is quite wrong to estimate a religion solely according to its conceptual content, or even according to this or that dominant idea alone, and not rather to regard the totality of the vital forms that spring from it in past, present and future. If this be true of religion in general, it is far more true of the life of Christ and of Christianity. As the history of Christianity shows, it is a life, which manifesting its power first in the Person of Jesus, not merely laid hold of the restricted group of His disciples, but in an incredibly short space of time gripped the whole ancient world and brought into being new civilisations, new peoples, new men, and which still alive and effectual among us, attests itself to our own day as a perennial source of spiritual life. We know of no spiritual movement on the earth which has worked upon men with such elemental power—and that of its own nature and being, and not through any external, foreign factors—so unitarily, comprehensively, fruitfully and vitally as has Christianity.

And since such is the case with it, since Christianity is not mere cold thought, but a unitary religious life, a fulness of life, it is therefore an obvious error to do as the critical theology is ever seeking to do, and to conceive this life in terms of certain stale notions and catch-words, such as that of the Fatherhood of God, or of inwardness, or the near coming of the Kingdom, and to talk of a Christianity of Christ, or the primitive community, of the Hellenistic communities, and of a Johannine or Pauline Christianity, as though these were not expressions and manifestations of the one original life of Christ, but rather complexes of new ideas, of their nature alien to Christianity and derived from external sources. In reality Christianity is an intimate organic unity, a vital unity, which unfolds itself indeed to its fulness progressively, and yet in all the stages of its unfolding is a unity and a whole, the Christianity of Christ. Just as I first appreciate the totality of that potential life which is in the acorn when I see before me the mature oak, fully developed in all its grandeur, in a way that no mere study of the embryology of the acorn can enable me to realise it, so can I first discern the width and depth of Christ's Gospel, the whole vast richness of His mind and His message, His "fulness," when I have before me the fully-developed Christianity, and then only in the measure in which I appreciate its inner unity. The history of dogma has established these three facts: First, that Catholic Christianity has developed in a direct line, without interruption and without violent distortion. Secondly, that this development has not been effected by individual enthusiasm or individual inspiration, but by the one spirit of the whole Christian community, guided by the apostolic teaching. The conception of the community fashioning dogma as so much fable and myth is an absurd one and there can be no room for such a wild phantom within the line of the apostolic succession and within the one living community spirit. And in the third place, it is evident that Catholic Christianity has throughout the centuries anxiously resisted all that appeared to its consciousness as innovation, that it has held fast doggedly and rigidly to that which was handed down, and that it has observed as a sacred trust the injunction of the apostle to Timothy, "Guard that which has been committed to thee" (2 Tim. i, 14). History attests with exactitude, from Ignatius onwards, the principle of apostolicity, of most rigid conservatism, of utterly scrupulous continuity with the traditional revelation. So there is in Catholic Christianity a unitary life-stream, a life of unity in fulness, a single mighty life. And if I would determine the content of the original cell of this life, the content of the Christianity of Christ, I must not approach the tree of Christianity with the knife of the critic and mutilate it in order to discover this original cell. On the contrary I must accept the Christian life as a whole and appraise it as a whole. Unlimited criticism, faulty and sterile historical or philological research: these things do not conduct us to the mystery of Christ. But we attain to Him by steeping ourselves lovingly in the abundance of life which has gone forth from Him, which has attested its inner organic unity throughout the centuries, and which to-day as in the beginning is nothing else, desires to be nothing else, than a life lived in the strength of Christ, a Christian life.

It is thus only that the whole revelation in general acquires meaning for me. If it be really true that there is a personal God—and there is such a God, for our whole spirit is rooted in Him—and if it be really true that this living God—for the very reason that He is a personal God

—willed to manifest Himself to be immediately and personally in Jesus Christ, then it cannot be that I should need, for the attainment of this infinitely important, saving reality, laborious historical and philological study, that I should have to appeal to the Higher and Lower Criticism in order to reach the divine mystery. For then the divine would not be simple and plain enough to penetrate into my heart and into the hearts of all men, even the least and simplest. But this simplicity and this plainness are found in the quiet, living faith, in the loyal and strong hope, in the devoted fellowship and love of the Church, which in her dogma, morals and worship breathes the Spirit of Jesus, and which in spite of persecution, sin and evil has for so many centuries with continually new strength borne testimony to Him. "Where two or three are gathered together in My name, there am I in the midst of them." Not three only, but millions of loving and loyal hearts—though there be tares among them—are united in this one Church in the name of Jesus. Therefore is Jesus verily in the midst of them.

ST. FRANCIS PREPARATORY SEMINARY
BETHANY, OKLA.

CHAPTER V

THE FOUNDATION OF THE CHURCH IN THE LIGHT OF THE TEACHING OF JESUS

"I am come, not to destroy but to fulfil" (Mt. v, 17).

WITH the experience of Pentecost the new faith and the new fellowship of the faith entered history. Must we therefore regard the Church simply as the creation of the Spirit of Pentecost, the offspring of the faith, ultimately as the work of the glorified Christ manifesting Himself in the faithful, or does the Church go back to a positive and immediate foundation by the "historical" Jesus Himself?

The question is important not only for the more accurate definition of the aims and intentions of Jesus and therefore for the complete understanding of His historical figure, but also and more urgently for the authentication of the claims of the Church. The Pentecostal experience of the disciples would have been without roots, had it not been preceded by their historical association with Jesus, which prepared the way for their faith. And, similarly, the authority of the Church would be without a secure historical basis, if it were derived only from purely supernatural experiences. "Grace presupposes nature," which in this case means that the supernatural experiences presuppose historical facts. Experiences which rest in no way upon natural facts, cannot lay claim to any absolute validity, because they cannot be tested and controlled. The Catholic Church is therefore vitally interested in the establishment of the fact that she was not called into

63

SPIRITUAL LIBRARY
ST. FRANCIS SEMINARY
OKLAHOMA CITY, OKLA.

existence exclusively by the Pentecostal faith of the disciples, but that she is rooted in the thoughts and intentions of Jesus, which may be historically ascertained. She is the creation not only of the glorified, but of the "historical" Jesus.

The so-called "critical" theology positively denies any direct connection between Jesus and the Church. It regards it as scientifically proved that "Jesus of Nazareth did not found the universal Church of later centuries. There is no inward connection between Jesus and the Roman Church; they are separated by a profound gulf." [1] Yet it does not wish to deny that the deep gulf between Jesus and the Church is "exiguous and narrow," and that it even 'seems in the end to close entirely." "The interval of time between Jesus and Catholicism is exceedingly small. The Christianity of the apostolic age is incipient Catholicism, and the catholicizing of Christianity begins immediately after the death of Jesus." [2]

Now that is a somewhat strange position. A mere historian might well be forgiven if he considered it odd that there should be a gulf between Jesus and the Church which is so narrow that it "seems in the end to close up entirely." It might well appear marvellous to him that the first disciples of the Lord, those who had seen and heard Him and must have known His mind, should "immediately after His death" set about catholicizing Christianity. And one might suspect, on *a priori* grounds, that there was some mistake in the "critical" argument. In order to get the matter clear, let us first examine our Lord's relations with Jewish worship and the Jewish Church, so that we may determine His attitude towards institutional religion. And, secondly, let us examine the fundamental ideas of His Gospel and see if they are really inconsistent with His foundation of a church. In this connexion we propose to examine the scriptural texts themselves which testify to a direct foundation of the Church by Jesus.

No historian denies that Judaism in the time of our Lord

[1] Heiler, op. cit., p. 43.   [2] *Ibid.*

possessed definite rites and an authoritative priesthood
which performed and safeguarded those rites.   Heiler is
correct in asserting that the Jewish society in which Jesus
lived and worked exhibited on its religious side "a striking
similarity to Catholic ecclesiasticism." *   What was our
Lord's attitude towards this Jewish Church?

On one point there is surely agreement, namely, that
Jesus should not be regarded—in the manner of many
romances of the past and present—as an aggressive reformer, who raised the standard of spiritual religion and
the love of God and attacked all external ordinances.   On
this point the evidence of the Gospels is too plain.   So
we are left to ask—and the question is in fact so formulated—whether Jesus did not by the novelty of His teaching, that is to say indirectly, undermine and uproot these
external ordinances, and so annul and abolish them.

The attitude of Jesus towards the authoritative teaching
of Judaism, as laid down in the Torah, is decisively indicated in His emphatic declaration (Mt. v, 17-18): "Do not
think that I am come to destroy the law or the prophets.
I am come not to destroy, but to fulfil.   For amen I say
unto you, till heaven and earth pass, one jot or one tittle
shall not pass of the law, till all be fulfilled."   We have in
this passage a genuine utterance of our Lord's, for St.
Luke also, who has in his whole attitude some of St. Paul's
hostility towards the Law, gives this important saying, and
puts it in the distinctive form: "It is easier for heaven and
earth to pass, than one tittle of the law to fall" (xvi, 17).

Therefore our Lord's attitude towards the Mosaic Law,
which comprehended both moral regulations and an abundance of liturgical ordinances, was by no means one of
indifference, or one of unwilling tolerance.   He is come
for this purpose, and regards it as an essential part of His
task, not to destroy the Law, but to fulfil it, down to its
last iota.   He explains in what sense He conceived this fulfilment in the verses which follow immediately, in which
He presses for a fully spiritual interpretation of the com-

* *Ibid.*, p. 25.

mandments of the Law. "It was said to them of old:
Thou shalt not kill. But I say to you that whosoever is
angry with his brother shall be in danger of the judgment."
So that He conceives the fulfilment of the Law as a moral
and religious deepening of it, or, more precisely, as its permeation by love of God and of one's neighbour. Nothing
whatsoever, He teaches, should be done in a merely external fashion, just because it is the Law. Everything should
be done on interior principle, under the inspiration of the
love of God and of one's neighbour. For on these two
commandments "dependeth the whole law and the prophets"
(Mk. xii, 29 = Mt. xxii, 40). The six examples which
Jesus gives all inculcate whole-hearted observance of these
commandments. Indeed, such is His insistence on the law
of love that He is compelled four times to break the letter
of the Mosaic Law. He sets Himself above even the
authority of Moses; yet not in order to deny or destroy
that law absolutely, but only to elucidate and fulfil it in its
innermost meaning. The fulfilment of the Law means, in
His eyes, that we should penetrate to the full depth of the
divine intention and that we should bring out the truest
and most profound meaning of the Law. Every legal
ordinance is to be tested by this whole-hearted fulfilment
of the two-fold law of love, and this is our Golden Rule.

Jesus subordinates the Mosaic law of the Sabbath to
this rule. So long as the love of one's neighbour is not
affected, this law remains obligatory; but if the two run
counter to each other, and His hungry disciples are forbidden to pluck the ears of corn because it is the Sabbath,
then the law must be subordinated to charity. "For the
Sabbath was made for man, and not man for the Sabbath" (Mk. ii, 27).

And the same is the case with the Jewish sacrifices.
Jesus twice cites the words of Osee (vi, 6): "I will have
mercy and not sacrifice" (Mt. ix, 13; xii, 7). But both
times His object is the same, namely, to spiritualise the
current practice. God is a God of mercy. The man who
offers God a sacrifice and yet is not merciful, does not

offer a sacrifice which is acceptable in the sight of the All-merciful. The same idea is developed and illustrated in the Sermon on the Mount: "If therefore thou offer thy gift at the altar, and there thou remember that thy brother hath anything against thee, leave there thine offering before the altar, and go first to be reconciled to thy brother; and then coming thou shalt offer thy gift" (Mt. v, 23). Jesus does not wish to abolish sacrifice. He says expressly: "Come and offer thy gift." But it must be a sacrifice inspired by love and performed in love. When our Lord attacks the Pharisees and with prophetic zeal scourges them for their merely external observance, we should expect, if the views of the critical theologians are correct, that His words would breathe hostility to the Jewish ecclesiastical system and to its ritual law. We find, on the contrary, that His revolt against the pharisaical spirit is inspired by the profoundest respect for the temple and its worship. "The temple that sanctifieth the gold is greater than the gold, and the altar that sanctifieth the gift is greater than the gift. Whosoever shall swear by the temple, he sweareth by him that dwelleth in it" (Mt. xxiii, 17 ff.). Indeed, He regards the temple and its service as so holy, that when He sees it profaned by the money-changers and sellers of doves, He is roused to anger and takes up a scourge of cords (Mk. xi, 17; Jn. ii, 15). True, the temple was not the most sacred thing, nor was it to endure for ever. "There shall not be left a stone upon a stone." He Himself was the manifestation of something greater than the temple. When His work was complete, then the Father would be no longer adored in Sion only, but "everywhere in spirit and in truth."

His attitude towards the temple and its sacrifices is in fact distinguished, like His attitude towards the Mosaic Law, by a striving after interior, spiritual values. He destroys only in so far as the inner law makes destruction necessary. And in so far as the rabbinical dogma that the temple of Sion was eternal and the only legitimate place of worship, was at variance with His spiritual teaching, He resisted this Jewish attempt to give the temple such an absolute position; but He did not quarrel with the temple itself or its worship.

The same fundamental emphasis on spiritual religion dominates His attitude towards the Jewish authorities. It is true that He is kindled to a holy indignation by the hypocrites and blind guides among the Scribes and Pharisees, who tithed mint and cummin, but neglected what was more important in the Law: justice and mercy and faith (Mt. xxiii, 4 ff.). Yet the very preface to this vehement attack makes it plain that His protest is directed, not against the chair of Moses itself, but against the blind guides who sit in it. Here Jesus distinguishes expressly between the teaching and the teacher, or, as we should say, between the office and the person. "All things therefore, whatsoever they shall say to you, observe and do; but according to their works do ye not" (Mt. xxiii, 3). Therefore Jesus intends to preserve the principle of a teaching authority as such, and attacks only the perverse manner in which the Scribes and Pharisees realised this principle. To be sure, so far as this perversity was rooted in the nature of pharisaism, His attack on the blind guides becomes an attack on the institution itself, but it is not an attack on the principle of a teaching authority as such. On the contrary He expressly adopts and commends this principle in the same context: "Let one only be your Master, Christ" (Mt. xxiii, 10). And in so far as the disciples have to spread the teaching of Jesus, they, and St. Peter especially, are the appointed teachers of the kingdom of heaven.

The more we examine the matter the clearer it becomes that our Lord's attitude towards the Old Law is neither abrupt rejection, nor unwilling tolerance, nor entire acceptance. It is rather the attitude of one who wishes to complete and fulfil this Law, that is to say, a conditional acceptance. Because in the Judaism of the Pharisees the Law, the worship of the temple, and the official teaching had become externalised and divorced from spiritual and moral values, therefore Jesus could oppose only a decisive "No" to this rabbinical perversion of the Mosaic Church. "No man puts a new piece to an old garment, no man puts new wine into old bottles." To that extent Jesus is a conscious reformer. But in so far as the Judaism of His time rested on ordinances which were sanctified by the authority of Moses and aimed at the moral improvement of men, He acknowledges their inner value unequivocally. "These things you ought to have done, and not to have left the other undone" (Mt. xxiii, 23). That is the formula in which He Himself describes His fundamental attitude towards the Law of Moses.

Therefore it is not true to say that Jesus inwardly rejected all ritual, liturgical and hierarchical elements, and merely suffered that sort of thing as so much "background," without positively accepting it. In saying this the "critical" theologians fall all too readily into the error of defining our Lord's teaching exclusively in terms of its novel elements. But the truth is that the new rests on the old and is not to be separated from it. The teaching of Jesus is incomplete without both old and new. The basis of His teaching is no purely spiritual one, but it is the broad basis of the Old Testament religion handed down from Moses and the prophets, a basis which included both sensible and supra-sensible elements, both worship and morality, both a hierarchy and the individual conscience. It was upon this basis that He erected His new things; or rather, He fulfilled the old and made it into the new. His teaching has a character of "unification, simplification and concentration"[4] in so far as He subordinated all external ordinances and regulations to the one thing necessary, the love of God and our neighbour. He restored to worship a guiding principle, gave it back its soul, its moral and religious significance. But, in doing that, He was restoring its original form and its true meaning as an expression and instrument of the supra-sensible. He did

[4] *Ibid.*, p. 35.

not destroy worship, but revived it. The old became new, and there was made one new thing.

We cannot, therefore, conclude from our Lord's attitude towards the Jewish Church, that He would have regarded the Catholic Church also as only so much background which had to be tolerated. For those very things which Jesus found lacking in rabbinical worship and teaching, namely, true spiritual religion and the love of God and of one's neighbour, these things are, as has been seen in the previous chapters, of the essence of the Catholic Church. The dogma, morality and worship of the Church are Christo-centric, are spirit and life, and her organism is nothing else than applied love. There is in the Catholic Church nothing that is, or may be, purely external, without inner connection with the love of God and of one's neighbour. By visible things to the invisible: that is the fundamental principle of the whole system of the Church, and it is the principle also which inspired our Lord's attitude towards Judaism.

But though it be granted that His hostility to the Pharisees is not incompatible with His founding a Church, yet is not the rest of His teaching inspired by ideas which cannot be reconciled with such a design? Did not Jesus believe that the end of the world was at hand and that the Kingdom of God would come down from heaven in His own generation? The so-called "eschatological" school in particular lays great stress on this idea. It regards this "recognition of the eschatological character of the Gospel of Jesus" as the "Copernican fact of modern theology." "It overthrows the dogmatic structure of Catholicism with a single blow and unhinges the colossal fabric of the Roman Church."[5] If Jesus believed that the end was near, He cannot have regarded His group of disciples as a lasting community, and He cannot have committed to them more than a purely personal authority. If, then, we wish to secure the historical foundations of the Catholic Church, we must face this eschatological question squarely. The

[5] *Ibid.*, p. 3.

problem may be resolved, for precision's sake, into two
particular questions. In the first place, we may ask, is the
Kingdom of God which Jesus announced a purely celestial
thing, which descends miraculously from heaven at a definite point in time, or a Kingdom which has its commencement and its roots in our world and in our time, but which
will reach its maturity and perfection only in the world to
come? It is obvious that Jesus can have intended to found
a Church, in the natural sense of those words, only in the
latter case. The second question is intimately connected
with this and is as follows: Did Jesus really share the
error of certain apocalyptic circles of His time and surroundings, and believe that the Day of the Lord was very
near at hand? If that be so, then again He cannot have
founded a lasting Church. Let us now consider the first
of these two questions.

Even the "critical" school must acknowledge that the
theory that Jesus had in mind only a purely celestial Kingdom, which was to come down from heaven on to this
earth—a theory first advocated by Reimar, then developed by Johannes Weiss and finally completed by Albert
Schweitzer—cannot be supported by scientific theology.
A glance at the Gospels is enough to convince any fair-
minded person that Jesus was not an apocalyptic. Weinel
is right in declaring that He belongs to the "main stream
of Jewish moral and prophetic thought, and not to any
eccentric movement or narrow coterie." * He is interested
in the accomplishment of the Kingdom of God in the
living man of the present. His thought is for the "poor,"
for those outside the law, for sinners, the sick, children
and for those who hunger for justice. He desired to sow
the seed of God's word in their hearts, the gospel of
absolute trust in the father, of love and humility even
to the sacrifice of one's life, of inwardness even to the
foundations of thought and desire. He regards the Kingdom of God as the incarnation on earth of purity, holiness
and inwardness; as a thing thoroughly ethical in character.

* H. Weinel, *Biblische Theologie des Neuen Testaments*, 1918, p. 82.

And so He tells the Pharisees expressly that the Kingdom of God cannot be observed and controlled like some astronomical phenomenon. "The Kingdom of God cometh not with observation. Neither shall they say: Behold here, or behold there." On the contrary, "the Kingdom of God is within you" (Lk. xvii, 20, 21). It is an inward spiritual force, it is a governance by God, which is already striking root all unheeded among the Jews, and which, in spite of its present smallness and in spite of all external obstacles, is asserting itself irresistibly like the mustard seed or the leaven (Mt. xiii, 31), or the grain which grows of itself (Mk. iv, 26 ff.). And Jesus is clearly conscious that the realisation of this divine governance on the earth, this incipient incarnation of holiness and purity, is essentially connected with His Person. Men cannot be born again by means of mere ideas, but only by the profound power of the original, personal and divine life itself. Jesus knows that this fulfilment is achieved in Himself, that He is more than Jona and a greater than Solomon (Mt. xii, 41, 42). The old era ends with John, the greatest of those born of women. The new era, the Kingdom of Heaven, has come. Therefore the least in this Kingdom of Heaven is greater than John (Mt. xi, 11). Jesus can testify: I saw Satan like lightning falling from heaven (Lk. x, 18). The strong man is bound and the Kingdom of Heaven has free passage (cf. Mt. xii, 29). To the doubters who asked for external proofs, He pointed to His deeds of power against the demons: "If I by the Spirit of God cast out devils, then is the Kingdom of God come upon you" (Mt. xii, 28). He Himself is the Kingdom. And this Kingdom is already beginning to send forth its first young shoots, men with trustful, childlike faith, the humble and loving souls of a Zacchaeus or a Mary Magdalen, and disciples who are ready to sell all to obtain the pearl of great price. And even the Scribe, who understands the law of love, is not far from this Kingdom (Mk. xii, 34). These and other Gospel texts place it beyond doubt that the Kingdom announced by Jesus is already present, not merely like "clouds that cast their shadows on the earth" (Johannes Weiss), but like a light that shines in the darkness (cf. Mt. iv, 16), which fights its way through to full day.   The light must break through, and it is precisely in this process that the true character of the present Kingdom of God is manifested.   For that Kingdom is not yet fulfilled.   It has still to struggle with the evil forces of the world.   It is like the field of wheat in which an enemy sowed cockle over night (Mt. xiii, 24).   It is like the net in which good and bad fish are caught together.   It is not yet finished and complete, but a compound of worthy and unworthy elements, which awaits the final selection, the harvest, the separation of spirits.

It is at this point that we meet that other aspect of our Lord's preaching of the Kingdom, its eschatological tendency and its preoccupation with the end of the world and the Judgment.   The present Kingdom of God, because it is essentially unfinished, points beyond itself to that consummation, when all tares shall be removed and when the Kingdom of God shall appear in all purity as the newly perfected Kingdom of those loving souls who in the Name of Jesus have fed the hungry and given drink to the thirsty.

When Jesus employs the phrase "Kingdom of God" in its full meaning, He is thinking of this future Kingdom wherein God's rule is perfected.   The beatitudes speak of this future Kingdom, and so does the prayer of the Paternoster, "Thy Kingdom come."   In many of His parables and in explicit promises He directs the hearts and minds of His disciples to this great thing that is to come.   Let your loins be girt, let your lamps be ready in your hands, the bridegroom cometh!   This hope gives His message an immense power to enkindle and stir men's souls.   It allows no easy acquiescence in the present, but requires us to be ever up and stirring, ready for the great hour.   Now, that our Lord's teaching, on its eschatological side, culminated in this emphasis on the future Kingdom and the Judgment, cannot be seriously debated.   But it is a far harder matter to determine from the Gospels His exact

conception of the coming of the Last Day. Did he conceive it as an abrupt and catastrophic event, or as the
gradual development of divine destructive forces which
effected the Judgment in their process?

But one thing is certain, that Jesus taught plainly that
the Kingdom which He had established in the immediate
present was as yet embryonic, the least of all seeds, a
tiny leaven, and that it was to pass from this embryonic
state into full life and strength only after His death and
because of His death, by a wondrous interposition of God.
"And I, if I be lifted up from the earth, will draw all
things to myself" (Jn. xii, 32). Not only St. John and
St. Paul, but the Synoptics also know of our Lord's promise that after His death a great new thing was to happen,
the visitation of the disciples by the Holy Ghost, "by the
power from on high," as St. Luke says (xxiv, 49), by the
"Consoler," as St. John calls Him. It is the plain conviction of early Christianity that this promise was fulfilled
in the "mighty wind" of Pentecost, and that the small,
embryonic Kingdom of God was then first awakened into
full and fruitful life, into a life that was to fill the whole
world.

From this we may conclude that our Lord's hope for the
future was not concerned with the Last Day as an isolated
event, but was concerned also with all those events which
are essentially and actually connected with it and which
lead up to the great separation of spirits: in particular,
with His death and resurrection, with the outpouring of
the Holy Ghost, with the founding of the universal Church,
and—as necessarily belonging to this—with the abolition
of the Old Covenant and the downfall of Jerusalem. Precisely because Jesus knew that the Kingdom of God was
already established in His own Person, because it was a
central fact of His consciousness that the great separation
of spirits, the judgment of the world, had already begun
in His Person, He necessarily regarded all the events that
depended upon His Person as particular moments of the
General Judgment which was fundamentally and practically

inaugurated with His Person. And so, regarding and valuing things in a prophetic manner, He made no distinction between to-day and to-morrow. He did not concern Himself with the position of events in time and history; but in a single, powerful intuition comprehended their essential character, their real inner unity and their connection with His Person. The whole future, the destruction of Jerusalem as well as the establishment and expansion of His Church, was to Him the present, the present of His judgment. So His expectation of the Last Day embraced future generations along with His own, and He could threaten His own generation with the Coming of the Son of Man.

When is the exact day, the precise hour of His coming? If we formulate the question thus, we feel at once that it is an idle question, and we realise how impossible it is to believe that the Lord Jesus depicted in the Gospels, whose mind was so concentrated on the essential and real, not on the "when" but on the "what," ever expounded a chronology.

On the contrary it is to His disciples that we must attribute the attempt to fix dates. The age was inclined to apocalyptic speculation, and the disciples, influenced by its curious anticipations, were especially interested in the "when," that is to say, in the external and chronological aspect of our Lord's eschatology. And so, when they heard Jesus talking of the Last Day, they were disposed to conceive the main elements of His announcement, not according to the inner and essential connexion in which He regarded them, but from a purely chronological standpoint, and so to weaken the whole force of His prophecy. And the evangelists manifest the simple fidelity of their record in nothing more plainly than in this, that in their manner of correlating our Lord's eschatological pronouncements with one another and with His other discourses, they represent the special interpretation, influenced as it was by traditional conceptions, which the disciples originally gave to the teaching of Jesus. Our Lord Himself expressly and finally refused to make any pronouncement regarding the day and hour of the Last Day. When the disciples asked Him when the sign of His coming and of the end of the world would appear (Mk. xiii, 4), Jesus declared without qualification: "Of that day or hour no man knoweth, neither the angels in heaven, nor the Son, but the Father alone" (Mk. xiii, 32). This is one of the most certain of all the sayings of our Lord. For a later generation, when theologians had already begun to develop a systematic christology, would scarcely have ventured upon a statement so liable to misconstruction, as that even the Son did not know the day of the Judgment. We should therefore interpret all other sayings of Jesus in the light of this certain utterance. Jesus does not, as He might have done, answer His disciples with a pure distinction. He does not say that the Son of Man will assuredly come soon, but that the exact hour of His coming depends on the Father. His answer is rather an unqualified and plain "I know not." And therefore that statement of His which immediately precedes these words, that "this generation shall not pass until all these things be done," cannot refer to the definite day and hour of the General Judgment, but only to the events mentioned in His discourse, to those events introductory to the Judgment which were to occur in His own generation, and especially to the destruction of Jerusalem. Had Jesus contemplated an immediate coming of the Last Judgment, He would not have mentioned in the same discourse another series of signs which could not possibly be fulfilled in His own generation, such as fierce international wars, famines, earthquakes, universal hostility to Christians, the appearance of many false prophets, the preaching of the Gospel in the whole world (Mt. xxiv, 5 ff.). A very short time before His death, when the sinner of Bethania anointed Him, He returned to the last of these prophecies: "Wheresoever this gospel shall be preached in the whole world, that also which she hath done shall be told for a memory of her" (Mt. xxvi, 13). So Jesus contemplates a universal crisis which will last a very long time and include a very large number of events. As to when these shall reach their end, that is a matter which depends upon the Father alone.

Several of His parables point in the same direction. The wicked steward maltreats the servants and squanders the property entrusted to him under the pretext that "My lord is long a coming" (Mt. xxiv, 48). The bridegroom "tarries" so long, that the virgins awaiting him, the wise as well as the foolish, slumber and sleep (Mt. xxv, 5). The industrious servants were able to double the talents committed to them, before their lord returned "after a long time" (Mt. xxv, 19). It is not sane criticism to cancel all these significant indications simply because they conflict with our eschatological preconceptions. If we judge all the eschatological utterances of our Lord according to their true meaning, in the light of that central point with which Jesus was concerned, we shall find that they are nothing but a vivid and imperative summons to constant watchfulness and readiness for the Day of the Lord, come it when it may. "Ye know not when the lord of the house cometh: at even, or at midnight, or at cock-crow, or in the morning. Watch ye, therefore, lest coming on a sudden he find you sleeping. And what I say to you, I say to all: Watch!" (Mk. xiii, 35-7; Lk. xii, 37 ff.) The point that Jesus emphasizes is this, that His coming cannot be calculated beforehand, that it breaks in suddenly as unexpected as a thief in the night (Lk. xii, 39), as instantaneous as a flash of lightning (Lk. xvii, 24), as quick as the snare that entraps an animal (Lk. xxi, 35). From a psychological standpoint we can readily understand how the disciples, haunted by the apocalyptic prepossessions of their time, and not so profoundly versed in the mind of their Master as were the twelve, interpreted the suddenness, speed and unexpectedness of the parousia to mean a proximate and imminent coming of the Lord, and how this misunderstanding long maintained itself among them, being supported by their personal desires and by the hopes of their time. Yet the apostles and evangelists were aware that our Lord Himself had not said that he would come

soon, but that He would come *suddenly.* The Acts of the
Apostles records the fact that the risen and glorified Christ
also expressly declined to say whether He would restore the
kingdom of Israel in that time (ἐν τῷ χρονῳ τούτῳ):
"It is not for you to know the times or the moments,
which the Father hath put in His own power" (Acts i,
7 ff.). It was this realisation that the notion of a proximate coming of the Judgment did not rest on the clear
promise of the Lord, but was derived only from their own
opinions and desires, which spared the young Christian
communities all those disappointments and troubles which
they must else have suffered when the return of the Lord
was delayed. The demolition of the old hopes was effected
without friction. In the Second Epistle to the Thessalonians
there is left but a faint echo of them, while in the Gospel
of St. John they disappear completely. But there is one
thing which did not disappear, and which abides even to
the present day, namely, the true declaration and plain
promise of our Lord, His great message: The bridegroom
cometh, therefore be ye ready!

And so, to conclude, an estimate of the nature of the
Church in the light of our Lord's eschatological teaching
yields these two points: In the first place we see that the
foundation of the Church is in the direct line of His
thought. For the very reason that the Kingdom of Heaven
is established in the immediate present and must by the
Father's will wait a long time yet for the Coming of the
Bridegroom, it is necessary that the pearl of great price
should be provided with a protective shell, that the new
spirit of God's governance should have a body, in order
to pass unscathed through history. But since this present
Kingdom is completed only in the future, therefore the
life of the Church also is ordinated towards that future.
The Church, founded on the one Peter, is a society awaiting
the parousia, and her nature is fundamentally eschatological. And so her dogma is in its purpose a preparation
for the future vision. "Now we see only in a mirror
. . . but then face to face." Therefore her creed closes

with the confession of belief in the life everlasting. Her liturgy seeks to adumbrate and anticipate by means of visible and transitory signs the glories of eternity. Her sacraments are anticipatory pledges of a future consummation. They convey that light of grace which is to pass one day into the light of glory. All her prayers and all her penance are inspired by the great hope: the Lord cometh. And so in her attitude she is not of this world, but of the next. Of course she recognises and uses the things of this world, but she does so only so far as they relate to the other world and to the life eternal. Just as her Lord and Master saw and valued all contemporary events only in their inward connexion with the great thing that was to come, so the Church also affirms in every present thing only its final and eternal value. She enlarges our life, and raises it from transitory values into eternity. She grasps the future in the present, and eternity in time. The Christian at prayer knows not time, as mere time. He does not allow himself to be governed by time and its movement. He is not the plaything of time, but lives in the eternal. His attitude is consciously supra-temporal. He "uses the world as though he used it not. For the fashion of this world passeth away" (I Cor. vii, 31).

And, therefore, the Church has no use for any merely human and temporal civilisation; her ideal is an eternal one, and consists in the establishment of God's Kingdom in the souls of men. Wherever a purely human ideal seeks to assert itself and men are taken captive by values less than the ultimate value, then the Church proves herself an irreconcilable opponent. This is the point in which she separates herself most profoundly from the world. She cannot rest in time. Whenever a purely worldly outlook shows itself, whether it be in the university, or in the busy market-place, or even in the home, she will never cease to cry her "Be ye ready!" to all and sundry. This is the vital centre of her being. Wherever the Church encounters the world, in philosophy and science, in politics and law, in art and literature, there the eternal impinges on the temporal, the divine on the human, and the Kingdom of Christ on the kingdom of this world.

That is the first point. And the second point is this, that the Church, in the light of our Lord's eschatological teaching, is seen to be necessarily incomplete and imperfect. The Church of the present is not as yet the whole and full Kingdom of God. It is a field of wheat in which there is still much cockle, a net that contains both good and bad fish. True, the spirit that dominates her is the Spirit of Jesus, and the forces that pulsate through her are the living forces of her risen Saviour. But the men in whom this divine reality is being accomplished are men confined within the bonds of their corrupt bodies, and therefore they are incomplete men and will remain so, until the Lord come. Moreover there will always be men in whom God's word does not take root, and who will be like the cockle and grow till the harvest. That is the tragedy of the Church and God's present Kingdom, that there should be this contrast between her temporal manifestation and her divine idea, between her actual state and that great and holy thing which liveth in her. But our hope is not illusory: this tragedy shall receive its happy solution on that day when Christ comes again. The Catholic turns his gaze away from all imperfection and wretchedness, from his own sins and the sins of his fellow Catholics, and looks forward with confident hope—exactly as did the first Christians of Corinth and Thessalonica—to the day when the Bridegroom shall come. Maranathâ—come. Lord Jesus!

CHAPTER VI

THE CHURCH AND PETER

"Upon this rock I will build my Church" (Mt. xvi, 18).

Our Lord's Gospel of the Kingdom pressed on to the foundation of a visible Church. The more definitely He opposed the ruling religious authority, and the clearer it became that He was dethroning the Law and setting His own word in its place, that the new Kingdom was bound up with His Person and with faith in Him, that it was His Kingdom (cf. Lk. xxii, 29, 30; xxiii, 42; Mt. xiii, 41), and that it was the New Covenant in His Blood, so much the more inevitable was the gradual detachment of His disciples from their previous religious fellowship. "No man putteth a piece of new cloth unto an old garment." And naturally the fellowship which held His disciples together was bound to become all the more intimate and conscious. How often had He not told them: "By this shall all men know that you are my disciples, if you have love one to another." They shall call one another brethren, they shall be His family (cf. Mt. x, 25), His marriage-guests, who cannot be sorrowful so long as the Bridegroom is with them (Mt. ix, 15), who drink together out of the same cup of the New Covenant. And one day they are to be His elect, and at His table and in His Kingdom to eat of the glad messianic feast (Lk. xxii, 29 f.; Mt. xiii, 41).

The messianic consciousness of Jesus necessarily led to the formation of a community. In His Person the Judgment was already begun, the contrast of faith and unbelief, the separation of spirits, the parousia. He told them quite plainly: "Do not think that I came to send peace upon earth; I came not to send peace, but the sword" (Mt. x, 34; cf. Lk. xii, 51). In Him the City of God invaded the earthly city, and at once there began the process of discrimination, the formation of the new out of the old.

The first step was taken when Jesus began gradually to gather "disciples" about Him, and the twelve are mentioned in twenty-nine passages of the Gospels. In St. Paul "the twelve" are already a recognised body. However much it may be disputed whether the twelve were named apostles by our Lord Himself, or whether this name became current first in Hellenistic surroundings, yet the fact that Jesus Himself selected the twelve is indisputable. They were to be twelve in number, no more and no less. By being twelve they were—so He plainly intended—to signify the new twelve-fold Israel, and to be the germ of that holy people which He, as the Son of man, foretold by the prophet Daniel, was come to establish.[1]   As the new Israel they were the kernel of the new Kingdom, its spiritual support, the authorised bearers of its message, the "salt of the earth," the "light of the world." They knew themselves as those who would one day judge the twelve tribes of Israel (Mt. xix, 28; Lk. xxii, 30). So deeply were the twelve permeated with the fundamental importance of their corporate union, that after the Ascension of Jesus they considered it their first business to fill the gap which the suicide of Judas had left in the apostolic college by electing Matthias (Acts i, 15 ff.). Therefore the twelve were the original form and foundation of the new Kingdom. That new Kingdom entered history as an apostolic Church, built, as the Epistle to the Ephesians says (ii, 20), "upon the foundation of the apostles." The character of apostolicity, this real historical connexion with the twelve, is essential to it and cannot be taken from it.

But already, at the election of Matthias, one of the twelve is distinguished from the others by his self-assur-

[1] Cf. F. Kattenbusch, *Die Vorzugsstellung des Petrus und der Charakter der Urgemeinde*, Festgabe für Karl Müller, 1922, p. 341.

ance. This is Simon Bar Jona, surnamed Peter. He pro-
posed the election and conducted it. On the day of Pentecost it was Peter again who by his stirring words brought
the first Christian community into being (Acts ii, 41).
Both in the temple (iii, 12) and before the Sanhedrim (iv,
8; v, 29) this same Peter was the spokesman of the twelve.
His miracles surpassed even those of our Lord. "The sin-
gular greatness of the marvels reported of him . . . shows
that Christian tradition raised him above the rest of the
twelve." [2] It was he, who by his reception of the Gentile
Cornelius, anticipated the decision of that question which
was so vital for the young Church, that is, whether the
Gentiles might be admitted directly into the Christian community. And he secured the general recognition of his
policy in spite of all opposition (Acts xi, 18). When the
question was raised later whether Gentile Christians were
under the law of circumcision, again his word was decisive
(xv, 7). And when the controversy threatened to break
out anew in Antioch, it was expected that his presence in
person would produce peace. But the prestige of St. Peter
was supreme, not only in the original community, but also
in those Hellenistic missionary churches where St. Paul
exercised his apostolate to the uncircumcised (cf. Gal. ii,
7). St. Paul tells us that St. Peter was accounted one of
the "pillars" of the Church, with James and John (Gal. ii,
9). He is one of the "authorities" (ii. 6). According to
St. Paul, St. Peter is entrusted with the gospel to the cir-
cumcised, as he himself is the apostle of the uncircumcised,
which means that St. Paul regarded him as the true founder
and head of the Jewish Christian community (Gal. ii, 7).
And so, on his first visit to Jerusalem, he sought out St.
Peter especially. His visit, after his three years' sojourn in
Arabia, was for the express purpose of "getting to know
Peter personally" (ἱστορῆσαι). And he abode fifteen days
with him (Gal. i, 18). Manifestly he considered it necessary to arrange matters with St. Peter and to be in
agreement with him. And even when he can say that he

[2] *Ibid.*, p. 335.

did not agree with Peter, but had to "withstand him to his face" because he had wrongly withdrawn himself from social intercourse with Gentile Christians and thereby practically belied his own principles (Gal. ii, 11-12), even then we discern his conviction that St. Peter's example is of especial authority even for Antioch, so that a public settlement with him is necessary.

And so St. Paul's attitude towards the apostles in general and towards St. Peter in particular confirms that picture of the Church which we derived from the original community in Jerusalem. It is clear that the governance of the Church appertained to the apostles, and that St. Peter was the most influential and esteemed of the apostles. The twelve governed the Church under the leadership of St. Peter. Jerusalem, as the seat of the apostolic college with St. Peter at its head, was the metropolis of the Christian churches. As Karl Holl has lately demonstrated against Sohm, Jerusalem had a special competence to decide questions that arose and a formal right to supervise the whole Christian mission and to accredit the missionaries.[3] St. Paul himself tells us with obvious satisfaction that the authorities in Jerusalem recognised his mission to the Gentiles and gave him "the right-hand of fellowship" (Gal. ii, 9), without laying more upon him (ii, 6). So the Pauline communities also were subject to the supreme control of Jerusalem. St. Paul adds: "Only that we should be mindful of the poor, which same thing also I was careful to do" (Gal. ii, 10). Not a few modern investigators see in these regular alms sent to Jerusalem a species of tax—Heiler even speaks of Peter's-pence—which the Christian communities of the diaspora had to pay in acknowledgment of their intimate dependence on Jerusalem, just as the synagogues of the Jewish diaspora were bound to contribute to the temple.

So if we consider the fundamental character of the original Christian Church we can understand how Heiler can call those early years the "formative period of Catholicism,"[4]

[3] *Sitz-Ber. der Preuss. Akad. der Wiss.*, 1921, p. lxxx.
[4] Op. cit., p. 61.

and in what respect he can say of the primitive community in Jerusalem that it displayed the "unmistakable germs and fundamental elements of the coming Catholicism." [8] The most outstanding of these is St. Peter's pre-eminence in the apostolic college.

How are we to explain this pre-eminence of St. Peter? According to Wellhausen and his followers it is simply due to the fact that St. Peter was the first to see the risen Christ. His faith awakened the faith of the rest, and so St. Peter's Easter faith was the creative cause and the root of all that Christianity which grew out of this Easter faith. Quite recently Holl has endeavoured to improve this theory by modifying it as follows: St. Peter is not precisely the creator and enkindler of the Christian faith, but its re-creator. The events of the Passion intimidated the disciples and extinguished their faith; that faith was re-enkindled by St. Peter's faith, and in that way the new faith is causally derived from St. Peter. Neither of these theories is admissible, because neither of them rests upon any secure historical basis. It is true that St. Peter was regarded by the primitive Christians as an important witness to the Resurrection of our Lord. And it is indubitable that his testimony was valued more highly than the testimony of the other apostles. When St. Paul, in his argument against those who denied the Resurrection, enumerates the most weighty witnesses to it, he mentions St. Peter first, and the twelve as a whole only after him (1 Cor. xv, 5). It is significant also that the angel at the tomb (Mk. xvi, 7) bade the women tell "the disciples and Peter" that Jesus would go before them into Galilee. So St. Mark also singles out St. Peter and distinguishes his testimony expressly from that of the other disciples. But nowhere, as Kattenbusch truly insists, is there any record of St. Peter's being the first to whom the Lord appeared. Nor is there any evidence whatever to show that the first disciples and the first communities expressly based their faith in the risen Christ on the testimony of St. Peter, that his faith begat

[8] *Ibid.*, p. 49.

theirs, and that their faith stood or fell with his alone. On the contrary the narratives of the Resurrection, and especially St. Paul's, are concerned to name a whole series of witnesses, and among them five hundred brethren "of whom many remain until this present" (1 Cor. xv, 6). Not St. Peter singly, but all the living disciples as a body, are the witness and guarantee of the Resurrection. The experience of Pentecost rests upon the basis of their common testimony.

Nevertheless St. Peter's testimony has a special value and is expressly invoked before and along with the testimony of the twelve. The reason is, not that St. Peter was the authentic and special, or the first witness, of the Resurrection, but rather that his word and his testimony in general were more highly treasured and that he enjoyed a higher prestige than the other disciples. In other words, St. Peter's pre-eminence as a witness is not to be explained by his being the first to believe in the Resurrection, but contrariwise it is by his already recognised pre-eminence that we must explain the special value which his testimony enjoyed. The high esteem and special consideration given to his testimony—as evidenced by St. Mark and St. Paul, and by St. Luke also (xii, 42)—compel the historian to conjecture the existence of some fact, existing before the Resurrection of our Lord, which gave St. Peter a special standing in the primitive community, and which caused that community to give his testimony, though not an exclusive, yet an exceptional value. Is there such a fact?

The evangelist, St. Matthew, records an event, which of itself is quite sufficient to explain St. Peter's pre-eminence in the primitive community and the high value set upon his testimony to the Resurrection. The scene is the neighbourhood of Caesarea Philippi, by the southern slopes of Mt. Hermon, in sight of the mighty range in which the Jordan has its source. Our Lord put this question to His disciples: "Whom do you say that I am?" Simon Peter made answer: "Thou art the Christ, the Son of the Living God." Jesus answered him: "Blessed art thou, Simon

Bar Jona; because flesh and blood hath not revealed it to thee, but my Father who is in heaven. And I say to thee: That thou art Peter [the rock], and upon this rock I will build my church. And the gates of hell shall not prevail against it. And I will give to thee the keys of the Kingdom of Heaven. And whatsoever thou shalt bind upon earth, it shall be bound also in heaven: and whatsoever thou shalt loose upon earth, it shall be loosed also in heaven" (Mt. xvi, 15 ff.). If we examine the linguistic idiom of these verses, it immediately becomes evident that they are Aramaic in origin. The play on the word Kephas is perfect only in Aramaic, for in the Greek petra (rock) has to be changed into Petros. The expressions Simon Bar Jona, gates of hell, keys of the Kingdom of Heaven, binding and loosing, and the antithesis of heaven and earth, are all Aramaic in character. Semitic scholars are therefore emphatic in their denial that the passage is a western, i.e., Roman forgery. On purely linguistic grounds that is an impossibility, and the hypothesis is now quite obsolete. The passage is native only to the soil of Palestine and to primitive Jewish Christianity. Is it genuine? That is to say, is it obviously an original part of the Gospel of St. Matthew, or does it betray the character of a later interpolation? In itself the whole passage is plainly very closely strung together and there is no sign of any artificial patch-work. St. Peter's confession: "Thou art the Christ" is balanced by our Lord's attestation: "Thou art the rock." Our Lord's searching inquiry: "Whom do men say that the Son of Man is?" and the exhaustive enumeration of the false opinions of the people lead up with psychological skill to St. Peter's correct answer and our Lord's commendation. "Other men judge falsely and in earthly fashion about me. But thou hast discerned my mystery: Blessed art thou, etc." The Protestant theologian Bolliger remarks of the verses that they "fit together as aptly as the members of a body. They have the quite inimitable flavour of a great historical moment. Moreover, they are expressed in words such as come only to the great ones of this world, and even to these only in the greatest moments of their life. No interpolator can write in this fashion." [•]

And if we consider the passage more broadly, in the light of the special tendency of St. Matthew's Gospel, its authenticity becomes manifest. It is the plain purpose of His Gospel to set forth Jesus as the Messiah foretold by the Old Testament, and in particular as the divine Law-giver and Teacher who reveals the deepest meaning of the Old Testament and brings it to fulfilment. His new and perfect doctrine corrects and amends the false doctrine of the Scribes and Pharisees, who strain out the gnat and swallow the camel (Mt. xxiii, 24). Therefore the special tendency of St. Matthew, though not anti-Jewish, is certainly antipharisaic. The true Teacher of the Kingdom of Heaven is Jesus alone. And in so far as His chosen disciples have to propagate His teaching of a justice superior to the justice of the Pharisees, they become a new teaching body and supplant the blind Scribes and Pharisees. And so we see that the wider purpose of St. Matthew's Gospel is the institution of a new religious authority, a new teaching body, and consequently the establishment of a new Church which should replace the Synagogue. And that disciple who grasped the mystery of the Kingdom of God beyond all the rest, and confessed it at Caesarea Philippi, is appointed to be the foundation stone of the new Church, to be its steward and instructor in the Kingdom, and is given the power of binding and loosing, that is of forbidding and permitting, not according to the manner of the Pharisees, but according to the mind of Jesus. Thus the anti-pharisaic tendency of the Gospel of St. Matthew culminates precisely at this point, in the foundation of a new Church and in the new authority granted to St. Peter. Our Lord's promise to St. Peter is undiluted anti-pharisaism. And for that reason the passage may not be expunged from the Gospel; it belongs to the evangelist's original plan. But is it not conceivable that St. Matthew himself—let us say in the

[•] Bolliger, *Markus, Der Bearbeiter des Mt.-Evangeliums*, 1902, p. 86.

Jewish and anti-Pauline interest—invented the words about the rock and the keys in order to secure St. Peter's teaching authority as against St. Paul, or the teaching authority of Jerusalem as against the pretensions of the Hellenistic communities? The passage would then be a product of Jewish Christians in Jerusalem, who wished to play off St. Peter against St. Paul; at the best a "pious fraud" of the author of our Gospel. It would take me too far were I to repeat the exhaustive proof adduced by Protestant as well as Catholic theologians to show that there is no evidence in the history of the primitive Church of any antagonism between St. Peter and St. Paul, or between Jerusalem and the Hellenistic communities. And the further demonstration that the Gospel of St. Matthew is inspired by no antagonism towards St. Paul is likewise quite unnecessary. It is decisive for our purpose to register the admitted fact that the fundamental word of our Lord's promise, His denomination of Peter as the "rock," was already current in primitive Christianity long before St. Matthew wrote his Gospel—i.e., shortly before the destruction of Jerusalem in A.D. 70—and that it was admitted and recognised not only among Jewish Christians, but also among the Gentiles, and not least of all in the churches founded by St. Paul. Not St. Matthew only, but St. Mark also (iii, 16) and St. John (i, 42) record that St. Peter was originally called Simon, and that our Lord Himself first gave him the name of Peter (Kephâ = Petros = Rock). Mark (iii, 16) tells us further that Jesus substituted also for the names of James and John the designation Boanerges. Now it is surely very significant—Holl has recently pointed this out— that the name Boanerges did not become current among the primitive Christians, whereas Simon's designation as Kephâ, or the Rock, did. Simon's surname became for all Christendom his proper name. St. Paul scarcely mentions him except as Kephas, the Greek form of the Aramaic Kephâ. In his Epistle to the Galatians (i, 18; ii, 7, 8) he introduces the Greek translation, Petros. And that form Petros prevailed in the Hellenistic communities to the exclusion of any other. His own proper name, Simon, fell completely out of use. The fact is all the more striking because neither the Greek Petros, nor the Aramaic Kephâ, had been employed as proper names before the time of Christ. Therefore the early Christian communities, several decades before St. Matthew wrote, and in any case already about the year A.D. 35, when St. Paul was converted, were interested in Simon's being called, not Simon, but Rock. "All the faithful were meant to know that he was the rock" (Kattenbusch). And why? For no other reason that can be discerned save that the whole Christian body recognised that surname (Kephâ = Petros = Rock) as the expression of St. Peter's special function and importance for the Church, and was aware that this special position rested upon the original intention, and deliberate, unequivocal decision of our Lord Himself. In other words the central substance of this passage of St. Matthew, Simon's designation as the foundation stone of the Church and the Church's establishment on him, belongs in the closest possible way to the texture of the common Christian tradition, and, indeed, to that tradition even in pre-Pauline times. And so it cannot have been the invention of narrowly Jewish and anti-Pauline circles towards the end of the first century. And thus we understand how not only the alleged "anti-Pauline" St. Matthew, writing for Jewish Christians, speaks of Simon the Rock, but also the Hellenistic Luke, writing for Gentile Christians and closely associated with St. Paul, records a saying of our Lord which reads like a paraphrase of St. Matthew's passage: "And the Lord said: Simon, Simon, behold Satan hath desired to have you that he may sift you as wheat. But I have prayed for thee that thy faith fail not; and thou being once converted, confirm thy brethren" (Lk. xxii, 31). So Christ prayed specially for Simon in particular that he should not fail in the faith and should "confirm" his brethren. The word "confirm" (στηρίζειν = support) reminds us of the rock of St. Matthew. It is the special function of Simon to be the support and prop of the young Christian faith. Therefore

St. Luke also implies Simon's vocation to be the rock. Nor is the case different with St. John. In the supplement to the fourth Gospel, which derives from the circle of St. John's disciples, the risen Christ asks: "Simon, son of John, lovest thou Me more than these?" (xxi, 15). Evidently our Lord expected a more faithful love from Simon than from the rest of His disciples. And on the basis of this more faithful love He deputed him, and him alone, to take His position as shepherd of His flock: "Feed My lambs, feed My sheep." We may turn these passages as we like, but we cannot escape the impression that the whole body of the early Christians knew that Simon bore a special relation to the stability of the Church, and derived this unique position of his from an express declaration of our Lord's. Consequently the words of our Lord reported by St. Matthew are not isolated and baseless, but they are in their substantial content rooted in and authenticated by the common tradition of primitive Christianity, a tradition which is earlier than St. Matthew's Gospel and earlier than St. Paul. It is therefore evident, and we need not labour the point, that we are not dealing here with a pre-eminence of St. Peter, which was confined to purely charismatic gifts, as for instance to a special capacity for the interpretation of Scripture or to special eloquence in the exposition of the faith. In fact, St. Peter counts not merely as one stone in the newly-founded Church, nor merely as the first stone, but as the rock, the foundation stone which supports the whole Church. He is therefore intimately connected with the whole being of the Church, not only with its teaching activity and its faith, but also with the fulness of that life which springs from this faith, with its discipline, its worship and its ordinances. The whole Church rests on Peter, and not merely its scriptural knowledge and its doctrine. Our Lord expresses this fact with even greater emphasis by the biblical image which he employs in the same context, promising Peter the keys of the Kingdom of Heaven. Peter is to be the steward of the house—the same figure is used by our Lord elsewhere

(Mt. xxiv, 45; Lk. xii, 42)—he alone has charge of the keys, and he has to supervise every department of the Church. The metaphor of binding and loosing points in the same direction. According to the rabbinical mode of speech from which it is taken, this signifies a power to forbid and to permit, to judge and to regulate, which is authoritative and valid in heaven, i.e., before God. Therefore the three images really describe that plenitude of power (plenitudo potestatis) of which the Vatican Council speaks, and which comprises full doctrinal and disciplinary authority, the complete governance of the Church in the most comprehensive sense. And, as we have seen, St. Peter's influence was not in fact confined to the doctrinal sphere alone.

But—and here we come to the last question—have we not to deal here with a purely personal relation of St. Peter to the Church? The passage of St. Matthew and the conviction of the early Church testify to the precedence of St. Peter. Can we claim their testimony for his successors also? Do they support the exclusive precedence of the Bishop of Rome?

A negative answer to this question can be given only by those who consider the scriptural texts in isolation and do not view them in relation to the divine Humanity of Jesus and His intentions. But those who really believe in Jesus, in His Divinity and in the necessarily imperishable character of His ideas and His works, in Jesus the Master and Lord of the future, cannot regard any of His works as transitory, or any of His words as spoken only for yesterday and to-day. All His words are instinct with eternal might, they are words of life, or creative power, they are promises which do not die until they are fulfilled.

And this is true of Matthew xvi, 18-19. What Jesus said and did on that occasion for His generation and His disciples, He said and did for all times, until He shall come again. When Jesus spoke the words: *Tu es Petrus,* He spoke them out of His triumphant messianic conscious-

ness that His Person and His work were imperishable.
True, He Himself is now at the threshold of death, the
"gates of hell"; but before His divine gaze all the dark
shadows of death melt away. Down the long vista of
time He sees the radiant picture of His eternal Church.
Peter's confession assures Him that Simon will be an
imperishable "rock" for His Church. He is certain of the
imperishableness of the Church. It will never perish, since
it will always be a Church founded on a rock. There will
always be a living Peter, whose faith will confirm his
brethren. It lies at the basis of His words that His Church
will never be without that strong foundation which He gave
it at Caesarea Philippi, because its continuance depends
upon this foundation. And so the continuance of St.
Peter's office is derived immediately from the triumphant
quality of the messianic consciousness of Jesus. Because
Jesus is sure that His Church, the most special creation of
His messianic consciousness, will never be overcome by the
gates of hell, therefore the original Petrine form, with
which He connected this imperishableness expressly and
emphatically, Peter's office as "rock," must last on until
He comes. So every successive generation of the disciples
will have, like the first generation, its living Peter, its rock,
which will enable it to triumph over all the assaults of the
gates of hell.

So much we know from faith in Jesus. And from history we know that St. Peter, according to the wise designs
of God's Providence, died a martyr in Rome, and that the
bishops of Rome have always regarded themselves, so far
as historical record reaches, as possessors of his episcopal
see. Nowhere throughout Christendom has another see
been established which has claimed in the same sense as
Rome to be the see of Peter. Though the theological basis
of the Roman primacy and the exact definition of its
meaning have been subject to some development, yet two
facts belong to the solid substance of the ancient Christian
tradition: first, that there has never been a Peter-less, non-
Roman Catholic Church, and that communion with Peter

and with the Roman church has been regarded from the earliest times as a fundamental necessity of the Catholic conscience; secondly, that Rome has been conscious from the most ancient times, from the days of Clement and Ignatius of its pre-eminence, and has exercised as "president in love," and "principal Church" (Cyprian), an authoritative and decisive influence on the development of doctrine, morals and worship. Whence we hold it as an historical certainty, a certainty which is ultimately founded on faith in the rational nature of our Lord's work and on the conviction that He guards His Church, that Peter lives on in the bishops of Rome. We know no other Peter in our community, and no man knows of any other. It is our belief that we have in the bishop of Rome the Peter upon whom Christ at Caesarea Philippi established His Church.

In the light of this faith our Lord's words to Peter: "Thou art Peter and upon this rock I will build my Church," become at once promise and fulfilment. Has not history taught us, and are we not seeking every day, that it was, and is, and will be this one rock which supports the Church of Christ, and with that Church a living faith in the Incarnation of the Son of God? There is a sacred and profound significance in the fact that Simon's appointment to be the rock of the Church was preceded by his confession: "Thou art the Christ, the Son of the Living God." For faith in Christ, the Church and Peter: these three things belong together. Where there is no Peter, where men have broken faith with him, there the fellowship of the faith perishes and along with it belief in Jesus Christ. Where there is no rock, there there is no Church, there there is no Christ.

And where Peter is, there of a truth the gates of hell rage against the fellowship of the faith. There Marcion comes, and Arius, and the renaissance and rationalism, and the gospel of worldly culture. But still we abide in the Upper Room, gathered round our Lord and Master. Where Peter is, there is Christ.

For us Catholics, faith in the Son of God, loyalty to the Church, communion with Peter: these things stand in an

intimate and necessary connexion.   And therefore since
we desire not to abandon Christ, we do not abandon Peter.
And therefore is it our quiet but confident hope, a hope set
in our souls by our Lord at Caesarea Philippi, that it cannot be otherwise, that it must be so again, that all who seek
Christ shall likewise again find Peter.   Heiler writes in
moving language of the longing for the "angelic pastor"
(*pastor angelicus*), to him a beautiful dream.'   But for us
it is no mere beautiful dream, but a certain expectation.
The divine life, the life full of grace and truth, has been
revealed and given to us once for all in Christ.   Nor can
there be any permanent and fruitful life of nations and of
men, which is not nourished on that original divine life.
There can be no unity of the West, no communion of souls,
which does not draw all its motives, yearnings and hopes
from this divine source.   Christ is and remains the heart
of humanity, its true and only native land, wherein it shall
find rest for its soul.   That is our faith, though western
civilisation should collapse—and the prophets of its downfall are already with us—or though it should be born again
in Him who is our life.   And the organ and instrument of
this Christian life will be that Church which He built upon
Peter.   For to her alone was made the promise that the
gates of hell should not prevail against her.   She alone
possesses the guarantee of permanence, to her alone belongs
the future.   Just as the Church by the compact unity and
strength of her Christian faith gave the Middle Ages their
inward unity and their strength of soul, and just as in her
severe and inexorable struggle with primitive pagan
instincts and with the forces of extravagant imperialism,
she defended the sublimity, purity and freedom of the
Christian faith and of Christian morality, so she alone is
able in our modern day to introduce again amid the conflicting currents, the solvent forces and growing exhaus-
tion of the West, a single lofty purpose, a constructive and
effective religious power, a positive moral energy and a
vitalising enthusiasm.   And she alone can reunite the severed threads which joined our western civilisation to that

' Op. cit., p. 334, ff.

great rich past whence it sprang. Whether we look forwards or backwards, we realize that without the Church of Peter there will be no inward dynamic unity, no further "history" for the West, but only a succession of experiences without goal or purpose, the convulsive movements of a body that has lost its soul. We need the Church that we may live.

I grant that there are many who do not see the matter so. Nor is that their fault alone. When dark clouds of prejudice and misunderstanding obscure the fair image of our Church, we Catholics often must admit our guilt: *mea culpa, mea maxima culpa*. It is due in no small measure to our imperfections and frailties and sins that those dark clouds arise and conceal the countenance of the Bride of Christ. When God allowed great sections of the Church, containing an abundance of most noble and valuable elements, to separate from us, He punished not them only, but also us Catholics ourselves. And this punishment, this penal permission of God, should, like all His permissions, cause us to look into ourselves and impel us to repentance. It should be an imperative "Do penance." The Spirit of Jesus is incarnate in the Church; we should all impress that Spirit on ourselves, and especially the spirit of love and brotherliness,[8] of loyalty and truth. And then it cannot be but that God, though after long wanderings and difficult inward crises of the western soul, will graciously grant that we may all unite again, that our inward union with Jesus may become an outward fellowship also, that we may be one flock under one shepherd. Then will be fulfilled the sacred prayer which Jesus offered to His Father on the eve of His death: "And not for them only do I pray, but for them also who through their word shall believe in me. That they all may be one, as thou, Father, in me, and I in thee; that they also may be one in us; that the world may believe that thou hast sent me" (Jn. xvii, 20, 21).

[8] Such is St. Augustine's admonition: *Habete igitur pacem, fratres. Si vultis ad illam trahere ceteros, primi illam habete, primi illam tenete* (Sermo CCCLVII, 3).

CHAPTER VII

THE COMMUNION OF SAINTS

(I)

"Now there are many members yet one body" (1 Cor. xii, 20).

THE true structural organs of the Body of Christ, as that is realised in space and time, are pope and bishops. Being born of that love which makes the Body of Christ one and maintains its unity, and being authorised by the special institution of our Lord, they exercise among the members of the Body the most important function for its stability, namely governing authority. But the organic activity of the Body is not confined to this administrative activity. The Church as the Body of Christ on earth does not consist merely of the authorities of the Church, of the pope and the bishops. "And if they all were one member, where would be the body? But now there are many members indeed, yet one body" (1 Cor. xii, 19 ff). By Him who is the Head, namely Christ, is "the whole body compacted and fitly joined together, by what every joint supplieth, and to every part is given its proper service, and so is accomplished the increase of the body, until it is built up in love" (Eph. iv, 16). Therefore there is a manifold abundance of functions in the one Body. In fact the course of St. Paul's thought implies that every faithful and loving member of the Body has a special function to fulfil within the Body. "For as in one body we have many members, but all the members have not the same office: so we being many are one body in Christ, and every one members one of another: having different gifts according to the grace that is given us" (Rom. xii, 4-6). And every one of these

particular functions has its importance for the well-being
of the Body. There is no grace that may be a purely personal possession, no blessing that does not belong to all.
"If the foot should say, Because I am not the hand, I am
not of the body: is it therefore not of the body? And if
the ear should say, Because I am not the eye, I am not of
the body: is it therefore not of the body?" (I Cor. xii,
15-16). The ultimate meaning of every vital Christian
function lies precisely in its close relation to the complete
organism, in its solidarity with the whole.

And so all the members of the Body are necessary to it,
although in different ways. Some, like pope and bishop,
serve its external structure, the statics of the Body of
Christ, whereas the rest serve its inward dynamics. When
we consider them all in the light of their ultimate purpose,
we cannot arrange their functions in any precise order of
rank and merit. "The head cannot say to the feet: I have
no need of you. Yea, much more those that seem to be
the more feeble members of the body, are more necessary"
(I Cor. xii, 21-22). And so it may happen that, though
for the external history of the Body of Christ the activities of the structural organs, the official activities of pope
or bishop, may be more manifest to the eye, yet the joyful poverty of a St. Francis of Assisi, the vigils of a St.
Ignatius of Loyola and the charity of a St. Vincent de
Paul may claim greater importance for its inner history,
for the realisation of the fulness of Christ.

Let us speak in the pages which follow of this constructive effectiveness of the "weaker" members of the Body of
Christ. Let us see how and in what measure the rest of
the faithful—and not only bishop and pope—work together
for the building up of the Body of Christ; and in what
degree the special gifts of the individual members benefit
the whole organism.

The key to this matter is the doctrine of the "Communion of Saints." By this doctrine the Church means a
community of spirit and of spiritual goods among the
saints on earth, that is among all those who are incor-

porated by faith and love in the one Head, Christ. More than that, she means also the vital communion of these faithful Christians with all those souls who have passed out of the world in the love of Christ, and who either as blessed souls enjoy in glory the Vision of their God, or as souls in the state of purgation await that Vision. The doctrine embraces therefore the whole mass of the redeemed, who in their various stages of development, as members of the militant, suffering or triumphant Church, are conjoined through their one Head, Jesus Christ, in one single family and fellowship, in one single sacred Body.

The Church Militant (*ecclesia militans*).—The "saints" of Christ, His "holy nation" (I Peter ii, 9) fight here on earth, not with loud clamour or great display, but in quiet and stillness. Their wrestling is not against men, but against sin; they seek the pearl of great price and the hidden treasure. They are depicted in the Sermon on the Mount, in the concise and graphic phrases of our Lord. They are the "poor in spirit," the "Cinderellas" of state and Church and society, the unappreciated and despised, who day by day go their inconspicuous way of duty, and cannot marvel enough that the great and holy God should wish to be with them also. They are the "meek" who never grumble at life and who ever accept with great content whatever God sends them. They are the "mourners" who in the lonely night cry plaintively to God: Lord, not my will, but Thine be done! and who at the last can thank their God with glad hearts that they are allowed to suffer with Jesus. They are those who "hunger and thirst after justice," those who reck nothing of comfortable piety and well-fed virtue, but on the contrary are pierced to the soul with the thought of their unworthiness, and put their whole trust constantly in the redeeming power of Jesus. They are the "merciful," for whom the need of others is their need, whom no obstacle, no sin or foulness can hinder from succouring their starving brother, and whose hands are closed by no ingratitude. They are the "pure of heart," men of a child-like simplicity and singleness of aim, kind-hearted, guileless and always cheerful, for whom life is all sunshine, a constant loving cry of Abba, Father! They are the "peace-makers," men of the Holy Spirit, of inward maturity and serene equipoise of mind, from whom quiet and peace flow forth as from a sanctuary, before whom all discord is ashamed and dumb. And lastly they are those who are persecuted "for justice sake," "for His sake," those apostolic souls and tireless workers in the vineyard, who proclaim His truth by speech and writing, by teaching and example, "in season and out of season" (2 Tim. iv, 2). They seek not their own advantage, neither recognition from the world, nor honours from the Church; they seek only souls. And commonly their lot is abuse, persecution and hatred. For their life is a special challenge to the world, and draws down the scorn and laughter of its wise ones.

The Church Suffering (*ecclesia patiens*).—The Church teaches, and her doctrine is abundantly supported by the Scriptures, that man can produce fruit for the eternal life only in this world, and not in the next world. "Work whilst it is day, for the night cometh when no man can work" (Jn. ix, 4; cf. I Cor. xv, 24 ff.) This earth alone is the field, wherein both good seed and cockle germinate and grow. The next life is the eternal harvest-time. In that life there is no "meritorious" activity, nothing that can elevate a man to a higher degree of grace and beatitude. When he stands before God in the Particular Judgment he sees himself by the judgment of his own conscience assigned once and for all either to the company of the damned or to the ranks of the blessed. And his soul will bear for ever those essential traits which it has acquired in the performance of its earthly task, in its wrestling with God, that is in fulfilling the duty which conscience illuminated by grace pointed out to it. The Catholic doctrine of Purgatory has no affinity with that Platonic and Origenist view, of Eastern derivation, whereby the human soul embarks after death upon a new stage of its development. On the other hand the Church teaches that not every

soul, even though it have passed out of this world in the
state of sanctifying grace, partakes at once of eternal bliss,
and of the Vision of God. It is true that sanctifying love
gives the soul a right to the possession of God, and is
already in germ a participation in the divine life. But
since, according to the Catholic conception, justification does
not consist in an external imputation of the merits of
Christ (see p. 177 ff.), but in the gracious operation of the
creative love of Christ within us, and in the supernatural
emergence of a new love for goodness and holiness, therefore justification of its nature demands sanctification and
perfection, and is only complete and finished in this sanctification. Strictly speaking, therefore, a man in a state of
grace is not already a saint (*homo sanctus*), not, that is,
until he has given this grace free scope in his life and
under its awakening impulse overcome every evil tendency,
even to his most intimate thoughts and most subtle inclina-
tions, and having brought all that is good to dominance
has become the perfect and unalloyed man. Only such a
one, whose being is in its every part transfigured by love
of God and his neighbour, only such a one will see God.
Are there such men on this earth of ours? "Who shall be
able to stand before the Lord, this holy God?" (1 Kings vi,
20). History testifies indeed that God has been pleased to
reveal His power in weak human vessels. There have
been, and there are saints, who have ripened even in this
life "unto the measure of the age of the fulness of Christ,"
though they may in outward form have remained the children of their time and have achieved their final perfection
only in their death. But experience also teaches us that
the great majority of the pious faithful who leave this life
have not attained that sublime ideal of being perfect "as
your heavenly Father is perfect" which our Lord puts
before us and which is prefigured and implanted in us
with the grace of our adoption as His sons. A great
many Christians, when they die, are united and devoted
to God, the absolute Good, only in the centre of their
being, but remain otherwise imperfect and immature. God's

rule is not yet supreme in every room and corner of their being. They have been subject to many erratic impulses and errors; they have fallen at times into transgressions, without full consciousness of the sinful character of their acts or omissions. Some sins there have been, which they rather suffered than deliberately committed, sins which are to be ascribed to unruly nature and not to the centre of their personal being, sins which theology therefore calls "venial sins." And there is no doubt that innumerable souls leave this world with a load of venial sin, and in consequence are unfit to "walk the holy way" (cf. Isaias xxxv, 8).

It is quite possible that the experience of death itself gives many their final purification. As the world of sense and its confusing turmoil grow still, as loneliness and helplessness press down upon them, as their awe deepens before the approach of the great reality and their sense of guilt is intensified by the coming Judgment, they cry in the terrors of death with purer inwardness and more profound trust to the merciful God. As a child in unquiet sleep reaches out for the loving hand of its mother, even so do they grope after God, the Life of their life. And so there springs up within them an ardent love for their Father, a love that is ready to relinquish life gladly, a perfect love. In such ardour all sin dies, every evil inclination is extinguished and every penalty. The soul enters into the joy of its Lord.

But such a happy death is not the lot of all who die in Christ, either because they are called away suddenly, or because they do not in their deaths achieve such a depth of inwardness and such a strength of love. Now, if we do not suppose that those who die thus without a perfect act of love are purified from their faults and prepared for the Vision of God without any act of theirs and so to speak in a purely magical way by a direct interposition of God's mercy—for that would be in conflict with God's justice and with His stipulation that man should co-operate with grace —and if we maintain on the other hand that such souls, being united to God in the centre of their being, cannot be eternally banished from His sight—for that would be contrary to His mercy—then there must be after death some possibility of a purification of the soul. This purification was present to the mind of Judas Maccabeus when he caused "sacrifices and intercessions" to be offered in Jerusalem for those heroic Jews who fell fighting for their faith against Gorgias and yet contrary to the Mosaic Law had idol offerings concealed in their garments, so that they might be "loosed from their sins" and partake of the "resurrection" (2 Macch. xii, 43 ff.). This possibility is alluded to also by our Lord, when He warns us of a certain sin that "shall not be forgiven, neither in this world, nor in the world to come" (Mt. xii, 32), and when He speaks of a prison whence no man shall escape "until he has paid the last farthing" (Mt. v, 25). St. Paul too was certainly thinking of the same thing, when he speaks of that teacher who builds on the one foundation, which is Christ, nothing but wood, hay and straw, and asserts that such a one, although his work be consumed in the fire of the Judgment, will himself be saved, yet "so as by fire," that is, not wtihout labour and pain (1 Cor. iii, 11 ff.). There is no apparent reason why these words of St. Paul should apply only to an unsatisfactory Christian teacher, and not to all Christians. For all such may base their lives upon Christ, and yet from moral frailty achieve only an imperfect work. Tertullian witnesses, and the evidence of early sepulchral inscriptions is constantly reinforcing the fact, that the early Christians, mindful of this salvation "so as by fire," were wont to offer prayers, alms, and particularly the Eucharistic Sacrifice, for the peace (*pax*), the refreshment (*refrigerium*), and the eternal rest (*requies*) of the dead.

On this foundation the Church in the Councils of Lyons, Florence and Trent, formulated the doctrine that there is a state of purification (*purgatorium*) after death, and that the souls consigned thereto may be helped by the prayers of the faithful (cf. Trent, Sess. 25 *De purg.*). The process of Purgatory is a negative one, a purification of the soul, a removal of those blemishes that remain in it because of the imperfection of its earthly life; it is not a positive process, an elevation and perfecting of the soul. And because death is the end of all creative moral initiative and meritorious activity, this removal of defects can be effected only by the way of passive punishment. It is not an active satisfaction for sin (*satisfactio*), but a satisfactory suffering (*satispassio*). And so the church calls the sufferings of Purgatory purifying and cleansing punishments (*poenae purgatoriae seu catharteriae*). The poor soul, having failed to make use of the easier and happier penance of this world, must now endure all the bitterness and all the dire penalties which are necessarily attached by the inviolable law of God's justice to even the least sin, until she has tasted the wretchedness of sin to its dregs and has lost even the smallest attachment to it, until all that is fragmentary in her has attained completeness, in the perfection of the love of Christ. It is a long and painful process, "so as by fire." Is it real fire? We cannot tell; its true nature will certainly always remain hidden from us in this world. But we know this, that no penalty presses so hard upon the "poor souls" as the consciousness that they are by their own fault long debarred from the blessed Vision of God. The more they are disengaged gradually in the whole compass of their being from their narrow selves, and the more freely and completely their hearts are opened to God, so much the more is the bitterness of their separation spiritualised and transfigured. It is home-sickness for their Father; and the further their purification proceeds, the more painfully are their souls scourged with its rods of fire.

Such is the character of Purgatory. It is not mere punishment and pain like Hell, but rather urgent love, glad hope and sure expectation. There is a sacred rhythm of pain and joy in the lives of the poor souls, the pain of sin, the joy of their blessed hope. And by that they are essentially different from those who "have no further hope." "Yet a little while and your hears will rejoice."

A moment will come, when for them Purgatory shall be
no more, but only the blessedness of Heaven. After all,
Purgatory is only a thoroughfare to the Father, toilsome
indeed and painful, but yet a thoroughfare, in which there
is no standing still and which is illuminated by glad hope.
For every step of the road brings the Father nearer. Purgatory is like the beginning of spring. Warm rays com-
mence to fall on the hard soil and here and there awaken
timid life. Even so Christ our Head sends grace upon
grace, strength upon strength, comfort upon comfort, in
ever richer abundance into His suffering members. The
blessed light of glory spreads and embraces an ever wider
extent of the suffering Church. Countless souls are already
awakening to the full day of eternal life and singing the
new song: "Salvation to our God, who sitteth upon the
throne, and to the Lamb" (Apoc. vii, 10).

The Church Triumphant (*ecclesia triumphans*).—Hosts
of the redeemed are continually passing into heaven,
whether directly, or mediately by the road of purification
in the Suffering Church. They pass into the presence of
the Lamb and of Him who sits upon the throne, in order
face to face—and no longer in mere similitude and image
—to contemplate the Trinity, in whose bosom are all possibilities and all realities, the unborn God from out of
whose eternal well-spring of life all beings drink existence
and strength, motion and beauty, truth and love. There is
none there who has not been brought home by God's mercy
alone. All are redeemed, from the highest seraph to the
new-born child just sealed by the grace of baptism as it left
the world. Delivered from all selfish limitations and raised
above all earthly anxieties, they live, within that sphere of
love which their life on earth has traced out for them, the
great life of God. It is true life, no idle stagnation, but a
continual activity of sense and mind and will. It is true
that they can merit no longer, nor bear fruit now for the
Kingdom of Heaven. For the Kingdom of Heaven is
established and grace has finished its work. But the life of
glory is richer far than the life of grace. The infinite

spaces of the Being of God, in all Its width and depth, provide a source in which the soul seeks and finds the satisfaction of its most intimate yearnings. New possibilities continually reveal themselves, new vistas of truth, new springs of joy. Being incorporated in the most sacred Humanity of Jesus, the soul is joined in most mysterious intimacy to the Godhead Itself. It hears the heartbeats of God and feels the deep life that pulsates within the Divinity. The soul is set and lives at the centre of all being, whence the sources of all life flow, where the meaning of all existence shines forth in the Triune God, where all power and all beauty, all peace and all blessedness, are become pure actuality and purest present, are made an eternal now.

This life of the saints, in its superabundant and inexhaustible fruitfulness, is at the same time a life of the richest variety and fulness. The one Spirit of Jesus, their Head and Mediator, is manifested in His saints in all the rich variety of their individual lives, and according to the various measure in which every single soul, with its own special gifts and its own special call, has received and employed the grace of God. The one conception of the saintly man, of the servant of Christ, is embodied in an infinite variety of forms. The Litany of the Saints takes us rapidly through this "celestial hierarchy." Beginning at the throne of the most holy Trinity and passing thence to Mary, the Mother of God, and then through the hosts of the angelic choirs to the solitary penance of the great Precursor, St. John the Baptist, it leads us to St. Joseph, the foster-father of the Lord, the man of quiet dutifulness and simplicity of soul. Next to them tower the figures of the Patriarchs and Prophets, primitive and sometimes strange figures, but men of strong faith, of sacred constancy, of ardent desire. Sharply contrasted with them are the witnesses of the fulfilment, the apostles and disciples of the Lord: Peter, Paul, Andrew, James and the rest. And while every name denotes a special gift, a special character, a special life, yet all are united in one only love and

in one gospel of joy and gladness. And around and
about these outstanding figures what a harvest and rich
crop of infinite colour and in infinitely diverse fields! All
holy martyrs—All holy bishops and confessors—All holy
doctors—All holy priests and levites—All holy monks and
hermits—All holy virgins and widows—All saints of God.
It is that "great multitude which no man can number, of
all nations, and tribes, and peoples, and tongues: standing before the throne and in sight of the Lamb, clothed
with white robes, and palms in their hands" (Apoc.
vii, 9).

But however wondrously glorious all these holy figures
are, each in his own way, yet all are outshone by one, by
the Queen of all angels and saints, Mary, the Mother of
God. Like every creature in heaven and on earth, she too
was called into existence out of nothingness. An infinite
distance separates her from the Infinite, from Father, Son
and Holy Ghost. And she has no grace, no virtue, no
privilege, which she does not owe to the divine Mediator.
Both in her natural and in her supernatural being, she is
wholly the gift of God, "full of grace" (κεχαριτωμένη,
Lk. i, 28). There is nothing, therefore, so misguided and
so preposterous as to decry the Mother of God as some
"mother goddess," and to talk of Catholicism having a
polytheistic character. There is but one God, the Triune
God, and every created thing lives in awe of His mystery.
But this one God is a God of life and of love. So great,
so superabundant is this love, that it not only raises man to
its own image and likeness by the natural gifts of reason
and will, but also, by the precious gift of sanctifying grace,
summons him from his state of isolation to an unparalleled
participation in the Divine Nature and in Its blessings, to a
sort of active co-operation in the work of God, to effective
initiative in the establishment of the Kingdom of God. It
is the profoundest meaning and the amazing generosity of
the redemption, that it raises the rational creature from the
infinite remoteness of its impotence and from the abysmal
ruin of its sins into the Divine Life, and thereby makes

it apt—while preserving its creaturely limitations—to co-operate in the work of redemption. The Scriptures tell us that the angels in their measure shared in the work of creation, and that they gave the Law to Moses (Gal. iii, 19; Hebr. ii, 2), thus co-operating effectively in the establishment of the Old Covenant. The new creation also and the New Covenant are not perfected without the co-operation of secondary causes (*causae secundae*), the blessed angels and men. So the whole of redeemed humanity enters in its measure into the circle of the Divine Life. To that extent it is not only the object of the divine work of salvation, but also subject and agent in that work. The true Kingdom, whence comes all blessing, is not God alone, not the divine "One" (ἕν) alone, but the "One and all" (ἕν καὶ πᾶν), or rather the totality of all the members whom Christ, their Head, introduces into the Divine Life of God, who is fruitful in His saints.

Here again we observe the essential difference between Catholicism and Protestantism. The special characteristic of Protestantism is isolation, abrupt separation and schism, not only in the sphere of Church government, but in that of religion generally. Protestantism separates reason from faith, justification from sanctification, religion from morality, nature from supernature, and so it introduces a cleavage into the domain of God's loving and gracious activity. When Luther narrowed the scriptural idea of God's all-efficiency into the doctrine of His sole-efficiency, he cut the native strength of the creature loose from its moorings in God, and delivered it over to total unfruitfulness. According to Luther's view, the stream of God's mercy flows only over the justified, and there is no creative radiance of His love within the soul, no bursting forth and concurrent flow of the soul's powers under the touch and stimulus of His love, no confluence of this new wealth with God's abundance, no living of Christ in His members. God alone is the agent and active force, God the supreme and infinite Spirit, and not the God who has taken our human nature, and who through that nature works and suffers, redeems and sanctifies, as though through His members. How different the belief of Catholicism! The Catholic cannot think of God without thinking at the same time of the Word made Flesh, and of all His members who are united to Him by faith and love in a real unity. The God of Catholicism is the Incarnate God and therefore no solitary God, but the God of angels and saints, the God of fruitfulness and abundance, the God who with a veritable divine folly takes up into Himself the whole creation that culminates in human nature, and in a new, unheard-of supernatural manner, "lives in it," "moves" in it, and in it "is" (cf. Acts xvii, 28). That is the basis upon which the Catholic veneration of the saints and of Mary must be judged. To the Catholic the saints are not mere exalted patterns of behaviour, but living members, and even constructive powers of the Body of Christ. They possess therefore, not merely a moral, but also a religious significance. Like the apostles and prophets, upon whom they are founded (Eph. ii, 20), they are essentially and for ever the fellow-workers of Christ (2 Cor. vi, 1), His servants (Mt. x, 24) and marriage guests (Mt. ix, 15), His friends (Jn. xv, 14) and His glory (2 Cor. viii, 23). They have all an abiding inward relation, a real and vital connexion with the whole Christ (*totus Christus*), and their importance for the welfare of the whole Body depends upon the special function which they have to fulfil within its organism.

That which is valid of the saints in general, holds in the highest measure of the Queen of all saints, Mary the Mother of God. The mystery of Mary's divine Motherhood does not merely comprise the bare fact that the Word took flesh and blood, our human nature, in her womb. The Catholic is not content merely to repeat with gladness the words of the inspired woman in the Gospel: "Blessed is the womb that bore thee, and the paps that gave thee suck." He listens with a far deeper attention to our Lord's answer: "Blessed are they that hear the word of God and keep it" (Lk. xi, 28). Mary's importance in the work of salvation does not lie chiefly in the purely bodily sphere, but in the sphere of morality and religion. It consists in this that Mary, so far as lay in her, gave the best of herself, even her whole being, to the service of God, and that, however infinitely small all human doing and suffering are in comparison with the Divine Perfection, she surrendered this infinitely small without limitation or stint to the visitation of Divine Grace, and so prepared herself to be the sublime instrument of the divine redemption. We know little or nothing of her early life; but from the moment that she appears upon the stage of history, Mary is irradiated with light: "Hail, full of grace, the Lord is with thee, blessed art thou amongst women" (Luke i, 28). No angel has ever spoken a greater or holier word than that of man or woman. For centuries now the Church has pondered this angelic salutation, prayerfully and lovingly, and has discovered continually in it new glories of Mary. And yet her mystery is still unexhausted. In the light of the same Gospel story we see her as one who in the deep consciousness of her lowliness (Lk. i, 48, 52, 53) is full of ecstatic joy and rejoices in God her Saviour and in Him alone (i, 46), and in the ardour of her maiden surrender and overmastering inspiration foresees and proclaims the amazing truth: "Behold, from henceforth all generations shall call me blessed" (i, 48). None other grasped as she did, at once and at the very beginnings of the Gospel, its revolutionary and triumphant power, and therefore the Church calls her "Queen of prophets." We know further that her whole subsequent life was lowliness and simplicity on the one hand, and on the other strong and joyful faith. Bethlehem and Golgotha are the two termini of a way of sharpest renunciation, of heroic resignation, of complete "self-emptying (*exinanitio*), such a way as our Lord himself travelled (Phil. ii, 7). The sword foretold by Simeon (Lk. ii, 35) pierced ever more sharply into her soul as the process of her self-abnegation advanced.

First it was at that scene in the temple when she listened to Simeon's prophecy (Lk. ii, 34-35), and then at the

marriage feast of Cana (Jn. ii, 4) and at that meeting in
Capharnaum (Mk. iii, 33—Mt. xii, 48—Lk. viii, 21) when
her Son said, "Woman, what is it to me and to thee?" and,
"Who is my mother?" and then finally beneath the Cross.
In all these experiences of her life, with ever deeper sorrow
and comprehension, she disengaged her divine Son from
her heart and surrendered Him to the Father: "Queen of
martyrs." But her faith was as strong as her humility.
She "kept all these words," which were spoken of her Son,
"pondering them in her heart" (Lk. ii, 19, 51). And so
she became the precious and pure source of the history of
His infancy, the faithful evangelist: "Queen of Evangelists." It was his mother's faith that produced the miracle
of Cana, the first manifestation of our Lord's glory among
men (Jn. ii, 1). And Mary was a blessed witness also of
His last revelation of His glory, in the fiery tongues of
Pentecost (Acts ii, 3). No apostle learnt the mystery of
Jesus so fully and so profoundly, or preserved his experience so faithfully, as did the "Queen of Apostles." It is
this radiant image of Mary, as portrayed by St. Luke and
St. John, which our Lord had in mind when He directed
the woman in the Gospel from the bodily motherhood of
Mary to her spiritual sublimity: "Blessed are they who
hear the word of God and keep it" (Lk. xi, 28). This
gives the scene its illuminating character and its importance in the history of our salvation. But all the sublimity
of Mary's moral personality, all the depth of her virginal
devotion, and all the strength of her faith culminate in the
word which she spoke to the angel: "Behold the handmaid
of the Lord, be it done unto me according to thy word."
These were no common, everyday words; no words such
as fall from men in the changing circumstance and casual
course of life. They were words out of the depths and
recesses of a soul that was pure and noble beyond all
earthly measure, words that were her being, her expression, her achievement. By them of a truth she consecrated her body to a "reasonable service" (cf. Rom. xii,
1 ff.), and that is the source of her blessedness. The

"Blessed" with which our Lord corrects that woman's praise, rings then like a conscious reference to the angel's "Blessed" in the same Gospel. "Blessed art thou that hast believed that those things shall be accomplished that were spoken to thee by the Lord" (1, 45). The gladness of redeemed humanity resounds in those words of St. Elizabeth. They are the first jubilee of the Gospel. And they are true of Mary beyond all others, for she by her "Be it done unto me" preceded all others along the way of redemption, yes even helped to prepare that way. Without her consent there had been no redemption, and therefore is she for us all the "Gate of heaven."

And so the wonderful fact that God is not alone in the work of redemption, but that creatures too, in their measure, truly share in that work, is illustrated nowhere more clearly than in Mary. It is true that the fact that Mary had such privilege was due to grace alone, that she was called from eternity to be the Mother of God and was from the beginning immersed in Christ's redeeming grace, so that she was conceived Immaculate, without stain of original sin. It was grace too, and grace alone, which gave her heart its ardent and complete devotion to the Saviour and its maiden resolution, so that she "knew no man" (Lk. i, 34) and as "Virgin of virgins" was that closed door "through which no man shall pass, because the Lord the God of Israel hath entered in by it" (cf. Ezech. xliv, 2). Yet the grace of God does not offer violence, but would be freely accepted. And therefore, however infinitely small Mary's own activity may appear in comparison with the activity of God, there remains a human strand in the divine robe of our salvation, the "Be it done unto me" of Mary. And the Catholic exalts Mary above all angels and saints (hyperdulia), because it has pleased God to give her decisive words this effective position in the work of redemption. The Fathers from the time of St. Justin Martyr continually urge this importance of Mary in the history of salvation, and contrast it with the sin of the first woman. Just as Eve's consent to the serpent's temptation brought sin and ruin, so did Mary's consent to the angel's message introduce redemption. So Mary possesses not only a personal relation to the Son of God and her personal salvation, but also a relation to the "many" who are redeemed by her Son. She is mother not of the Redeemer alone, but also of the redeemed; and so she is the mother of the faithful. The Catholic acknowledges in heaven not only a Father, but also a mother. Though by her human nature she is infinitely distant from the Father, yet her special graces have raised her to a wonderful nearness to God, and as mother of the Redeemer she reflects God's goodness and bounty with an inwardness and a truth that are possible to no other creature. When the Catholic speaks of his Heavenly Mother, his heart is full with all the strength of feeling that is contained in that word. Mary is as it were a gracious revelation of certain ineffable and ultimate traits in the nature of God, which are too fine and too delicate to be grasped otherwise than as reflected in the mirror of a mother. Ave Maria!

CHAPTER VIII

THE COMMUNION OF SAINTS

(II)

If one member glory, all the members rejoice with it
(1 Cor. xii, 26).

THE way of the saints leads from earth through the place of purification to heaven. It is no lonely way. We travel it in the fellowship of the body of Christ, growing and blossoming in the fulness of Christ, giving and taking one from another "according to the grace that is given to each member." We have already pointed out that the saints in heaven and on earth win their positive and proportionate importance in the organism of the Body of Christ by this reciprocal give and take. When the Church speaks of the Communion of Saints she is thinking primarily of this interaction, of this confluence of the powers of Jesus that work in His saints, of this supernatural interchange of graces, of this solidarity of life and movement. For it is important to note that the Communion of Saints does not simply mean that every member of the Body exercises its own special function faithfully for the good of the whole, and that every saint practises this communion simply by fulfilling his personal task. St. Paul says: "If one member suffer anything, all the members suffer with it. If one member glory, all the members rejoice with it" (1 Cor. xii, 26). All the saints are bound together, over and above their personal functions, by a close community of life and sentiment, by a fellowship and sympathy in sorrow and joy. Being members of Christ, their souls do not stand before God as isolated units. However individual may be the character of their sanctity, yet it is still the life of a member of Christ and as such belongs to all. Consequently, although the doctrine of the Communion of Saints was not inserted in the Apostles' Creed until about the middle of the fifth century, yet it is substantially contained in St. Paul's teaching. In effect the doctrine represents the practice of the early Church in its prayer, and does no more than set forth the full meaning of the Christian fellowship. We shall in the following pages consider the various aspects of this close fellowship, and in so doing we shall realise anew how world-wide and even God-wide is the Catholic outlook, and how it comprehends both God and man in one mighty circle of life, so that God may be "all in all"; and yet, on the other hand, stands silent in lowliest reverence before the majesty of God and anxiously observes the limits imposed upon every creature by the nature of its being.

The Communion of Saints comprises, and is made fruitful by, three great vital movements. A stream of ardent love flows from the Church Triumphant to the members of Christ on earth, and thence returns in countless rushing brooks to the blessed in heaven. A similar traffic of love takes place between the members of the Church Suffering and the Church Militant. And thirdly that same communion operates between the several members of the Church Militant, producing those fruitful centres of life whereby the earthly fellowship is continually renewed.

The Church Triumphant and the Church Militant.—The relations of these two consist in the veneration of angels and saints on the one hand, and on the other in their intercession for us and application to us of their merits. It is a fundamental principle of the Church's teaching that adoration belongs to God alone. From the account of St. Polycarp's martyrdom (xvii, 3), which is our earliest evidence for the veneration of the martyrs, through St. Augustine and St. Jerome, both eloquent advocates of the veneration of the saints, down to St. Thomas Aquinas, who has defined with unequalled lucidity the nature of this Catholic practice, the theology of the Church is plain, and emphatically insists that the veneration which we give to angels and saints is essentially (*specifice*) different from the worship which we offer to God. The difference is in fact the whole difference between the creature and the Creator. To God alone belongs the complete service of the whole man, the worship of adoration, that worship and prayer which are inspired by awe before the mystery of God (*cultus latriae*). To God alone do we cry, "Lord, have mercy on us!" since God alone is the All-perfect, the Infinite, the Lord. But so pervasive and so creative is God's glory that it does not shine only in the face of His Only-begotten Son, but is reflected also in all those who in Him have become children of God, and therefore illuminates with unfading radiance the countenances of the blessed. So we love them as countless dewdrops in which the sun's radiance is mirrored. We venerate them because we find God in them. "Their name liveth unto generation and generation. Let the people shew forth their wisdom and the church declare their praise." (Ecclus. xliv, 14-15). And because God is in them, therefore are we confident that they can and will help us; for where God is, there is our help. They do not help us through any strength of their own, but through the strength of God, and they help us only so far as creatures may. They cannot themselves sanctify us. For sanctification, the new life in God, is to be obtained only from Him who is Himself the divine life, that is from our divine Redeemer. St. Augustine tells us that the power of awakening souls to this life belongs to God alone.[1] So the Catholic knows that he belongs to God alone, is related only to Him and lives only in Him, and that not only in the substance of his natural being, but also in his supernatural life. In comparison with our intimate and vital conjunction with God, and with that marvellous contact with the Infinite Being, where difference is annulled and where the Divine Life

[1] *Propria majestas Dei suscitantis* (Sermo XCVIII, 6).

penetrates our souls and continually pervades them anew, the activity of even angels and saints pales into insignificance.   For it is God and God only who redeems us and gives us life.   Yet angels and saints have the power to accompany the great work of our redemption with their fostering love and by their "intercession" (*intercessione*) to elevate our prayers for help into the great solidary prayer of the whole Body of Christ.   It is true that God knows our necessities, and needs no saints to tell Him.   And it is true also that His Only-begotten Son by His sacrifice on the Cross merited His grace and mercy for us once and for all, so that they are ever near us.   Yet, for the very reason that Jesus Christ, the God-man, is the Mediator of our redemption, the saints also have a share in it.   For they are members of our Redeemer.   He is not without them, and they are not without Him.   No help comes to us, but that the members of Christ in their manner co-operate with their Head.   We say "in their manner," that is, otherwise than the Head.   This is the fulfilment of the law of love, the great structural law of the Kingdom of God.   God redeems men in such a way that every love-force in the Body of Christ has its proper share in the work.   The Body of Christ of its very nature implies communion and co-operation, and so the divine blessing never works without the members, but only in and through their unity.   God can help us without the saints; but He will not help us without their co-operation, for it is His nature and will to be communicative love.

Therefore, although the veneration of the saints has undergone some development in the course of the Church's history—in so far as the primitive veneration of apostles, prophets and martyrs expanded about the middle of the third century to include all the saints, and then in the fourth century, not uninfluenced by that veneration of our Lady which was promoted by the Nestorian conflicts, was deepened into faith in their intercession—yet such veneration was from the beginning germinally contained in the nature of the Church as the Body of Christ, in the Christian conviction of the fellowship and solidarity of His members, and ultimately in the comprehensive validity of the Christian commandment of love. It is no pagan growth, but indigenous to Christianity.[*] It has this much in common with pagan hero-worship, that it venerates the historical achievement of the saintly figure and reverences the manifestation of the divine in human form. But that is an impulse which is not specifically pagan, but belongs to our common humanity and is therefore of universal validity. But the special characteristic of paganism was to obliterate the boundaries between the divine and human and to cultivate polytheism. In that respect the influence of paganism upon the development of the veneration of the saints was rather to impede than to promote, for it was the fear of polytheistic instincts which prevented the earlier blossoming of this veneration. It was not until the Christian conception of God and the worship of our Lord were deeply and firmly rooted in

[*] Heiler (p. 183 ff.) distinguishes between popular piety and the official theology of the Church, thus making the road easy for an elaborate analysis in which he characterises popular devotion to the saints as veiled polytheism. But the alleged distinction between Catholic theory and practice does not really exist, since the devout Catholic has recourse to the saints because of his very faith in God who is "wonderful in his saints," and because of his reverence and awe before the mystery of God. So that popular devotion to the saints is in line with dogma and is utterly monotheistic in its character. Nor does that devotion, as it might appear from Heiler's presentation, comprise the whole of popular piety. If the devout Catholic turns to the saints in special need, yet, for the ordinary and fundamental concerns of his soul, he practices after the pattern of the saints and supported by their intercession an immediate intercourse of prayer with God, especially in the reception of the sacraments and in the use of those private devotions, such as devotions to the Blessed Sacrament and the Sacred Heart, which cultivate a direct child-like relation with God. It is true that special needs may become manifold and frequent, and that devotion to the saints may occupy what seems a disproportionate space in the religious life of this or that individual. Yet the Church rightly avoids restricting in any way the satisfaction of these individual religious needs, in order not to endanger the freedom of religious movement within the limits of dogmatic truth and so imperil the fertility of the religious life. And, after all, no Catholic is formally bound to venerate the saints. His faith requires him only to recognise that it is "good and useful" to appeal to their intercession. (Trent, Session 25.)

the consciousness of the masses, that the ground was ready for the specifically Christian form of hero-worship.

The intervention of the saints is effected especially in their intercession with God, that is, in the special love with which, as they see us in God, they follow up our fortunes and recommend them to Him. Like Onias, the High Priest, and the prophet Jeremias, who "as friends of the brethren on earth pray much for the people and for the holy city" (cf. 2 Macch. xv, 14), so does the great company of the saints supplicate for the struggling members of Christ on the earth. Their intercessory prayer manifests their ardent longing that the name of God should be sanctified and His will accomplished on earth as well as in heaven. And so it is nothing but living and active love, and a true expression of their blessed life. The Church is not deaf to the pulsation of this life, and therefore continually commends herself anew to their intercession. She cannot think of her Head, without also naming His holy members. Her whole liturgy is a going "to Mount Sion and to the city of the living God, the heavenly Jerusalem, and to the company of many thousands of angels, and to the church of the first-born, who are written in the heavens, and to God the judge of all, and to the spirits of the just made perfect, and to Jesus the mediator of the new testament, and to the sprinkling of blood which speaketh better than that of Abel" (Hebr. xii, 22-24). Above all she turns to Mary, in trustful prayer. The Catholic regards Mary's intercession as all-powerful with God, and Catholic Christianity is becoming more and more clearly conscious that as mother of the Redeemer and as aware of every pulsation of her Son's heart, Mary is the mother also of all His grace.

If Mary is the mother of all the faithful, the influence of the other saints is defined by the position which they occupy in the whole organism of the Body of Christ. This belief that angels and saints have special spheres and special tasks of love is the foundation of Catholic doctrine concerning the Guardian Angels, abundantly attested in the

Scriptures (Tob. xii, 12; Zach. i, 12; Hebr. i, 14), and of
Catholic faith in the special help of Patron Saints.

But the ministry of the saints to the faithful on earth is
not limited to loving intercession. It is also a love of self-
sacrifice and service, a love which is ready to share its own
wealth with all the struggling members of the Body of
Christ, to the widest extent that it can so share it. The
saints during their mortal life amassed beyond the measure
of their duty a store of wealth and of sacrificial values
made precious by the Blood of Christ. The superabundance of their love and penance forms a rich deposit.
United with the superabundance of the merits of Christ,
and derived from those merits, this wealth of the saints is
that "treasure of the Church" (*thesaurus ecclesiae*), that
sacred family inheritance, which belongs to all the members of the Body of Christ, and which is at the service
especially of its sick and feeble members. "If a member
suffers, all the members suffer with it." When a member
has not made sufficient reparation for his sins, when after
the forgiveness of sin and the remission of its eternal punishment, there yet remains a debt of "temporal" punishment, which the just God in His wise ordinance attaches
still to forgiven sin, then all the members of the Body help
to bear this burden of punishment, and then the Church
in virtue of her power of binding and loosing may supplement the poverty of one member out of the wealth of
another. And thus she grants "indulgences," that is to
say, supplements the insufficient reparation of her weaker
members by means of the vicarious superabundance of the
merits of Christ and His saints. So that the indulgence
not only attests the seriousness of sin and teaches that
guilt must be expiated "to the last farthing," but is also
an illustration of the blessed potency of the Communion of
Saints and of the vicarious expiation which is interwoven
with it. All the main ideas upon which the doctrine of
indulgences is based—the necessity of expiation for sin,
the co-operative expiation of the members of the Body of
Christ, the Church's power so to bind and loose on earth

that her action is valid in heaven—all these ideas are contained in holy Scripture. So that although the historical
form of the indulgence has undergone some change—
from the vicarious expiatory suffering of the martyrs
and confessors, and the penitential "redemptions" of the
Middle Ages down to our modern indulgenced prayer—
and may in the future undergo further change, and
although the theology of indulgences has only been gradually elaborated, yet in its substance the doctrine is in
line with the pure thought of the Scriptures. Here, as
in no other practice of the Church, do the members of
the Body of Christ co-operate in loving expiation. All
the earnestness and joyfulness, humility and contrition,
love and fidelity, which animate the Body are here especially combined and manifested. For that reason, as the
Council of Trent says, "the use of indulgences is very
salutary for the people of Christ" (Sess. 25 *De indulg.*)
But, because indulgences are based upon truths which are
not easy for the rude and uneducated, distortion and
abuse are very possible, especially where the people are
not well instructed in religion and where Church authority is not vigilant. There were many abuses during the
period before the Council of Trent, and we are still suffering their evil consequences. But it is a proof of the
permanent value of indulgences that abuses have not been
able to kill them, but have only purged them with cleansing fire and aroused them to a new and deeper life.
They have become in our day, more than ever, a valuable adjunct to pastoral work. Every instructed Catholic knows that an indulgence is not a remission of sin,
but only of the temporal penalties attached to sin. He
knows that it belongs therefore not to the centre and
core of the life of grace, but only to its outermost cir-
cumference. The granting of an indulgence is not a
sacramental or priestly act, but an act of Church authority. Every indulgenced practice has meaning and value
in so far as it is at the same time a simple prayer in the
Holy Ghost. A man who would want to use prayer, not

for loving converse with God, but merely for the gaining of indulgences, would misuse it and would display a bad misunderstanding of its meaning and nature. The supreme aim of all Christian piety, the one absolutely necessary thing, is to live a new life in God and to be delivered by the power of this life from the guilt of sin and from eternal punishment. No indulgence can exempt from this duty. Indeed the gaining of an indulgence presupposes this one necessary thing, for there can be no remission of temporal punishment where there is no remission of guilt and eternal punishment. So that indulgences may be said to operate at least indirectly towards this purification from sin and towards the establishment of the new life in God. The indulgence, therefore, of its nature is not instituted for the externalising of the religious life, but for its deepening and enrichment. It is an emphatic summons to repentance, a strong impulse to vital incorporation in the Body of Christ, so as to obtain His blessing. And as an indulgence does not simply abolish the whole burden of temporal punishment, but remits it only so far as your works, exactly prescribed by the Church, unite with the merits of Christ and His saints, it may serve also to arouse the sluggish conscience and to make it sensitive, not only to the infinite seriousness of sin, but also the unparalleled blessings contained in the fellowship of the members of Christ.

The Church Suffering and the Church Militant constitute in their relations a second circle of most vital activities. Having entered into the night "wherein no man can work," the Suffering Church cannot ripen to its final blessedness by any efforts of its own, but only through the help of others—through the intercessory prayers and sacrifices (*suffragia*) of those living members of the Body of Christ who being still in this world are able in the grace of Christ to perform expiatory works. The Church has from the earliest times faithfully guarded the words of Scripture (2 Macch. xii, 43 ff.) that "it is a holy and a wholesome thing to pray for the dead that

they may be loosed from their sins." The suppliant cry
of her liturgy: "Eternal rest give to them, O Lord, and
let perpetual light shine upon them," can be heard already
in the Acts of the martyrdom of SS. Perpetua and Felici-
tas (A.D. 203) and is represented in numerous sepulchral
inscriptions of the most ancient period, while theologians
and Fathers of the Church, beginning with Tertullian, have
supplied its substantial proof. The theology of the schismatical Greek Church agrees with Latin theology in its
belief in the efficacy of prayers for the dead. So fundamental indeed and so natural to man's hope and desire and
love is this belief, that historians of religion have discovered it among almost all non-Christian civilised peoples: a striking illustration of Tertullian's saying that the
human soul is naturally Christian.

The Catholic, therefore, is jealous to expiate and suffer
for the "poor souls," especially by offering the Eucharistic
Sacrifice, wherein Christ's infinite expiation on the Cross
is sacramentally re-presented, and stimulating and joining
itself with the expiatory works of the faithful, passes to
the Church Suffering according to the measure determined
by God's wisdom and mercy. So the saying of St. Paul
that the members of the Body of Christ "are mutually
careful one for another" (1 Cor. xii, 25) is nowhere more
comprehensively and luminously fulfilled than in the
Church's suffrages for her dead children. When, in the
Memento of the Mass, in the presence of the sacred Oblation and under the gaze so to speak of the Church Triumphant, she cries to heaven: "Be mindful also, O Lord,
of thy servants and handmaids . . . who have gone before
us with the sign of faith and rest in the sleep of peace,"
then truly heaven and earth greet each other, the Church
Triumphant, Suffering and Militant meet in a "holy kiss,"
and the "whole" Christ with all His members celebrates
a blessed love-feast (agape), a memorial of their communion in love and joy and pain.

The relations between the Church of this world and the
Church of the next are many and various; scarcely less

rich and fruitful is the loving and vital fellowship that exists between the earthly members themselves of the Body of Christ. When the Fathers, beginning with Nicetas, bishop of Remesiana at the commencement of the fifth century, speak of the Communion of Saints, they are thinking especially of this earthly fellowship, and it was this that St. Paul also had specially in mind. It is the mysterious inner life of the Church, the mysterious exchange and commerce in functions and graces between its members, the mysterious process whereby the fellowship of Christ grows up organically into a "holy temple in the Lord," into the "habitation of God in the Spirit" (Eph. ii, 21-22).

The communion of the members of Christ with the priesthood of their Head is of fundamental importance for their mutual commerce of love. There is but one priesthood in the Church, the priesthood of the God-man, who redeemed us by His whole life, but especially by the sacrifice of His death. But because this invisible priesthood of Christ needs visible instruments and organs, so that Christ's grace may be ministered to His people in sacramental words and signs, there rightly exists in the Church a visible priesthood. And that visible priesthood has existed from the beginning, though its full significance was not at first manifest to the consciousness of the faithful, nor expressed in a precise terminology. Whenever the most holy Eucharist was celebrated and whenever sins were forgiven, whenever the grace of Christ was imparted under visible forms, then instrumental agents were employed, and were called sometimes "presbyteri" or priests, sometimes presidents, sometimes overseers (*episcopi*). The visible priesthood is nothing else than a visible attestation of the continual living and working of Christ in the world.

However manifold and various its names and duties were and are, there is nevertheless but one single priesthood, since the priesthood of Christ is but one. The priesthood is always only the visible manifestation and mediation of the one grace of the one High Priest. Nevertheless the visible priesthood must have its inner differentiation, according to the intimacy with which its holders are incorporated into the priesthood of Christ, and consequently, according to their sacramental authority to realise that priesthood. It is in this sense only that Catholic theology distinguishes the specific priesthood from the priesthood of the laity, and not as though these two forms of the priesthood were fundamentally different. On the contrary they have their substance in common, namely, the priesthood of Christ. A consideration of the Church's teaching with regard to the character which is given by some of the sacraments, may make this point clearer.

It is one of the profoundest truths of Catholic theology that besides the purely personal, the religious and moral relation of the Christian to Christ, as manifested in faith and sanctifying love, there is also an extra-personal and wholly factual relation, which consecrates the Christian abidingly to Christ independently of his subjective life in grace, which gives him Christ irrevocably for his own, which incorporates him once and for all into Christ's high priesthood, and which thereby establishes that indissoluble religious basis upon which the loving intercourse and mutual commerce of Christ and His members is founded. Even the most delicate relation that exists within the Body of Christ, the relation that is of the individual human soul to Christ, is determined by a system of sacred ordinances, of fixed and indissoluble form and of unalterable interconnexion. As in the natural world all free movement of powers is based upon the determinate statics of natural being and its laws, and as all the activity of our subjective powers presupposes the objective world and its stable ordinances, so also in the supernatural world the life of grace with all its striving is closely knit to a permanent basis, to the fixed and inward relations and laws of the Body of Christ. Here once more we recognise the trend of Catholicism towards reality, its complete and fundamental preference for the objective fact and the fixed form. The ultimate basis of this is the fundamental dogma that it is God, and not man, who is the author of natural and supernatural reality, that the new order of being is determined not from below, but from above, and that in the world of religion we have to deal with supernatural facts, which man must simply accept and which do not depend upon him. As God alone is the eternal "form" of all beings, so is Christ, the Head, the eternal form of the Body of Christ, and from this eternal form does the Body of Christ acquire its determinate form and its inward structure, by the purely sacramental way, and so quite independently of the activity of the human subject. Man can effectively realise the grace which is imparted to him only on the basis of this sacramental order and within it. Now there are three sacraments which give the Christian his fixed and definite place within the Body of Christ, his fundamental relation to the whole Body, and thereby to the high-priesthood of Christ which supports and pervades the whole. They are the sacraments of Baptism, Confirmation and Holy Orders. Each of these three sacraments not merely confers grace, but also imparts to the soul of the Christian an abiding religious character, whereby the soul is incorporated in the high-priesthood of Christ in a greater or less degree according to the substance and nature of the sacrament, and remains permanently incorporated therein (*character indelebilis*), even though—as in the case of the damned—this impersonal and objective relation to Christ never results in the subjective and personal relation of grace and blessedness. The highest form of this sacramental incorporation into the high-priesthood of Christ is contained in the sacrament of Holy Orders. This sacrament confers the ineffaceable aptitude and full faculty of conveying the redeeming grace of Christ to the faithful in its widest extent, by word as well as by sacrament. By the priestly character the Christian is consecrated a "minister of Christ" in the full sense of the words, and in so far as the Church is Christ living on in the world, he is consecrated the "minister of the Church." As the external unity of the members of Christ culminates in pope and bishop, so their inner sacramental unity, the unity of their powers and graces, culminates in the priest.

That priesthood which is imparted to the Christian along with the sacramental character of Baptism and Confirmation is not so inward as this, nor so comprehensive, and therefore it is specifically different from the priesthood in the narrow sense of the word. It does not, as the full priesthood does, confer on the Christian the special position of a minister of the Body of Christ, and for that reason it comprises only a limited number of priestly powers. Nevertheless it is a true priesthood, for it, just as really as the special priesthood, gives the Christian a genuine participation in the one identical priesthood of Christ.[*] Every baptism is a consecration to the priesthood of Christ, for baptism removes the man from the profane world, appropriates him to Christ and sanctifies him for the performance of those most general acts of worship which belong to the vocation of the child of God. And the sacramental character of Confirmation intensifies this priesthood, since it fits the Christian to take an active share in the building of the temple of God, and equips him for the apostolate and for its "evidences of the spirit and of power." Therefore the Catholic conception of the priesthood of the laity is very far from being a making void of the original doctrine of the priesthood of all Christians. On the contrary the beautiful words of St. Peter in his First Epistle (ii, 9-10) still hold good in all their original freshness and force: "But you are a chosen generation, a kingly priesthood, a holy nation, a purchased people: that you may declare his wondrous deeds, who hath called you out of darkness into his marvellous light, Who in time past were not a people, but are now the people of God. Who had not obtained mercy, but now have obtained mercy."

---

[*] St. Thomas Aquinas, *Summa Theologica, Pars tertia*, Q. LXIII, A. 3; *Sacramentales characteres nihil aliud sunt quam quaedam participationes sacerdotii Christi ab ipso Christo derivatae.*

This priestly conjunction of all with the high-priesthood of Christ, an utterly sacred conjunction, is the source whence springs the close fellowship of all in their prayer and faith and love.

If we exclude some very rare and really necessary exceptions, such as the communion prayers of the priest, there is no liturgical prayer of the earthly Church which is not a prayer of all for all. As our Lord, in the great prayer which He taught His disciples, joined all who pray into a single unity and directed them to appeal out of this unity to their common Father, and as St. Paul especially enjoined prayer for one another (Rom. xv, 30; 2 Cor. i, 11; Eph. i, 15, etc.), so the Church prays, not in the name of any individual, nor as the mere sum of all individuals, but as a fellowship, as a priestly unity, as the visible priesthood of Christ.

It is not I and you that pray, but the mystical Christ. And so the fruits of this prayer belong to all those who in Christ are consecrated to the Father, to the "chosen generation" and "kingly priesthood." And the Church is desirous that her children should remember their priestly character, and in their private life, as well as in the liturgy, pray, offer and suffer, not for their own needs only, but also for the great and holy fellowship of all the redeemed in Christ. The genuine Christian prayer has the priestly quality of the great High Priest: it is offered "for all" (ὑπὲρ πολλῶν, Mk. xiv, 24), a quality which is so strongly marked in ancient Christian prayer (cf. *Martyrium Polycarpi*, v, 1; viii, 1). And this priestly communion in prayer and sacrifice is nowhere more clearly and strongly emphasised than in the Eucharistic Sacrifice, wherein Christ our High Priest sacramentally re-presents the sacrifice which He once offered on Calvary. It is true that it is the specially consecrated priest who by his instrumental ministry makes the invisible sacrifice of Christ visible, and he performs his service in liturgical vesture and in a liturgical tongue, which, sanctified by the use of the See of Peter and of so many Fathers of the Church, is raised above the vicissitudes of time and is especially suitable for the enactment of the Mystery. But the priest does not offer for himself alone. Nor does he merely offer as the people's representative, so that as in the ancient sacrifices there is only a moral unity between priest and people. On the contrary the unity between priest and people is a mystically real unity, the unity of the priesthood of Christ, in which both priest and people share, though in different degrees. The liturgy of the Church expresses this wonderful fact, when it causes the priest to pray thus after the Consecration: "We thy (priestly) servants, O Lord, but also thy holy people, mindful of the blessed Passion of Christ thy Son, our Lord, as also of his Resurrection from the dead and his glorious Ascension, do offer to thy glorious Majesty, of thy gifts and presents, a pure sacrifice, a holy sacrifice, an immaculate sacrifice, the holy Bread of eternal life and the Chalice of everlasting salvation."

The common faith of the members of Christ is most intimately bound up with their priestly fellowship in prayer. The Catholic fellowship in faith does not mean merely that all the members of the Church loyally profess one and the same faith, presented to them by apostolic authority, that they share the same luminous ideal, the same effective rule and the same fruitful sources of spiritual life. It means more than that. It means that there is a solidarity and partnership of the faith, a reciprocal interaction and fruitful influence, which by intimate and pervasive action make their external union an inward communion in the faith, a communion which out of the depths of the common experience of the faith is ever expressing itself anew in a single "credo" of the mystical Christ. This solidarity of Catholic belief manifests itself in two ways. On the one hand it communicates the inwardness and strength of your personal faith, the "power of God" that you experience in your own conscience, to other members of the Body of Christ, in ever new impulses and stirrings, and makes them the vital experience of ever wider circles. On the other hand, this solidarity of the faith, returning so to say upon itself, becomes a fertile soil and fruitful womb, which impregnated by the infallible teaching of the Church produces a constantly deeper insight into the marvels of the faith and a constantly richer appreciation of supernatural truth. In its first aspect—as an evidential force—the solidarity of the faith manifests itself in the Catholic practice of the apostolate. The true and most eminent bearers of the apostolate are the successors of the apostles, those bishops who are united together and with the one Peter, and who are "set by the Holy Ghost over the whole earth" (Acts xx, 28). The preaching of the Gospel has been committed to them, the chosen disciples, ever since that hour when the risen Christ sent them out into the whole world and made them the promise that He would be "with them all days, even unto the consummation of the world" (Matt. xxviii, 18). Christendom, in all periods of its history, has recognised in their concordant testimony, but especially in their harmony with the See of Peter, the guarantee and sign of the true apostolic faith as contrasted with all individual "gnosis" and sectional opinion. They incarnate the "teaching Church" (*ecclesia docens*), and in relation to their authentic teaching the rest of the Church can only be a "learning Church" (*ecclesia discens*). No layman, priest, teacher, or theologian of the Church may preach the Word of God unless he be commissioned to do so by the apostolic authority of the Church (*missio cano- nica*). For, "How shall they preach, unless they be sent?" (Rom. x, 15). But however true it is that the authorita- tive preaching of Christian truth appertains exclusively to the apostolic teaching authority, it is equally true that the living of this truth, its realisation in deed and in truth, is the business of the individual Christian conscience and of the grace which visits that conscience. And therefore the life of faith, that life which is the supreme goal of the Church's preaching, the one thing necessary, the super- natural fruitfulness of the faith, all intimate experience, all consolation, all confidence, all nobility and lofty courage: these things do not belong to any privileged individual, but to the community, to the fellowship of all those who by baptism have been born again in Christ. Faith becomes living, and the seed of preaching strikes root and grows and bears fruit in the fellowship of the members of Christ. The spirit of the faith is never an isolated or an isolating thing, but always a spirit that presses towards fellowship, because it is derived from the Spirit of God, the Spirit of union and love. If the authorities of the Church are the instruments and bearers of the truth, it is by means of the community that the truth becomes life. It is the special task of the community to attest the truth which is proclaimed by the Church in living it, and to live it in attesting it. It is the special mission and apostolate of the community, in St. Bernard's pregnant words, to "experience the faith in prayer." [4] Being finally incorporated into Christ, its Head, by baptism, and being obliged to confess Him by confirmation, the community has its fundamental duty in this, that it gives testimony to Christ by the superabundant wealth of its life, a duty from which no man can absolve it. Living by the faith, its gives testimony to the faith. Every life that is lived in faith is necessarily a persuasive and inspiring life, an incarnation of the apostolic message, a building of the temple of God in oneself and in others. It is that "shewing of the spirit and of power" in the face of which all unbelief is dumb, and by which all weakness is made strong. It is the most convincing proof of Christianity, more effective than all the "persuasive words of human wisdom" (1 Cor. ii, 4).

Every individual member of the community should have this living faith and should exercise this confessorship. It will be exercised in infinitely various ways according to each one's particular qualities, according to his bent of mind, the graces he receives, his special vocation, his environment and fortunes. For the one revealed truth may be expressed and applied in an infinite variety of ways. And every one of these various expressions reveals new vistas of its hidden beauty and power, displays new types of the

[4] *Experimur orantes (In Cant. XXXII, 3).*

Christian ideal and sets before us new incentives to imitation. The characteristic types of the Christian life—confessor, martyr, prophet, hermit, monk, virgin, widow—change into ever new forms, and each new form contains a creative tendency to further forms, until the whole content of the Christian life is exhausted. The most fundamental, the simplest, and the most effective form in which living faith becomes inspiring testimony will certainly always be found in the Christian family. The family reflects, as no other social institution does, the mystery of the Church, her real union with Christ, her Head (Eph. 5, 32). The family illustrates, as it is illustrated nowhere else, the priesthood of the laity and shows it in all its beauty. For bride and bridegroom, in virtue of their priestly character, are themselves the ministers of the sacrament of their union, and, entering upon the life so consecrated, propagate in their children and children's children their own devout faith. The Christian family is the nucleus of the lay apostolate, of that faith which awakens and enkindles faith, which continually flames up anew and through whole generations gives testimony to Christ.

Besides speaking of that Church authority which guides the stream of the Christian life of faith in a sure course and protects it from all contamination, we ought also to consider the stream itself The two things cannot in fact be separated, because the life of faith is nourished by the truths of faith, and the truths of faith are attested in the life. Authority guards the truth, and the community manifests the life, and therefore these two stand in a close reciprocal relation and must not be separated. Not only does Church authority mould the life of the community with the truths of faith, but the life of the community reacts on the authority itself, protects it, and illuminates with ever new radiance the truths which it conveys. It is because of this essential union of truth and life, of authority and community, that when Church authority has sometimes and in some places failed in its trust, the life of the community has been the fresh source whence the life of the Church has been renewed. In fact history testifies that when truth has seemed barren and authority overcome by human frailty, the grace of Christ, its Head, has brought forth from the womb of the living community members who by the power of their faith have given new life, not only to their own immediate environment, but to the whole Church. It is in this that the providential and salutary influence, and the historical importance of so many saints are manifest. St. Bernard and St. Francis, St. Catharine of Siena, St. Clement Maria Hofbauer and so many others —what else did they do but bring forth from within themselves "streams of living water"? (cf. Jn. vii, 38). Did not the living ardour of their faith give to wide regions of the Church new growth, new youth, a second spring?

But the blessing of the close fellowship of the faith goes deeper still. It does not merely out of its abundant fruitfulness, as a shewing of the Spirit and of power, attest the Gospel before the world and communicate its own living faith to the weak members of the Body of Christ. It plays an important part also in the begetting of the faith and in the development of particular truths. We have already shown that the community co-operates in the begetting of supernatural faith, and that in particular it is by living contact with the church fellowship that faith acquires its absolute certainty (cf. p. 56 ff.). Let us speak here only of those delicate influences whereby the fellowship of the faith, in its mysterious co-operative action, brings about the formulisation of a truth of the faith, the definition of a dogma.

There is no revealed doctrine (*dogma explicitum*) proclaimed by the Church which is not contained in its exact substance (*formaliter*) in the sources of revelation, that is, in Scripture and Tradition. But it is not always expressly (*explicite*) revealed in its specific content, and is often contained so to say wrapped up (*implicite*) in other truths. As the history of dogma shows, it sometimes needed a long process to free such truths from their wrappings and to make them plain and visible. More than six centuries passed before the Church set forth the central Christian dogma of Jesus, God and Man, in all its aspects and formulated it exhaustively. The doctrine of transubstantiation was not defined as a revealed dogma until the year 1215, nor the infallibility and plenary jurisdiction of the pope until 1870. This dogmatic development, fulfilled under the assistance of the Holy Spirit and under the supervision and guidance of the Church's teaching office, is not always effected in a purely logical manner, by mere juxtaposition of revealed truths, or by philosophical methods, by demonstrating that a truth is attested by Scripture and Tradition, however indispensable may be the labours of theologians in elucidation and demonstration. For the legacy of the faith as left us in the revelation has not been transmitted to us in the form of a clear logical system, but is wrapped up rather in the forms of its time; nor was it always so lucidly and plainly set forth in those forms, that its inner content and irresistible external proof were immediately obvious. And sometimes, when the source of a doctrine is to be sought, not in holy Scripture, but in that age-long tradition which is represented in the most various documents, the discriminating eye of the theologian has the greatest difficulty in determining clearly what is the pure gold of revelation and what the product of purely human wisdom and purely human faith. Often enough he will find Fathers and theologians expressing views which impair their unanimous witness (*unanimis consensus patrum*). And so the exegesis and argument of the theologians are not able unaided to prepare the way effectively for the definitive decisions of the Church's teaching authority. Indeed, were they such a decisive factor in the construction of dogma, then—to mention only one of the latest of dogmas—the beautiful truth of our Lady's Immaculate Conception might never have been defined. For two most distinguished Mariologists, St. Bernard and St. Thomas, expressly questioned its revealed character, nay even denied it. How then, in spite of all obstacles, was the dogma ultimately defined? And how was the dogma of Papal Infallibility defined?. Certainly it is Church authority under the guidance of the Holy Ghost which by its ordinary and extraordinary teaching strews the seeds of revealed truth in the field of the Church, and like a careful gardener protects their sprouting, guards the tender shoots from foreign growths and prunes away all evil tendencies. The teaching authority, guarded by the Holy Ghost, is therefore the decisive *active* factor in dogmatic development. But—to keep to our metaphor—the gardener does not do the whole of the work. For the very reason that the seed of revealed truth is a living and organic thing, it requires for its progressive growth a fertile field, a maternal soil, which may foster the seed committed to it and bring it to maturity. The living community is this fertile soil. Theologians speak of a passive infallibility of the faithful, and in the same way the community may be called the *passive* factor in the formation of dogma. The living community of the faithful, hearing and obeying the revelation which the teaching authority proclaims, itself shares in the infallibility of the Church as it accepts this revelation, cherishes it and bears fruit. Such is the nature of the influence which the community exercised in the development of the dogmas above mentioned, especially that of the Immaculate Conception of our Lady. It was the Catholic body, the fellowship of the faithful, in its vital movement, and with its vivid sense and profound instinct for the faith, which refused to abandon these truths, even when authoritative theologians sought to deprive it of them. All these truths germinated in the soil of the community, like living seeds, to be protected and fostered by pope and bishop until their time came. And even though these truths—as for instance the particular one of the Immaculate Conception of Mary—circulated originally among the faithful in distorted and legendary forms which will not bear historical criticism, yet the living community grasped their substance and inner value too intimately, vitally, and immediately to be able to sacrifice their eternal content along with the imperfect forms and expressions to which the theologians objected. The divine spirit of its faith was too sensitive, the moral and religious experience produced in so many of its members by that truth was too rich, manifold and profound, and the Church's custody of the deposit of faith too vigilant, to allow of such a consummation. Because of the solidarity of its life, this common experience of a truth, new and yet old, belonged to the whole community, and became deeper and stronger the more widely it spread, until all shared it. And since this life of faith was not a spasmodic and fortuitous phenomenon, but was steadily evolved under the purifying and promoting influence of the teaching authority, and thereby drew strength and guidance from its profound connexion with the whole mass of supernatural revelation, it became for that reason a life full of divine clarity and purity. It is not the sectional belief of this or that group of the faithful, but a life in the whole and of the whole infallible Church, of the whole Body of Christ, a life inspired by Christ. It would be by no means difficult to show that the compact fellowship of the faith exercised this quasi-maternal function in the growth and ripening of most of our dogmas, from the consubstantiality of the Son to the infallibility of the pope, and that it is exercising it at present in respect of that belief in the universal intercessory mediatorship of Mary, which is beginning to become ripe for definition. It is the teaching authority of the Church which proclaims the revelation in its complete fulness, together with the truths which are contained only germinally (*implicite*) in it; and it is the same authority which watches over the process of the unfolding of these implicit truths and by the help of the theologians excludes all spurious elements. And lastly it is the teaching authority alone that gives the final solemn decision regarding the revealed character of a truth. We should grievously misconceive the absolutely pre-eminent and decisive authority of the "teaching Church" if we supposed that its function was merely one of registering and ratifying the unanimous belief of the "learning Church" and that it played no inde-

pendent and decisive part in the formation of dogma.[8] Yet
on the other hand it is the maternal organism of the compact fellowship which, fertilised by the Church's teaching,
brings dogmas to maturity, until they receive their definitive form in the Church's authoritative definition.

According the development of the faith originates in
the Church's teaching authority, not only as regards that
deepening which it receives at the hands of the theologians,
but also as regards that extension in the dimensions of
length and breadth which it receives from the compact
living fellowship of the faithful.   There is therefore no
piece of dogmatic knowledge which is the knowledge of
individuals and not at the same time an experience and
love of the many in the Holy Ghost.   In this sense every
new dogma is the child not only of authority, but of love,
of the love of the fellowship of the faith, of the heart of
the praying Church.   Every dogma is consecrated by the
reverence and earnestness, by the conscientiousness and
loyalty, by the inwardness and devotion, with which the
fellowship of the members of Christ "rooted and grounded
in love" (Eph. iii, 17) "confirms the testimony of Christ
in itself" (cf. 1 Cor. i, 6).   As a rule the *"lex orandi"* the
unwritten law of prayerful, lived faith, precedes the *"lex
credendi,"* the authoritaive formulisation of a truth as a
dogma.   Whenever any dogma has been attacked in the
name of historical criticism, its impugners have overlooked
this vital power of the living fellowship and its function
in the formation of dogma.   When Döllinger (28 March
1871) wrote to Archbishop Scherr of München-Freising:
"We have to do, in the present distracted state of the
Church, with a purely historical question, which, therefore, must be handled and decided by means only of those
resources which are at our command, and according to
the rules which govern every historical enquiry, every

---

[8] Pope Pius X condemned the modernist proposition that *"in defini-
endis veritatibus ita collaborant discens et docens ecclesia, ut docenti
ecclesiae nihil supersit nisi communes discentis opinationes sancire* (Decree
Lamentabili, 1907, n. 6).

manipulation of things in the past," [*] he overlooked the fact that the Church is not a dead, but a living organism; and he failed to recognise that vigorous life of faith which pulsates in the Church and which as a living thing cannot be found in dead documents but only in the hearts of the faithful, in the compact fellowship of the faith united with pope and bishops. Such was the tragedy of his intellectual development: he could not see the surging life of the present, he saw only the petrified life of history.

The fellowship of prayer and faith is perfected in the fellowship of love. This love is love towards one another and for one another; it is the strong consciousness that we are bound to one another in prosperity and in misfortune, not merely by natural bonds, but by a supernatural kinship through communion in the Body and Blood of Christ, our Head. This love produces a feeling of mutual responsibility in sorrow and in joy, a warm sympathy, a magnanimous generosity, an absolute loyalty of service to others, as St. Paul so beautifully depicts it (1 Cor. xiii). This love is that solidarity of Christian sentiment which ever first envisages the whole and comes back to the individual and to itself only from the whole; which with deep reverence of soul sees in every member of Christ, even in the least, a brother or sister of the Lord, yes, Christ Himself. This love is the most precious fruit of the Communion of the Saints on earth. It is this love that gives to the external and visible organism of the Body of Christ, to papacy and episcopacy, the vital inspiration of Christ (see p. 42 ff.) and it is this alone that creates and maintains its inner wealth. In truth and in fact this love is therefore the life-blood of the Body of Christ, which, welling forth out of the heart of the God-man, flows through the whole Body and gives it form and strength and beauty. Without this love the Body of Christ on earth would be a rigid corpse, and all Church ordinances and offices, all sacraments, all

[*] See *Döllinger on the Infallibility of the Pope. A Letter addressed to the Archbishop of Munich*, London, 1871, p. 18.

dogmas, all faith would be stale and unprofitable, like "sounding brass or tinkling cymbal," or, in the words of St. Augustine, mere "forms of piety." Moreover the inner history of the Body of Christ, the course of its ills and difficulties, of its progress and development, is determined by the sincerity, inwardness and fertility of this love. There is no more perilous crisis for it than when its love is in jeopardy. When it can no longer be said of the majority of its members: "See how these Christians love one another!" then will be the most dangerous crisis of all, that time when, in our Lord's words, "the charity of many shall grow cold" (Matt. xxiv, 12). For there is nothing so essentially alien to the Body of Christ, nothing so inimical, as that its members should abandon their mutual love. For Christ our Lord is love incarnate, nor is the Body of Christ anything else but an incarnation of that same love, in all those who are incorporated into Christ. Wherever Christianity is, there is love. According to St. Augustine's striking saying, love is the motive weight of the Christian being.[7] It can be manifested nowhere else in such purity, inwardness and power as in Christ and His Body. And so the development of the Body of Christ on earth is characterised by nothing so plainly as by the growth of this love. All development of dogma, of worship, of government and of law, is profitable to the Body of Christ only because it produces this growth of love. And the Body of Christ will not be fully mature and perfect, until love, as the soul of all the virtues (*forma virtutum*), has become not merely in some members but in all, both in the shepherd and in the flock, the fundamental and dominant principle of all living, suffering and dying. By not other mark shall men know that they are the disciples of Christ than by this, that they have love one to another.

Communion of Saints—what a glad and blessed light illumines it! It is the hidden treasure, the secret joy of the Catholic. When he thinks on the Communion of Saints his heart is enlarged. He passes out of the solitariness of

[7] *Pondus meum amor meus.* Conf. XIII, 9.

here and of there, of yesterday and to-morrow, of "I" and "thou," and he is enfolded in an unspeakably intimate communion of spirit and of life, far surpassing his needs and dearest wishes, with all those great ones whom the grace of God has forged from the refractory stuff of our humanity and raised to His height, to participation in His Being. Here are no limitations of space and time. From out of the remote ages of the past, from civilisations and countries of which the memory is now only faintly echoed in legend, the saints pass into his presence, and call him brother, and enfold him with their love. The Catholic is never alone. Christ, the Head, is ever with him, and along with Christ all the holy members of His Body in heaven and on earth. Streams of invisible, mysterious life flow thence through the Catholic fellowship, forces of fertilising, beneficent love, forces of renewal, of a youthfulness that is ever flowering anew. They pass into the natural, visible forces of the Catholic fellowship, especially to pope and bishop, completing and perfecting them. He who does not see and appreciate these forces, cannot fully understand and expound the nature and working of Catholicism. And, indeed, it is simple, child-like faith alone which perceives these forces; and therefore that faith alone discovers the road to sanctity. For such is the prayer of Jesus: "I praise thee, O Father, Lord of heaven and earth, because thou hast hidden these things from the wise and prudent, and hast revealed them to little ones. Yea, Father, for so it hath seemed good in thy sight" (Lk. x, 21).

CHAPTER IX

THE CATHOLICITY OF THE CHURCH

I became all things to all men, that I might save all (1 Cor. ix, 22).

THE Church is the Kingdom of God thoroughly leavening all mankind in slow but irresistible process, the Body of Christ embracing the whole of fallen humanity in a supra-personal unity. Therefore of her nature she rests upon faith in the divine Redeemer, in Christ. As the supra-personal unity of mankind reunited to God she obtains in Peter's office the perfect expression of this unity and its guarantee, while her inward life, with the loving commerce which characterises it, is realised in the Communion of Saints. Such is the sequence of thought developed in the previous chapters.

The "notes," or characteristic marks of the Church, follow directly from her essential nature. Let us investigate first her most outstanding and most obvious attribute, that which is meant when one speaks of the "Catholic" Church: her catholicity. Ignatius of Antioch is the first witness for this title of "catholic" (Smyrn. viii, 2) and he indicates at the same time the reason why the Church must be catholic, that is to say, must have an essential aptitude for propagating itself over the whole earth (καθ᾽ ὅλον) and embracing all humanity. "Where Christ is," he says, "there also is the Catholic Church." Since Christ came to redeem all mankind, therefore His Body is essentially related to all mankind. The whole of redemption-needing mankind is potentially present in it. And so the Church is not complete until she has in pro-

gressive process embraced all mankind. This trend towards
the whole of mankind is native to her.

The Church's attractive power, her appeal to all men,
has its source in the missionary injunction of the risen
Christ: "Go ye and teach all nations, baptizing them in the
name of the Father and of the Son and of the Holy Ghost"
(Matt. xxviii, 19). This command represents in the broad-
est outline the fundamental motives of our Lord's Gospel
of the Kingdom. His Kingdom of God had in it "from
the start the tendency to become a universal religion"
(Holtzmann). For it is a great spiritual creation, that
stands above all national interests or other worldly consid-
erations, and that is of a purely moral and religious character. Its gifts are forgiveness of sin and grace, and its
requirements are those moral imperatives which apply to all
men and are set forth in the Sermon on the Mount. The
citizens of this Kingdom are the children of God, and they
pray in the *Our Father* to the common Father of all men.
The preachers of this Kingdom have their mission not only
to the Jews, but also to the whole world, for they are the
salt of the earth and the light of the world. Jesus Himself,
in His messianic consciousness, takes His stand above all
merely national aspirations. He is not merely the Son of
David, but the Son of Man. He belongs to all men and
not to the Jews alone. Even if He had not after His Resurrection expressly given His apostles this great missionary
injunction, yet in view of the supra-national and fundamentally universal aim of His Gospel of the Kingdom, we
should have to say at the very least that He displayed a
potential universalism. But if we turn from His Gospel to
the living Jesus Himself, if we remind ourselves of the
open repugnance and strong distaste with which He criti-
cised and rejected all the caste prejudice, narrowness, petti-
ness and pride of the Pharisees, if we think of the boundless generosity with which He welcomed every trace of
nobility, purity and goodness which He encountered, though
it were in publicans and sinners, and if finally we observe
that in His parables of the prodigal son, of the Pharisee

and publican, and of the marriage feast to which beggars and the lame and blind are invited, the radiance of His redeeming love penetrates to the most wretched and for- saken corners of our humanity: then we realise that it is a psychological monstrosity to say with Harnack that "the Gentile mission cannot have lain within the horizon of Jesus."[1]   It is an incontrovertible fact that the mission of the Gentiles not only lay within the horizon of con- temporary Judaism, where it degenerated into a dreary proselytism (cf. Matt. xxiii, 15), but that it also gave a special colour to the promises of the prophets. Jesus lived and moved in the world of the prophets. Therefore their hopes—even if we ignore His messianic consciousness— could not have been unknown to Him, and their spirit must have had its effect upon His large-hearted and liberal attitude. And in fact He never avoided pagans when they came to Him. He healed the sick daughter of the Syro- phenician woman (Mk. vii, 24) and the sick servant of the pagan centurion (Matt. viii, 5 ff.; Luke vii, 1 ff.). On both occasions He does what He does with a hearty good- will and undisguisedly expresses His appreciation of their dispositions: "O woman, great is thy faith." "Amen I say to you, I have not found so great faith in Israel. And I say to you that man shall come from the east and the west and shall sit down with Abraham and Isaac and Jacob in the kingdom of heaven" (Matt. viii, 10-11). Our Lord here expressly confirms the promises of the prophets in their full scope. The parable of the Good Samaritan, which contains a severe rebuke to the Jews, teaches that practical charity was to be found rather among the hereti- cal Samaritans than among the orthodox priests and levites. And we know also that Jesus frequently (Matt. viii, 28; xv, 21) entered heathen territory, and that there- fore He did not shun the heathen, but rather sought contact

---

[1] *Die Mission und Ausbreitung des Christentums in den ersten 3 Jahrh.,* 1916; Vol. I, p. 39, note 3. Eng. tr., Jas. Moffatt: *The Mission and Expansion of Christianity in the First Three Centuries,* 2nd ed., London, 1908; Vol. I, page 38, note 1.

with them. Yet if, despite this fundamental friendliness towards the Gentiles, He deliberately confined His own and His disciples' preaching to the people of Israel, there were sound practical reasons for that course. It was important that the forces at hand for the preaching of the Gospel should not be dissipated, and the preachers had to take account of natural and religious facts. Of natural facts, in so far as their own people, with their special history and with their ethico-religious monotheism, provided the strongest natural foundation on which to build the Kingdom of God. Of religious facts, in so far as Jesus, like the prophets before Him and like Paul after Him, regarded Israel as the chosen people who because of their covenant with Jehovah seemed to be especially called to deepen the faith which they had carried through the centuries into faith in the Triune God. No doubt we may here trace in our Lord's attitude a strain of nationalism. But it is far from being an exclusive nationalism. It did not exclude, but included, the conversion of the Gentiles. Israel—as the prophets conceived the matter—was to be the foundation and nucleus of the new Kingdom of God, a Kingdom which was to embrace all peoples and nations, and therefore also the Gentiles. So long as the Jewish people had not forfeited this claim, they had an historical and religious right that the Kingdom, germinally contained in the whole of their age-long development, should be fulfilled and completed in them.

Therefore while Jesus lived on the earth He belonged to His own people. From among them He called the twelve apostles, in order to fashion the new Israel. And when He had by His Resurrection proved Himself the "Son of God in power" (Rom. i, 4) and as such had bidden His disciples evangelise the whole world, it was from this Jewish sapling that the mighty tree grew, in whose branches dwell the birds of the air. The catholicity of the new society, which was to embrace all languages and all men, was manifested at the very beginning in the pentecostal miracle of tongues. The life of the young plant, in its early days needed a protective sheath of Jewish custom; but this sheath was not able to hinder or restrict further development, and it was decisively set aside by St. Peter and St. Paul. St. Peter was the first to admit a pagan, the centurion Cornelius, into the Christian community; and St. Paul, by his vigorous reasoning as much as by his strong action, finally demolished the barriers of Jewish legalism and gave Christianity free course into the world. The universal character, which is implicit in our Lord's preaching, was made explicit by St. Peter and St. Paul. It has been maintained recently that by making Christianity co-terminous with the Church, St. Paul was unfaithful to our Lord's fundamental thought.[*] But that is to overlook the fact that St. Paul conceives the Church, not as one particular sect, but as a society embracing the whole of redeemed humanity. The Church is not an institution to be established within humanity, which for that reason introduces new lines of division and produces a sectional organisation and a sort of new synagogue. On the contrary, it is so world wide in its nature that it breaks down all barriers and all divisions. It is as big and as wide as humanity itself.

This world-wide spirit, rooted in the preaching of our Lord, has been taken over in its full breadth and depth by the Catholic Church, and by her alone. The Church is not one society or one church alongside many others, nor is she just a church among men; she is the church of men, the church of mankind. It is this claim that gives her action its persevering determination and its grandeur. The interests of the Church have never been subordinated to purely national interests, nor has the Church ever put herself for long in bondage to any state. Her members belong to 'this or that nation, and national interests are bound to exert some influence on the Church's action. There have even been times when the Church seemed to be no more than a handmaid of the German Emperor or the French king. But those were only episodes, only brief

[*] Kattenbusch, op. cit., p. 351.

and passing checks in her world-wide mission. She had
to fight hard for it again and again, in bitter struggles, but
she won for herself, in virtue of her mission to all mankind, her spiritual freedom from princes and peoples, and
so secured the sovereignty of the Kingdom of God and the
independence of Christian faith and morals. As such a
supra-national power which assembles all men and all
peoples in one Kingdom of God, she is able, far more than
any national organisation, such as the Anglican, Swedish,
or Russian churches, to evoke the best that lies dormant
in the individual peoples and to make it serviceable for
the propagation of the Kingdom of God. All peoples, each
with their special aptitudes, are her children and all bring
their gifts into the sanctuary. The elasticity, freshness of
mind and sense of form of the Roman combine with the
penetration, profundity and inwardness of the German, and
with the sobriety, discretion and good sense of the Anglo-
Saxon. The piety and modesty of the Chinaman unite
with the subtlety and depth of the Indian, and with the
practicality and initiative of the American. It is unity
in fulness, fulness in unity.* The individual life of men
and peoples—the most precious thing in the world and
unique in character—flows with its rich and sparkling
waters in all the innumerable courses and channels dug
by missionaries in far lands; and those countless tributaries
flow into the Church, and purified in the Holy Spirit by
its infallible teaching, merge into a single mighty stream,
into one great flood which flows through all humanity,
fertilising and purifying as it goes. That is the true conception of the Catholic Church. It is a great, supra-
national tidal wave of faith in God and love of Christ,
nourished and supported by the special powers of every
individual nation and of every individual man, puri-

---

* St. Augustine emphasises this unity in fulness: *Corpus ipsius ubi
jacet?* . . . *Extende caritatem per totum orbem, si vis Christum amare,
quia membra Christi per orbem jacent* (*In. Ep. Joann.* Tr. X, 8). The
Catholic may proudly claim: *Ego in omnibus linguis sum: mea est
Graeca, mea est Syra, mea est Hebraea, mea est omnium gentium, quia in
unitate sum omnium gentium* (*En. in Ps.* CXLVII, 19).

fied and inspired by the divine spirit of truth and love.

How is this catholicity of the Church realised? The internal catholicity of the Church, its essential aptitude for the whole of mankind, is of fundamental importance for its world-conquering power, its external catholicity. This internal catholicity of the Church is based upon two particular qualities, and first on a resolute affirmation of the whole of revelation in all its living fulness. Unlike all non-catholic communions, the Church affirms, completely and entirely, the whole of holy Scripture, both the Old Testament and the New. She affirms therefore not only the theology of St. Paul, but also the mysticism of St. John, not only St. Matthew's teaching concerning the Church and doctrinal authority, but also the faith and works of St. James and St. Peter. There is no thought in holy Scripture which is for her antiquated or unseasonable. Nor does she allow one truth to be obscured or garbled for the benefit of another. And by the side of holy Scripture stand extra-scriptural Tradition. The Gospel itself is based upon oral teaching, upon the preaching of Christ, of His disciples and of that apostolic succession of teachers which began with the first pupils of the apostles. Therefore the formation in the Christian communities of a living stream of tradition was natural and inevitable. The New Testament is certainly an important expression, but it is by no means an exhaustive expression, of this apostolic tradition which filled and permeated the whole consciousness of the Church. Oral tradition, the apostolic teaching alive and active in the Christian communities, that is prior to and more fundamental than the Bible. Nay, it is even the basis which sustains the Bible, both in its inspiration and in its canon. It is more comprehensive than the Bible, for it attests a mass of ritual and religious usage, of customs and rules, which is only slightly indicated in the Bible. And it possesses a quality which the Bible as a written document has not and cannot have, and which constitutes its pre-eminent merit, namely, that living spirit of revelation, that vitality of revealed thought, that "instinct of the faith" which stands behind every written and unwritten word, and which we call the "mind of the Church" (φρόνημα ἐκκλησιαστικόν). This spirit of revelation lives in the living hearts of the faithful, and is quickened and promoted by the apostolic teaching authority under the guidance of the Holy Ghost. It is the most genuine, primary and precious heritage from the preaching of Jesus and His apostles. It is by means of this spirit that revelation acquires its inward unity, its inter-connexion and its ultimate meaning. Now, because the Church accepts as revelation the whole of holy Scripture and the whole of that extra-scriptural Tradition which has come down from the teaching of Christ and His apostles, without restricting herself to particular revealed thoughts, such as the notion of the Fatherhood of God or of the certainty of forgiveness, and because the Church accepts and affirms that full Christian life and experience which originated in Christ was by the apostles conveyed to mankind, therefore she is able out of her abundance to be something for all men and to give something to all men. She is become "all things to all men." Like St. Paul at Corinth, she gives the "little ones in Christ" milk and not meat, for they "are not yet able" for meat. To those who are not yet delicate enough of hearing and perception to appreciate the profound spirituality and delicate inward power of the Christian message, and to understand the "liberty of the children of God," those who are not ready for St. Augustine's rule, "Love and do what you will," the Church in her sermons and instructions indicates the stern commandments of the Decalogue, insists upon the obligations of Christian morality and holds up the aweful majesty of that Judge who condemns to everlasting fire all those who fail in mercy and in love. If love of God cannot achieve it, at least fear of His justice will deliver them from their earthliness and self-seeking and give them a spiritual life based on a fear of God which for all its imperfection is yet supernatural. And when souls are alive to her voice and can understand her doctrine of inwardness and love, then she allures them by the sweetest methods, by the Mystery of the Tabernacle, by devotion to the Sacred Heart, by the Stations of the Cross and by her Rosary. Thus she leads the simplest and rudest of souls to a height of spiritual life wherein the cry "Abba, Father!" is experienced in its full meaning, to the heights where St. Paul and St. John abide. And it may happen that a man is so penetrated with love of Christ and zeal for His Kingdom that his soul is stirred to its depths by those words of the Gospel: "If thou wilt be perfect, go sell what thou hast and give to the poor; and come, follow me" (Matt. xix, 21). Then deserts and great cities alike are peopled with hermits and monks. There is no stage of religious development which the comprehensive influence of the Church cannot grip and mould. It is impossible to describe the infinite variety of forms in which the religious and moral life of Catholics is expressed. In this region individualism is the rule and an unrestricted freedom of religious self-expression the dominant law.

Yet, however various these expressions may be, they have all sprung in their fundamental forms from the living tradition, from that abundance and variety of life which is our inheritance in Scripture and Tradition. For here, in Scripture and Tradition, yes in Scripture alone and even in St. John and St. Paul alone, we have not merely the spiritual, but the sensible also, though it be the sensible transfigured into the spiritual. We have not only certainty of forgiveness, but also the severe imperative, the commandments and the doctrine of merit. We have not only personal spiritual experience, but also service of the community and official authority. And above all we have mysticism; for wherever there is genuine religion, there you must have mysticism. The fundamental forms of Catholicism may be determined without difficulty or dialectic from the Scriptures and even from St. Paul alone. For revelation does not consist merely in this or that inspiring idea. On the contrary, it is original, comprehensive, mighty life. It is something holy and but half-expressed, "a reality, which is fruitful in resources; a depth, which extends into mystery." [4]

So the fulness of Catholicism wells out of the fulness of the revelation of the Old and New Testaments, out of the fulness of Scripture and Tradition. But it is a fulness in unity, for it is animated by one spirit and by one soul. The life of Catholicism grows, but it does not outgrow itself. The Church has advanced, past all hesitation and reverses, "till the whole truth 'self-balanced on its centre hung'." [5]

There are, indeed, apparent disturbances of this inward equipoise, especially when heresies have arisen and compelled the Church to withdraw a truth which has been abused or to emphasise another which has been denied. But a mere attitude of antagonism to heresy, whether it be to Gnosticism, Arianism, Lutheranism or Modernism, is not the proper attitude of Catholicism.

Such an attitude, on the contrary, is the creature of its time and represents a temporary shifting of the balance in order to meet and discomfit heresy. And Catholicism displays its vitality, its inner unity and truth, most clearly in the fact that it always ultimately regains its balance, after such temporary disturbances, though it may take it centuries to do so. The strong force which gives it back its inner equipoise is the vital spirit of revelation transmitted in its teaching authority, or, more profoundly, the Holy Spirit living in it. The Holy Spirit gives that secret energy which infuses new life into the weakened parts of the organism and repairs all unnatural dislocations in the Body of Christ. It could be shown in detail how Catholicism has sometimes repelled and rejected outright an heretical position with all its implications, reasons and consequences in order to prevent any contamination of revealed truth, and then, when the danger of such contamination was past, has taken over those elements of

[4] Cardinal Newman, *University Sermons*, XV (1872, p. 318).
[5] *Ibid.*, p. 317.

truth which heresy had grasped but wrongly emphasised, and moulding them into harmony with the whole of revelation, has consciously built them into her teaching and maintained them. The Church alone, says Cardinal Newman, "has succeeded in thus rejecting evil without sacrificing the good, and in holding together in one things which in all other schools are incompatible."[*] It is the spirit of revelation living in the Church, the vitality and consistency of Catholic thought, that "active tradition," as the schoolmen call it, which prevents any injury to the Catholic whole and ever restores its massive unity and inward harmony.[†] It is the same living spirit of revelation, manifested in the teaching authority, which gives the Church its flexibility and power of expansion, and enables it to adapt itself to every age, to every civilisation, and to every mental outlook. It is indeed the propelling and progressive principle in Catholicism. All other Christian bodies, in so far as they have maintained a positive belief, have attached themselves to a fixed and rigid principle. In Lutheranism and Calvinism it is the letter of the Bible; in the schismatical churches of the East it is the Bible and "passive" tradition, that is to say, the tradition of the ancient Fathers and most ancient Councils. Therefore these churches are in danger of treating revelation as so much dead capital, as a store of gold which must be passed on to future generations in a merely external fashion, and of overlooking the vital energies that lie in the revelation and work for the further development of its germinal content. To this danger of petrifaction and ossification the Orthodox Church has succumbed. Or there is the opposite danger, that in an effort to accommo-

---

[*] *Development of Christian Doctrine*, VI, §2 (1846, p. 352).

[†] St. Augustine repeatedly speaks of the importance of heresies in the development of the Church's teaching. *Plurimum prosunt, non verum docendo, quod nesciunt, sed ad verum quaerendum carnales et ad verum aperiendum spiritales catholicos excitando.* (*De vera religione*, VIII, 15.) *Improbatio quippe haereticorum facit eminere, quid ecclesia tua sentiat et quid habeat sana doctrina. Oportuit enim et haereses esse, ut probati manifesti fierent inter infirmos* (*Confes.* VII, 19, 28).

date religion to modern needs and requirements, its inner connexion with revelation is sacrificed, and an entirely novel Christianity, the religion of German idealism, or what you will, is summoned into life. This is the danger that menaces Protestantism. But Catholicism is safe from both possibilities. The vitality of the spirit which inspires her teaching authority is manifested constantly in this, that acting as a living power it lays hold of the revelation enshrined in Scripture and passive Tradition, and discloses as it advances the fruitful energies that they contain. In the Catholic Church alone may we discern an organic growth in the consciousness of the faith. There is no petrifaction here; yet there is on the other hand nothing erratic or abrupt, but an organic development. Thus the Church has a message for the men of every age. For the dogmatic development is no fortuitious one, but corresponds to the needs and problems of the contemporary Church. Since they who bear the spirit of the revelation are themselves living men and living members of the body of the faithful, they are in constant sympathy with the questions and needs of the "learning Church," of the community of the faithful. They are able to bring revealed truth into connexion with those needs and questions, and from its store to provide those answers for which the faithful look. So there is a constant movement in the exposition of the faith, and a continual dispensation of the store of revelation for the benefit of hungry souls. The revelation does not grow old, but remains ever new and full of life. It is timeless, it is immediate present, though century succeed century.

.   .   .   .

Not to lose the thread of the argument, let us summarise what has been said. We have laid it down that the external catholicity of the Church, her world-conquering power, rests upon her internal catholicity. And we have pointed out that the first element in this internal catholicity is a comprehensive affirmation of the whole of revelation, and a vitalising of this revelation by that living spirit of revelation which resides in the teaching authority of the Church.

The second element in her internal catholicity is her comprehensive affirmation of the whole man, of human nature in its completeness, of the body as well as the soul, of the senses as well as the intellect. The mission of the Church is to the entire man. According to the teaching of the Church—as that was formulated at Trent against the Lutheran conception—original sin by no means destroyed the natural structure of man's being, nor is it synonymous with what St. Paul calls the law of our members, that is with concupiscence. It is true that the understanding is darkened by it and the will weakened; but these effects are not the direct and immediate consequences of original sin. They are the direct results of the loss of our original, supernatural union of life and love with God, whereby we were in our whole being diverted from our original, supernatural end. Consequently the natural structure of our being remains fundamentally unimpaired. Though original sin brought a weakening of nature, it did not bring as well a physical deterioration or corruption of our bodily and mental powers.

So the Church, starting from this basis, is able to enlist man's entire nature, his body and its sensitive life, his reason and his will, in the service of the Kingdom of God. Since man's nature is not essentially damaged in its natural powers, but only by diversion from its supernatural end, that is to say by a false orientation, therefore so soon as this false orientation is mended and man is replaced by baptism in his original, living union with God, that nature can be gripped in all its powers by the Church's preaching. The Church as the Body of Christ lays hold of all that is of God, and therefore of man's body, his senses and his passions, just as much as of his intellect and will. And in redeeming his body and senses and passions by sanctifying grace from their earthliness and selfishness and reclaiming them for God, she not only wins them back for His Kingdom, but also ennobles and deepens them. So the Church destroys man's old earthly structure to its foundations, but she takes over the old stones for the new building and gives them for the first time their true positions, their proper meaning, their full beauty and their glory. Therefore the conception of nature, so far from being destroyed by Catholicism, is enormously deepened. As man came from the hand of God, in the beauty of his body, in the ardour of his sense life, in the storm and stress of his passions, with keen intellect and mighty will, even so does the Church affirm him and even so would she have him be. She would mould this man of ardent, stormy passions and clear-sighted strength so that he may belong to God, and that he may by union with the original basis of his life bring all the greatness and the glory of his natural gifts into inward harmony and perfection.

Hence two further elements in that catholicity which gives the Church her comprehensive power of attraction. The first of these is that she loves and understands man's nature, his bodily and sensitive structure, as well as his mental powers. In acute and prolonged conflicts with Gnostics, Manicheans, Albigenses, Bogomili, and other similar sects, she has guarded the rights and the dignity of the human body, and in particular the rights and dignity of marriage. She does not regard the body as a "garment of shame," but as a holy and precious creation of God. And she teaches that this gift is so precious and so necessary for man, that the body that is dissolved in death will one day be raised again by God, to be the ministering organ of the immortal soul. Therefore the Church loves this body so related to God, and inspires her artists to represent, in its nobility and beauty, the unspeakable beauty of divinity and holiness. She adorns the humblest village churches with images of our Lord and our Lady and the saints, in order to raise her children by visible things to things invisible, from the beauty of this earth to the beauty of heaven. Art is native to Catholicism, since reverence for the body and for nature is native to it.

This reverence for the body leads the Church further to

a careful consideration for man's sensible needs. Since we are not pure spirits, but spirits enmeshed in body, we grasp spiritual things by means of things visible and sensible. Hence the whole sacramental system of Christianity and the Church. Our Lord Himself submitted to baptism. He has granted us communion in His Body and Blood by the visible signs of bread and wine, and in other ways conjoined spiritual blessing with sensible means. He bade His disciples anoint the sick with oil, He never ate bread without first blessing it, He never dismissed a child without laying His hand upon it. Even so, the Church joins her spiritual benefits to sensible signs. Besides the sacraments she employs the sacramentals. In distinction from the sacraments, they rest upon ecclesiastical ordinance and not upon the institution of Christ. Their efficacy is not derived therefore from a positive act of our Lords' will, but from the intercession of the whole Church and from their devout employment. They are supplications for blessing and grace made by the faithful and by the whole Church, and objectively manifested in visible signs. When the Catholic uses Holy Water, or makes the sign of the Cross on the forehead of one he loves, or fixes on his wall blessed palms and blessed flowers, his action signifies a devout communion with the intercessory prayer of the whole Church, that God may help him in all his needs. Each and every element of his mundane life, from marriage ring and bridal bed down to the blessed salt which he gives to a sick beast, is drawn by the blessing of the Church into a supernatural relation with God. By this means the whole activity of the Catholic in all its aspects is directed towards heaven—by visible things to things invisible. It is true that abuses are possible and that the sacramentals may be degraded into magical charms. But wherever there are men there will be abuses, nor should we judge a good thing by its abuse, but contrariwise. In elevating men by these sensible means to appreciate the suprasensible, the Church obtains religious influence over those whose minds are as yet wholly immersed in the things of sense. She is able to bring a ray of divinity and holiness even into their small and poor lives. So she is not only the Church of the nations, she is the Church of the people.

As the Church affirms man's sensible nature, so does she also affirm and lay hold of his spiritual nature, and especially human reason. She aims deliberately at conquering the world of the mind. Her whole theology, from the apologists and the schools of Alexandria and Antioch, through early and late Scholasticism down to our own day, is dominated by confidence in the illuminating power of reason. Her conception of faith presupposes that human reason can of itself recognise the so-called *praeambula fidei*, i.e. the spirituality of the human soul and the existence of God—realities which transcend sensible experience—and that reason can establish the credibility of revelation on historical and philosophical grounds. The supernatural certitude of faith is the gift of God, but in so far as it is built upon these rational presuppositions, philosophy becomes the handmaid of faith (*ancilla fidei*). The Church does not in this propose to interfere in any way with the independence of the profane sciences in their own proper sphere. Indeed, the Vatican Council expressly renounces any such intention (Sess. III, cap. 4). What she wishes to establish is the fact that human reason, while remaining true to itself, can by its own principles advance to a point where God becomes visible as the fundamental basis and ultimate meaning of all reality, and where knowledge passes over into faith, philosophy into theology. Whenever men have doubted or denied the capacity of the human mind to transcend the limits of experience, whenever they have attempted to paralyse or kill man's profound yearning for absolute truth, then the Church has come forward in defence of reason, whether against Averroes and Luther, or against Kant. And the more our own age becomes weary of subjective idealism and seeks to rediscover the objective world, the more grateful will it be to Pope Pius X that in his much-abused anti-modernist Encyclical "Pascendi" he denounced all positivism, pragmatism and phenomenalism and defended the power of reason to transcend and surpass experience, thus exorcising those twin bugbears of solipsism and scepticism which menace all knowledge. The catholicity of the Church is manifested not least in this, that she does not allow knowledge and faith to be separated and set in an unhealthy antagonism, but conjoins them in intimate harmony, making knowledge accessible to faith and faith to knowledge. Her greatest minds, Origen, Augustine, Aquinas and Newman, made it their life's task to establish this synthesis of faith and knowledge. Nor do the theologians of our own day know of any more important task than that of making modern knowledge fruitful for the faith. Catholicism lays its hand on every branch of knowledge, seeking everywhere the golden grains of truth, that it may adorn its sanctuary with them.

We have described the first consequence which follows from the high value which the Church sets upon our human nature and indicated its relation to her world-wide influence. The second consequence shall be treated very briefly. It is her definitely affirmative attitude towards all that is natural, genuine and incorrupt in the pre-Christian and non-Christian world. So far as paganism is genuine paganism, that is to say, revolt from the living God, self-deification or the deification of nature, it has no more resolute foe than Catholicism. But there is more in paganism than revolt. There break forth even in paganism, from out of the uncorrupted sources of human nature, noble and pure impulses, thoughts and resolves, not only in philosophy and art, but also in religion and morality. The seeds of truth, as the Fathers constantly declare, are to be found everywhere, among Romans as among Greeks, among Indians as among Negroes. What we have to do is to free these seeds from the non-Christian growth that chokes them and to redeem them for the Kingdom of God. The Church is pursuing this task of purification and redemption when she takes the wisdom of the pagan philosophers, of Plato, or Aristotle, or Plotinus, or the Stoics, and makes it minister to the Incarnate Word. She does not hesitate even to take over pagan ritual and pagan symbols, whenever such things can be Christianised and reformed. This is not weakness, or unprincipled accommodation, but practical catholicism. It is a direct consequence of that fundamental Catholic conviction that every genuine value, everything that comes from pure and uncorrupted nature, belongs to God and has citizen rights in His Kingdom. Therefore the Church sets up no barrier against non-Christian culture, and no barrier against antiquity. She sets up her barrier only against sin. It was her loving hand that preserved for us many of the treasures of antiquity when the ancient world collapsed under the assault of the Germanic peoples. And were those same treasures, and the whole spiritual achievement of antiquity to be in danger, in our own time, of being frittered away and squandered by modern vandals in their greed for gold, and were some frigid instinct for the practical and useful, for the idols of our time, to deprive men of sympathetic feeling for the spirit of antiquity and to destroy our humanist institutions, then the Church would stand forth once again, as she did in the Middle Ages, and taking the "gold of the Egyptians" hand it on to her sons and daughters.

Such is Catholicism: an affirmation of values along the whole line, a most comprehensive and noblest accessibility to all good,[8] a union of nature with grace, of art with religion, of knowledge with faith, "so that God may be all in all." Let others be "ever hunting for a fabulous primitive simplicity; we repose in Catholic fulness."[9] Catholicism knows no other watchword than the sentence of St. Paul: "I became all things to all men that I might save all. And I do all things for the gospel's sake" (1 Cor. ix, 22-23).

[8] F. von Hügel (*The Mystical Element in Religion*, II, 118) speaks of the "all-welcoming" spirit of Catholicism.

[9] Cardinal Newman, *Essays Critical and Historical*, Vol. II, Essay XI (1873, p. 233).

CHAPTER X

THE CHURCH NECESSARY FOR SALVATION

And if he will not hear the Church, let him be to thee as the heathen and publican (Mt. xviii, 17).

THE Catholic Church as the Body of Christ, as the realisation in the world of the Kingdom of God, is the Church of Humanity. Of her essential nature she aims at the incorporation of the men of all times and all places in the one Body of Christ. Hence inevitable her external and internal catholicity, her accessibility and comprehensiveness. And hence also her exclusiveness, that is her claim to be *the* Church of Humanity, the exclusive institution wherein all men shall attain salvation. Because the Church is conscious that she is the Church of Humanity and that Kingdom of God to which all men whatsoever by the will of Christ fundamentally belong, she cannot admit that men can be saved by membership in other societies established by the side of and in antagonism to the primary Church of Humanity founded by Christ. Even Heiler cannot deny the cogency of this position. "So far as Catholicism is genuinely universal and represents fully all religious values, it must be exclusive. But this exclusiveness is not the exclusiveness of narrowness, but of inexhaustible wealth."[1] The Church would belie her own deepest essence and her most outstanding quality, namely her inexhaustible fulness and that which guarantees and supports this fulness, her vocation to be the Body of Christ, if she were ever to recognise some collateral and antagonistic Christian church as

[1] Op. cit., p. 614.

her sister and as possessing equal rights with herself. She can recognise the historical importance of such churches. She can designate them as Christian communions, yes, even as Christian churches, but never as the Church of Christ. One God, one Christ, one Baptism, one Church. There can never be a second Christ, and in the same way there cannot be a second Body of Christ, a second manifestation of His Spirit. When some American Christians went to Rome in the Spring of 1919 to invite Pope Benedict XV to take part in a "World Conference on Faith and Order," they misunderstood the Catholic conception of the Church and this its fundamental claim. The Catholic Church can and will appraise generously, and will countenance, all the communities of non-Catholic Christendom. She can and will recognise in them the first rudiments of a preparation for that re-union of all Christians which is demanded by the present state of Christendom in general and of the West in particular. But she cannot recognise other Christian communions as churches of like order and rights with herself. To do so would be infidelity to her own nature, and would be the worst disloyalty to herself. In her own eyes the Catholic Church is nothing at all if she be not *the* Church, *the* Body of Christ, *the* Kingdom of God. This exclusiveness is rooted in the exclusiveness of Christ, in His claim to be the bringer of the new life, to be the way, the truth and the life. The fulness of the Divinity was revealed to us in Christ. The Incarnate God is the last and most perfect self-revelation of God. God's wisdom, goodness and mercy became incarnate in Him. "Of His fulness we all have received, and grace for grace" (Jn. i, 16). And therefore there is no other road to God except through Christ. There is "no other name under heaven given to men, whereby they must be saved" (Acts iv, 12). But we can grasp Christ only through His Church. It is true that He might, had He so willed, have imparted Himself and His grace to all men directly, in personal experience. But the question is not what might have been, but what Christ in fact willed to do. And in fact He willed to give Himself to men through men, that is by the way of a community life and not by the way of isolation and individualism. He willed that His grace should come to men who were conjoined in a single compact fellowship, and that it should come to them through this fellowship, not without it, and still less in opposition to it. It was not His will to sanctify a countless multitude of solitary souls, but a corporate kingdom of saints, a Kingdom of God. And this method of communicating Himself corresponds entirely to His fundamental requirement, the commandment of fraternal love. For that commandment implies a community, implies the union of the brethren, and there can be no fraternal love without such a community. And it corresponds fully also to the essential character of the Divine, which belongs, wherever it appears, to all men at once. The power of God in its manifestation is a catholic power, comprehending and grasping all men. So that it cannot manifest itself otherwise than in absolute unity. There can be no contradiction, or dissension, or schism where God is. His truth cannot be otherwise than one truth, one life, one love. And therefore it can be realised in but one form, in a comprehensive fellowship that binds together all men in intimate unity.

From the very beginning, as St. Matthew testifies (xviii, 17) the necessity for salvation of belonging to the one fellowship was established on the basis of an express saying of our Lord's: "If a man will not hear the Church, let him be to thee as the heathen and the publican," that is, regard him no longer as a Christian. St. Cyprian afterwards expressed this conviction of primitive Christianity in those clear-cut sentences which have impressed themselves on the memory of Christendom: "To have the one God for your Father, you must have the Church for your mother" (Ep. lxxiv, 7). "No man can be saved except in the Church" (Ep. iv, 4). "Outside the Church there is no salvation" (Ep. lxxiii, 21).

Thus was formulated that sentence which puts the

Church's claim to be the only source of salvation in the most concise form: "Outside the Church no salvation" (*Extra ecclesiam nulla salus*). The Fourth Lateran Council (A.D. 1215) adopted this formula verbatim. In the so-called Athanasian Creed, which the Church admits among her confessions of faith, it is fully paraphrased: "Whosoever wishes to be saved, before all things it is necessary that he hold the Catholic faith. And if a man do not keep this faith inviolate and intact, without doubt he will perish." More unmistakable still is the declaration of the Council of Florence that all pagans, Jews, heretics and schismatics have forfeited eternal life and are destined to everlasting fire.

Now there is no doubt, that if her catholicity gives the Church a world-wide and comprehensive character, her claim to be the only source of salvation turns her in upon herself and makes her aloof and exclusive. In contrast to her unlimited devotion to all values wherever they may be found, is her equally strong and unlimited assertion of and insistence on her own claims. The one is a necessary counterpoise to the other. Without her rigid and deliberate self-assertion, and without her immense concentration on herself, the catholicity of the Church, in its acceptance of all humanity, of the whole world and its values, would bring her dangerously near to a gradual decomposition of her true supernatural being, and induce a fusion of her essence with alien elements, that is to say syncretism. For the very reason that the Church, with the same vigour and momentum with which she devotes herself to the world, remembers her supernatural origin, her essential connexion with Christ, and her exclusive possession of the power of salvation, she maintains the supernatural substance of her gospel and so preserves her capacity to elevate all the natural values which she takes over from the world into supernatural values, to permeate them with Christ and to uplift them to God. If her catholicity is a centrifugal force, then this exclusiveness of hers is a centripetal force. And the secret of her remaining true to herself in her fulness is that these two forces are maintained in exact equipoise, so that she is at once catholic and exclusive.

So there is no doubt about this matter. There is only one answer to the question whether other Christian communions have not also a vocation and a power to save men, and the Church is quite intolerant about it. For the very reason that these communions have set themselves up against the original unity of the brethren in faith and love, they appear to the Catholic consciousness as institutions which have not arisen out of the spirit of Jesus, and therefore as purely human and even anti-Christian creations. The Church cannot but anathematise them and she will continue to do so until the Lord comes.

It is psychologically quite intelligible that the adherents of non-Catholic communions should be grieved by the Church's dogmatic intolerance and disposed to regard it as the manifestation of a spirit which is foreign and even hostile to the spirit of Jesus, a spirit of uncharitableness and harsh severity. When the critic speaks of the Church's "fearful exclusiveness and intolerance"[1] he forgets that truth must always be "fearfully exclusive and intolerant." In the very same book he asserts that "a straight road leads from belief in Jesus regarded as the sole means of salvation to belief in the exclusive claim of the Church,"[2] which means that if we believe that Christ is the only name in heaven and on earth whereby we may be saved, we must believe also that true salvation is to be found only in the one Church which He founded. The one Christ and the one Body of Christ belong indissolubly together. He who rejects the one true Church is all too easily brought, as by an inexorable logic, to go astray also about Christ. As a matter of fact the history of revolt from the Church is at the same time a history of the progressive decomposition of the primitive faith in Christ.

So the truth stands fast, rigid and inexorable in its compact solidity, that there is but one Christ and but one jus-

[1] Heiler, op. cit., p. 613.   [2] Ibid., p. 48.

tifying Church of Christ. But, we may ask, does that mean that all heretics and non-Catholics are destined to hell?

If we would interpret correctly the Catholic doctrine that there is no salvation outside the Church, that is to say if we would understand it as the Church would have it understood, we should grasp its history and its connexion with the rest of her teaching. For no Catholic doctrine is an isolated mass of thought, but has on the contrary its proper place and meaning in the whole unitary system and cannot be fully appreciated except through this whole system.

To begin with, it is certain that the declaration that there is no salvation outside the Church is not aimed at individual non-Catholics, at any persons as persons, but at non-Catholic churches and communions, in so far as they are non-Catholic communions. Its purpose is to formulate positively the truth that there is but one Body of Christ and therefore but one Church which possesses and imparts the grace of Christ in its fulness. Stated otherwise the declaration would run: Every separated church which sets itself up against the original Church of Christ stands outside the communion of Christ's grace. It cannot be a mediator of salvation. So far as it is a separate and antagonistic church, it is essentially unfruitful as regards the supernatural life. So that that spiritual unfruitfulness which is predicated in the doctrine is not to be affirmed of the individual non-Catholic, but primarily of non-Catholic communions as such. By that which constitutes their separateness and differentiates them in faith and worship from the Catholic Church, they are able to awaken no supernatural life. Therefore, in so far as they are un-Catholic and anti-Catholic, that is to say in regard to their distinct character, they are not able to claim the honourable title of a "mother" church.

In saying so much we have already indicated the second dogmatic qualification which the proposition receives within the system of Catholic doctrine. For non-Catholic communions are not merely non-Catholic and anti-Cath olic. When they set themselves up against the original Church of Christ, they took over and maintained a considerable amount of the Catholic inheritance, and also certain Catholic means of grace, in particular the sacrament of Baptism. They are therefore, if we regard them as a whole, not mere antithesis and negation, but also to a large extent thesis and affirmation of the ancient treasure of truth and grace that has come down to us from Christ and the apostles. Their churches are built not only of their own un-Catholic materials, but also of Catholic stuff from the original store of salvation. And in so far as they are genuinely Catholic in their faith and worship, it can and will and must happen that there should be, even outside the visible Church, a real growth and progress in union with Christ. So is the promise of Jesus fulfilled: "And other sheep I have that are not of this fold" (Jn. x, 16). Wherever the Gospel of Jesus is faithfully preached, and wherever baptism is conferred with faith in His Holy Name, there His grace can operate. When the disciples would have forbidden a man who had not attached himself to Jesus from casting out devils in His Name, Our Lord declared: "Forbid him not. For there is no man that doth a miracle in my name and can soon speak ill of me. He that is not against you is for you" (Mk. ix, 38-39). The Church acted entirely in harmony with these words of our Lord when in her severe struggle with St. Cyprian and the African tradition and afterwards in prolonged controversy with the Donatists, she upheld the validity of baptism in the Name of Jesus conferred by heretics. And it was Rome, Rome that is so violently attacked for her intolerance, and Pope Stephen, who even at the peril of an African schism would not allow heretical baptism to be impugned. The Church practises the same toleration with regard to all those sacraments the administration of which was entrusted by Christ exclusively to the limited circle of the apostles. In those non-Catholic bodies in which the apostolic succession has been maintained by means of valid episcopal ordinations, as in the schismatic churches of the East, and in the Jansenist and Old-Catholic churches, she still recognises the validity of all those sacraments which of their nature require only valid orders and not the power of jurisdiction. It is Catholic teaching, therefore, that in all these churches the true Body and the true Blood of Christ are received in the Holy Eucharist, not because they are schismatical churches, that is to say not because of their own special character, but because in spite of this they still preserve a part of the original Catholic heritage. It is that which is Catholic in them that still has power to sanctify and to save.

And—to pass to a third point of doctrine which illustrates the proposition we are discussing—we are not to regard these sacraments thus administered outside the Church as being objectively valid only, and not also subjectively efficacious. St. Augustine seems to have held such a view regarding the efficacy of these sacraments. He supposed, apparently, that the grace objectively provided in these non-Catholic sacraments was not subjectively effective in the heretics and schismatics who received them, because they were all in bad faith, or, more profoundly, because they were in deliberate and obstinate antagonism to the spirit of unity, and therefore to the Holy Ghost. The Jansenists in the seventeenth century followed St. Augustine and advocated the same erroneous opinion, setting it up as their principle that "outside the Church there is no grace" (*extra ecclesiam nulla conceditur gratia*). But again it was Rome and a pope that expressly rejected this proposition.[4]

The assertion that the Catholic Church of later centuries has developed the ideas of St. Cyprian and St. Augustine, that she has "continually sharpened the principle of exclusiveness and so continually narrowed Catholicism"[5] is in contradiction with the plain facts of history. For the truth is that the later Church corrected the original rigourism of the ancient African theologian and maintained that God's grace worked even outside the Catholic body. Non-Cath-

[4] Pope Clement XI in the year 1713.
[5] Heiler, op. cit., p. 614.

olic sacraments have the power to sanctify and save, not only objectively, but also subjectively.   It is therefore conceivable also, from the Church's standpoint, that there is a true, devout and Christian life in those non-Catholic communions which believe in Jesus and baptize in His Name. We Catholics regard this Christian life, wherever it appears, with unfeigned respect and with thankful love.   We regard with deep esteem our Protestant deaconesses,[6] and such noble figures as Wichern and Bodelschwingh.[7] We admire the loving manifestations of the "Home Mission."

The songs of a Paul Gerhard, the St. Matthew Passion of a Sebastian Bach and the oratorios of a Handel affect us almost as "sweet melodies from our old family home."[8] And not merely a Christian life, but a complete and lofty Christian life, a life according to the "full age of Christ," a saintly life, is possible—so Catholics believe—even in definitely non-Catholic communions.   It is true that it cannot develop with that luxuriance which is possible in the Church, where is the fulness of Jesus and His Body; and it will never be anti-Catholic in its quality.   Yet it will be a genuine saintly life; since, wherever grace is, the noble fruits of grace can ripen.   Such saintly figures have appeared and do still appear, especially in the Russian Church, which has preserved the fullest measure of the ancient inheritance.   Consider the saintly characters of a Dmitri, an Innocens, a Tykhon, a Theodosius.[9]   Nor are saints and martyrs impossible, on Catholic principles, even in the Protestant churches.[10]   Nay, it is Catholic teaching that the grace of Christ operates, not only in the Christian

[6] "Diakonissin," women living in small communities and devoting themselves to works of charity. They wear a quasi-religious dress.

[7] Two remarkable social and religious workers. Friedrich Bodelschwingh (1831-1910) was a man of great force of character and originality who sought in his work for the poor and outcast to provide them not with "institutional" charity, but with a real personal and private life on an independent, family basis.

[8] Knöpfler, a Catholic professor in the University of Munich.

[9] Cf. D'Herbigny, *Theologica de ecclesia*, 1921, Vol. II, p. 110.

[10] See in the Catholic monthly, *Seele* (1924, p. 7 ff.), an appreciative and sympathetic picture by L. Pfleger of the Anglican, Florence Barclay.

communions, but also in the non-Christian world, in Jews and in Turks and in Japanese.[11] Every Catholic catechism, when it explains the ordinary form of baptism, lays emphasis also on that extraordinary form which is called baptism of desire. By that is meant that perfect love, evoked and supported by the redeeming grace of Jesus, has power to sanctify the soul, and that that soul so decisively affirms the will of God that it would at once receive baptism, if it knew of that sacrament or could receive it. As God sends His rain and His sunshine upon all, so does He send His conquering grace into the hearts of all those who hold themselves ready for it, who do what in them lies, who perform what their conscience bids them. Since Christ appeared on earth and founded His Kingdom of God, there is no longer any purely natural morality, however much such a natural morality may be possible in itself. Wherever conscience is astir, wherever men are alive to God and His Holy Will, there and at the same time the grace of Christ co-operates and lays in the soul the seeds of the new supernatural life. Heiler himself, without observing the violent contradiction with his assertion that the later Church has narrowed Catholicism, cites that distinguished Catholic theologian, the Jesuit Cardinal Juan de Lugo, as summarising Catholic teaching in this manner: "God gives light, sufficient for its salvation, to every soul that attains to the use of reason in this life . . . the various philosophical schools and religious bodies throughout mankind all contain and hand down, amid various degrees of human error and distortion, *some* truth, *some* gleams and elements of divine truth . . . the soul that in good faith seeks God, His truth and love, concentrates its attention, under the influence of grace, upon these elements of truth, be they many or few, which are offered to it in the sacred books and religious schools and assemblies of the Church, Sect, or Philosophy in which it has been brought up. It feeds upon these elements, the others are

[11] See Père Maréchal's attractive account of the Mohammedan mystic, Al Hallaj (*Recherches de science rel.,* 1923, Vol. XV, p. 244 ff.).

simply passed by; and divine grace, under cover of these elements, feeds and saves this soul." [11]   It is therefore de Lugo's precise opinion—and it is the opinion of the Church's theologians in general—that all those elements or "seeds" of truth which are dispersed in the most multifarious sects, philosophical schools, and religious communions can provide a basis and starting point for the grace of Christ, so that the natural man may be elevated into the new supernatural man of faith and love.   The Church rightly maintains and continually reiterates, in decisive and uncompromising fashion, her claim to be the sole true Body of Christ; but at the same time she holds a generous and large-minded view regarding the activity of Christ's grace.   That activity has no bounds or limits, but is as infinite as the love of God.

If we consider the Church's claim to be the only Church wherein men may be saved in the clear and radiant light of her belief that God's grace knows no bounds or limits to its operation, we at once see the true and profound meaning of that claim.   The Church understands it to mean that by virtue of the express institution of Christ she represents in the economy of salvation the ordinary proper institute of the truth and grace of Jesus on the earth.   In the Catholic Church the saving power, which was revealed in Christ, flows into the world with original force, in untroubled purity, and in complete and exhaustive fulness. With original force—for while non-Catholic bodies owe such Christian truth and grace as they possess to the Catholic Church, the Church receives it through no intermediary but direct and fresh from our Lord Himself.   She is in fact nothing else but His body of disciples, expanded in space and time.   In untroubled purity—for she has not, like the various sects, contaminated her Christian heritage with novelties and modernisms, but has in the unbroken series of her bishops maintained it as immaculately pure

[11] De Lugo, *De fide*, Dispp. XIX et XX, as cited by F. von Hügel, *Essays and Addresses on the Philosophy of Religion* (first series, London, 1921, p. 252), and by Heiler (op. cit., p. 612) from him.

as she received it from Christ. In exhaustive fulness—for she does not choose only this or that precious jewel, but she calls her own the whole inheritance of revealed truth contained in Scripture and Tradition. Therefore the Church is the true and ordinary institute of the grace and truth of Jesus. But that does not prevent there being, alongside this ordinary institute, extraordinary ways of salvation, or hinder the grace of Christ from visiting particular men without the mediation of the Church. But because and in so far as the Body of Christ comprehends all those who are saved by Christ, those also who are visited by His grace in this immediate way belong to His Church. It is true that they do not belong to its outward and visible body, but they certainly belong to its invisible, supernatural soul, to its supernatural substance. For the grace of Christ never works in the individual in an isolated fashion, but always in and through the unity of His Body. And thus it holds good, even for those brethren who are thus separated from the visible organism of the Church, that they too are saved through the Church, and not without her or in opposition to her.

But, it may be objected, how can there be true Christians who belong to the soul of the Church and yet are separated from her visible body? How can a man belong to the Body of Christ and yet not belong to the body of the Church? In supplying a brief answer to this question, we shall pass from the theological to the psychological explanation of the dogma under discussion. From the purely theological standpoint, in the light of the dogmatic idea of the intimate and necessary connexion between Christ and the Church, the only possible conclusion regarding all heretics and schismatics, Jews and pagans, is that judgment of condemnation which the Council of Florence pronounced upon them. In so far as they stand, and will to stand, outside the one Church of Christ, they stand according to strict theology outside the sphere of Christ's grace and therefore outside salvation. It is thus, from this purely theological standpoint, that we are to understand the sharp anathemas pronounced by the Church against all heretics and schismatics, as also those contained in that Borromeo Encyclical of Pope Pius X which was so much impugned.[18] In these pronouncements the Church is not considering individuals as individuals, but regarding them as representatives of ideas antagonistic to the Church. When ideas are in conflict, when truth is fighting against error, and revelation against human ingenuity, then there can be no compromise and no indulgence. If our Lord had exercised such indulgence, He would not have been crucified. When He called the Pharisees whited sepulchres and a brood of vipers, and Herod a fox, He was not inspired by any sort of hatred against individuals, but by the tremendous earnestness of truth. It was His defiant and vivid conviction of responsibility for eternal truth that caused Him to use such strong words towards error and its representatives. And if we do not fight thus for the truth, then we lose all moral and spiritual power, we become characterless, we disown God. Dogmatic intolerance is therefore a moral duty, a duty to the infinite truth and to truthfulness.

But so soon as it is a question, not of the conflict between idea and idea, but of living men, of our judgment on this or that non-Catholic, then the theologian becomes a psychologist, the dogmatist a pastor of souls. He draws attention to the fact that the living man is very rarely the embodiment of an idea, that the conceptual world and mentality of the individual are so multifarious and complicated, that he cannot be reduced to a single formula. In other words the heretic, the Jew and the pagan seldom exist in a pure state. What we actually have before us is living men, with their fundamental outlook influenced or dominated by this or that erroneous idea. Therefore the Church expressly distinguishes between "formal" and "material" heretics. A "formal" heretic

---

[18] An encyclical of Pope Pius X concerning St. Charles Borromeo, issued in the year 1910, which by its unfavourable references to the leaders of the Reformation raised a storm in Protestant Germany.

rejects the Church and its teaching absolutely and with full deliberation; a "material" heretic rejects the Church from lack of knowledge, being influenced by false prejudice or by an anti-Catholic upbringing. St. Augustine forbids us to blame a man for being a heretic because he was born of heretical parents, provided that he does not with obstinate self-assurance shut out all better knowledge, but seeks the truth simply and loyally.[14] Whenever the Church has such honest enquirers before her, she remembers that our Lord condemned Pharisaism but not the individual Pharisee, that He held deep and loving intercourse with Nicodemus, and allowed Himself to be invited by Simon. The spirit of the Church in her dealings with souls may be stated in St. Augustine's words: "Love men, slay error!"[15]

It is true that heretics were tried and burnt in the Middle Ages. But that was not done only in Catholic countries, for Calvin himself had Servetus burnt. And capital punishment was employed against the Anabaptists, especially in Thuringia and in the Electorate of Saxony. According to the Protestant Theologian, Walter Köhler, even Luther after 1530 regarded the penalty of death as a justifiable punishment for heresy.[16] The fact that the persecution of heresy was approved as a justifiable thing by non-Catholic bodies, and in certain cases carried out in practice, goes to show that such persecution did not spring from the nature of Catholicism, or in particular from its exclusive claims. The origin of such persecutions is to be sought rather in the Byzantine and medieval conception of the state, whereby every attack on the unity of the faith was regarded as an open crime against the unity and stability of the state, and one which had to be punished according to the primitive methods of the time.

Besides this political cause, the mentality of the period played its part. The religion of the medieval man embraced his whole life and outlook. There was as yet no

[14] *Ep.* XLIII, i, 1.

[15] *Diligite homines, interficite errores, sine superbia de veritate praesumite, sine saevitia pro veritate certate. Orate pro eis, quos redarguitis atque convincitis* (Contra litteras Petiliani, iii, Lib. I, 29).

[16] *Reformation und Ketzerprozess,* 1900, p. 36.

unhappy cleavage between religion and morality.   So that
every revolt against the Catholic faith seemed to him to be
a moral crime, a sort of murder of the soul and of God,
an offence more heinous than parricide.   And his outlook
was logical rather than psychological.   He rejoiced in the
perception of truth, but he had little appreciation of the
living conditions of soul by which this perception is
reached.   He lived and moved in the dialectical antithesis
of Yes and No, of Either and Or, and hardly considered
the fact that life does not express itself in the sharp con-
trasts of Yes and No, Truth and Error, Belief and Unbelief, Virtue and Vice, but in an infinite wealth of transitional forms and intermediate stages; and that in dealing
with the living man we have to take account not only of
the logical force of truth, but also of the particular quality of the mental and spiritual endowment with which he
reacts to the truth.   Because they were not alive to the
infinite variety of such spiritual endowment, they were all
too ready, especially when truth was impugned, to conclude at once that it was a case of "evil will" (*mala fides*)
and to pass sentence of condemnation, even though there
were insuperable intellectual obstacles (*ignorantia invincibilis*) in the way of the perception of the truth.   This pre-
eminently logical attitude of mind is characteristic of the
Middle Ages.   That epoch had no feeling for life as a
flowing thing with its own peculiar laws, no appreciation
of history, whether within us or without us.   And this
attitude was not to be overcome and corrected, until the
spirit of the time had changed, until in the course of centuries and by a long evolution a new outlook took its place.
Therefore the persecutions of heretics did not proceed
from the nature of Catholicism, but from the political and
mental attitude of the Middle Ages.

So with the passing of the Middle Ages such persecutions gradually ceased.   The new Code of Canon Law
expressly forbids any employment of force in the matter
of faith.[17]   The great conception of a single Emperor and

[17] "*Ad amplexandam fidem catholicam nemo invitus cogatur*," Canon
1351.

a single Empire has gone. And the theologian has by means of psychological and historical studies attained a wider understanding and become increasingly cautious in attributing an "evil will" to the heretic. He has become more alive to the thousand possibilities of invincible and therefore excusable error. "It must be regarded as true," declared Pope Pius IX in an allocution of the 9th December, 1854, "that he who does not know the true religion is guiltless in the sight of God so far as his ignorance is invincible. Who would presume to fix the limits of such ignorance, amid the infinite variety and difference of peoples, countries and mentalities, and amid so many other circumstances. When we are free from the limitations of the body and see God as He is, then we shall see how closely and beautifully God's mercy and justice are conjoined." Wherefore the Church's claim to be the Church of salvation by no means excludes a loving and sympathetic appreciation of the subjective conditions and circumstances under which heresy has arisen. Nor is her condemnation of a heresy always at the same time a condemnation of the individual heretic. As an instance of the generosity of the Catholic attitude, take the words of the celebrated Redemptorist, St. Clement Maria Hofbauer, regarding the origins of the Reformation: "The revolt from the Church began," he wrote, "because the German people could not and cannot but be devout." Hofbauer was a convinced Catholic, who condemned all heresy as a moral and religious crime, as a violation of the unity of the Body of Christ. He was fully aware also that the causes of the Reformation were by no means exclusively religious. But that knowledge did not prevent him from appreciating those religious forces which contributed in no small degree to its success. The fact that Hofbauer has been canonised suggests that the Church did not disapprove of his utterance, but regarded it as a confirmation of her constant belief in the possibility of invincible error and perfect good faith in the heretic.

Unless we understand that, we shall not grasp the meaning of her proposition, that there is no salvation outside the Church. True there is only one Church of Christ. She alone is the Body of Christ and without her there is no salvation. Objectively and practically considered she is the ordinary way of salvation, the single and exclusive channel by which the truth and grace of Christ enter our world of space and time. But those also who know her not receive these gifts from her; yes, even those who misjudge and fight against her, provided they are in good faith, and are simply and loyally seeking the truth without self-righteous obstinacy. Though it be not the Catholic Church itself which hands them the bread of truth and grace, yet it is Catholic bread that they eat. And, while they eat of it, they are, without knowing it or willing it, incorporated in the supernatural substance of the Church. Though they be outwardly separated from the Church, they belong to its soul.

So that the non-Catholic of good will is already fundamentally united to the Church. It is only that he sees her not. Yet she is there, invisible and mysterious. And the more he grows in faith and in love, the more plainly will she become actually visible to him. Many have already seen her, and many more yet will see her. There is a special possibility of such reunion with the Catholic Church wherever Protestantism has remained faithful to Christ and believes truly in the Incarnate God. And it is because we believe that very many non-Catholics are already thus invisibly united with the Church, that we do not abandon our conviction that this invisible union will one day be made visible in all its beauty. The more consciously and completely we all of us exhibit the spirit of Christ, the more certainly will that hour of grace approach, when the veils will fall from all eyes, when we shall put away all prejudice and misunderstanding and bitterness, when we shall once again as of old extend to one another the hand of brotherhood, when there shall be one God, one Christ, one shepherd and one flock.

CHAPTER XI

THE SACRAMENTAL ACTION OF THE CHURCH

Christ loved the Church and delivered himself up for it, that he might sanctify it, cleansing it by the laver of water in the word of life (Eph. v, 25-26).

THE purpose of the Church is the establishment of the Kingdom of God in the world, and therefore it is the sanctification of men. St. Paul sets forth this purpose in the words: "Christ hath loved the Church and delivered himself up for it, that he might sanctify it, cleansing it by the laver of water in the word of life. That he might present it to himself a glorious Church, not having spot or wrinkle, or any such thing, but that it should be holy and without blemish" (Eph. v, 25-27). In those words the apostle sketches an ideal which can never attain complete fulfilment in the Church on earth. For the words which our Lord spoke to His disciples at the Last Supper are true of her: "Ye are clean, but not all" (Jn. xiii, 10). Our Lord foretold only too plainly that there would be cockle among the wheat, bad fish among the good, and that scandals must come. So long as the Church abides in this world, awaiting the coming of the Lord, her prayer will have to be, not only "Hallowed be thy Name, thy Kingdom come!" but also "Forgive us our trespasses, lead us not into temptation!"

But however little the Church of this world can be called a society of saints—and the New Testament too refrains from speaking of a "holy Church" in that sense—yet her whole nature as the Body of Christ aims at that consummation. She seeks to redeem men, all men, in slow but steady process, from their self-centredness, and to form them into new men, children of God, "fellow-citizens with the saints, and the domestics of God" (Eph. ii, 19), into a "kingly priesthood and a holy people" (1 Peter ii, 9). It is from this her essential task that the Church wins that venerable name of "Holy Church," a title used by the apostolic Fathers and incorporated into the ancient Creeds.

In this and the next chapter we shall ask how the Church merits this title and wherein lies the sanctifying power of her action. Since "the end of the commandment," as the apostle tells us (1 Tim. i, 5), "is charity, from a pure heart and a good conscience and an unfeigned faith," does she really show herself, in her doctrine and worship, to be the great school of charity, to be the institute of salvation in a special and comprehensive sense?

If we would appreciate the sanctifying power of the Church, it is of fundamental importance to understand her dogmatic teaching concerning the character and development of the regenerate man, the *homo sanctus*, to understand therefore her conception of justification.

The Church's doctrine of justification is based upon the presupposition that man is not only called to a natural end, to the fulfilment of his natural being, to the development of his natural powers and aptitudes, but also beyond that, to a supernatural elevation of his being which entirely surpasses all created aptitudes and powers, to sonship with God, to participation in the divine life itself. Such is the central fact of the glad tidings of Christianity: "To as many as received him, to them he gave the power to become the sons of God" (Jn. i, 12). "Dearly beloved, we are now the sons of God, and it hath not yet appeared what we shall be. But we know that, when he shall appear, we shall be like to him" (1 Jn. iii, 2). This likeness consists, according to the Second Epistle of St. Peter, in an enrichment by grace, in a fulfilling and permeation of our being by divine and holy forces. We shall be made "partakers of the divine nature" (2 Peter I, 4). We win a "share in His sanctity" (Hebr. xii, 10). Therefore man's end lies, not in mere humanity, but in a new sort of superhumanity, in an elevation and enhancement of his being, which essentially surpasses all created powers and raises him into an absolutely new sphere of existence and life, into the fulness of a life of God. God shows Himself most luminously as the absolute Personality, sufficient for Himself and independent of the world, in the fact that He reveals Himself personally to us, as one person to another. And He shows that He is absolute Goodness in the fact that He reveals Himself to us as our Friend, nay, as our Father, so that by the power of His love we become His sons and may cry "Abba, Father." Wherefore the Church, in her educative effort, cannot be contented with developing any mere humanity, or perfection of humanity. That is not the object of her work. On the contrary her ideal is to supernaturalise men, to make them like to God. It is of the essence of the Church's character that she should press on towards that which is better and pursue the best and highest that is to be found in heaven and on earth, that she should move in the unsearchable depths of the divine mystery and therefore love the heroic, the incomprehensible and inconceivable, the wide spaces of infinity. That which was naturally and finally enacted in the life of Christ, namely the incarnation of God in man, is constantly repeated by grace in the life of the individual Christian.

This incarnation, this raising of man to the fulness of the divine life, cannot be effected by man himself. It can be merited by no human effort. It is the work of God alone. God gives Himself to those to whom He wills to give Himself, with the most gratuitous mercy and love. So it is the Church's doctrine that every movement of man towards God, every holy thought, every good resolution, and every pure affection is initiated and supported by God's grace—the theologians speak here of "actual" grace; and further, that the definitive establishment of the new life in the soul, the state of direct communion of life and love with God—which the theologians call "sanctifying" grace —is effected in the soul by God alone without human merit. We are made sons of God solely by the eternal love of God, by a mysterious operation of His power effected supernaturally.

The child of God, the saint, is therefore according to the Church's view essentially a creation of grace, a child of the eternal Love. And since it is the function of Christ and of Christianity, as being the incarnation of the divine, to bring the love and grace of God to sense-bound man under the veil of visible and evident signs, therefore the first and chief duty of the Church's educative activity is the sacramental mediation of the grace of Christ. The seven sacraments are God's appointed means whereby man shall ordinarily (*ordinario modo*) experience the action of the grace of Christ, the elevation of his being into the stream of God's life and love. This does not mean that extraordinary ways and activities of grace are excluded, as was shown in the last chapter.

On the other hand—and here is the chief distinction between the Catholic and the orthodox Lutheran conceptions of justification—man is not purely passive under the action of grace like some lifeless stone or log. As the Church conceives original sin, the natural religious and moral endowment of man was not destroyed by that sin so that as the Lutheran "Formula of Concord" expresses it "no spark of spiritual power was left him for the knowledge of truth and accomplishment of good." Man's religious and moral faculties are not impaired in their natural substance, but weakened in their operation, inasmuch as original sin deflects them from their supernatural course and gives them therefore a false direction. The effect of grace, as the up-surging of the eternal love within him, is to bring a man's faculties back again into their original course, and so to disengage them completely and set them free. Therefore grace is not merely compassionate mercy, nor is it like some brilliant cloak of gold thrown over the human corpse. On the contrary the Church conceives of it as a vital force, which awakens and summons the powers of man's soul, understanding, will and feeling, inspires them with a new love, with a new fear of God and His judgments, with a new yearning for transcendent holiness and infinite goodness. When grace thus works on the sinner, continually urging him on with its secret goad to the heights, it produces in man those spiritual acts of faith, fear and trust which are the preparation on the human side for justification. The justification itself which follows these acts is the sole work of God. In the sacrament of Baptism or Penance God answers the appeal of the penitent with His kiss of forgiving love: "I baptize thee, I absolve thee."

But—and here we see again the special quality of the Catholic doctrine of justification, the dynamic character of the Church's conception—God does not merely forgive. At the same time as He forgives He sanctifies. So that justification is not a mere covering over of sin, a mere external imputation of the righteousness of Christ. It is the communication of a true inward righteousness, of a new love which re-makes the whole man; it is sanctification. Justification and sanctification are not to be separated the one from the other, as though sanctification were merely a happy consequence of justification. On the contrary, God's justifying word of forgiveness is an omnipotent word which re-makes the man, not only forgives the penitent but inwardly sanctifies him; nay, forgives him for the very reason that it has already inwardly sanctified him. The first effect of God's mercy in the penitent is the awakening of this new life, of this new love. Theologians call it the "infusion of love" (infusio caritatis), which produces a new sense of sonship, so that the man cries "Abba, Father." Therefore, according to Catholic doctrine, the grace of justification not only puts the man into a new relation with God, but also produces a new attitude. It creates a new heart and a new love.

This new heart, this new state of righteousness and holiness is not produced fortuitously and in a magical manner. For the man is already inwardly ordinated to this life by his preparatory acts of faith, fear and love, acts supported

This page was omitted in the original book.

fore the merit which is won by grace does not exclude humility, but includes it.

If we look at the matter more broadly, this point becomes still plainer. When we define justification as an "infusion of charity" it follows, in the fourth place, that this love can be lost again, and that even the justified are amenable to the apostles' words: "Work out your salvation with fear and trembling" (Phil. ii, 12). The justified man has indeed an absolute certainty of faith, but he has no unconditional certainty of salvation, that is to say that he does not know with unconditional certainty whether he is permanently worthy of love or of hatred. It is true that he can by certain subjective signs and by earnest self-examination ascertain with moral certainty whether he is at the moment impelled by the new love, and so whether he is a child of love and a child of God. But without a special divine revelation he has no unconditional guarantee that he is at any given moment in the grace of God, nor has he any unconditional certainty that he may not in the future, by misusing his freedom, by his own fault, be deprived of the love of God. However solid his piety may be, however magnanimous and courageous, yet he avoids above everything spiritual pride and overweening presumption. His piety gives him humility, the vivid consciousness that he abides wholly in the hands of God and must always pray humbly with the publican: "Lord, be merciful to me a sinner!" The accusation is levelled against the Church that by this teaching of hers concerning the uncertainty of salvation she harasses the Catholic conscience, and that she has made the malady of scrupulosity endemic in Catholicism.[1] This reproach is a gross exaggeration. It is true that there are pathological states, especially at the time of adolescence, which feed for choice on religious conceptions. And such states are especially dangerous when religious instruction is defective or where it is in the hands of clumsy directors. But Protestantism also has such scrupulous souls. Goethe himself laments the

[1] Heiler, op. cit., p. 261 ff.

religious scruples of his youth. And generally speaking such people are not scrupulous because this or that truth of faith terrifies them, but they allow themselves to be terrified by them because they are already scrupulous. Scrupulosity is in fact a condition of psycho-physical infirmity, which is not created, but only disengaged by religious conceptions. The condition shows itself particularly in a lack of vitality and confidence on the one hand, and on the other in an exaggerated self-centredness. Milder cases will yield to the treatment of the spiritual director, but the more difficult cases require the mental specialist. Catholic pastoral theology, while warning us against presumptuous trust in God's mercy, insists with quite as much vigour on the immeasurable riches of His goodness—"for He is good." It is the fault of the invalid, and not of the Church, if he hears only the warning, and neglects the assurance.

To sum up: the special quality of the Catholic doctrine of justification lies on the one hand in its clear and consistent emphasis on grace, on the unmerited nature of the new life and the new love, and on the other hand in its decisive summons to man's religious and moral powers to play their part in the work of grace. The unmerited character of justification is manifested in the Church's sacramentalism. The decisive word of sanctification is not spoken by man, but by God, in the sacrament's visible sign of grace. On the other hand grace is a dynamic force which sets free all man's religious and moral powers to take their share in the work of salvation. So that the sacramental and divine factor is joined by the moral and human factor, that is to say by man's personal initiative set free and controlled by grace. In the work of salvation God and man, grace and nature, sacrament and moral effort are united. We have therefore in justification a repetition of the fundamental mystery of Christianity, the incarnation of the divine in human form. The acts of a justified man are neither purely divine nor purely human, but a compound of divinity and humanity.

And from this we may understand how far the sanctifying action of the Church apparently moves along two distinct lines, being sacramental and mystical on the one hand, and moral and ascetical on the other. In reality these two lines do not run parallel to each other, still less in opposite directions; they run in each other, and are mutually interlaced. There is no sanctity in the Church which is not sacramental, and there is no sacramental act which is not at the same time a striving after sanctity. In the next chapter, when we describe the sanctifying powers and means of grace to be found in "Holy Church," we shall note that point. In accordance with the Catholic conception of justification these powers and means will be found to lie partly in the religious and sacramental sphere, and partly in the domain of the ethical and ascetical. For the present let us be content to describe the sacramental effectiveness of the Church.

We have already shown how the seven sacraments of the Church embrace the whole of human life, and how they sanctify all its heights and depths. The soul at peace with God is sanctified in Confirmation and Holy Eucharist; the soul burdened with sin in Baptism and Penance; the afflicted soul, in the awful hour of death, in the Last Anointing. The community life also is sanctified by the sacramental blessing: on its social side by the sacrament of Matrimony, on its religious side by the sacrament of Holy Orders. It is before all else the realism of its sacramental thought which gives the sacramental worship of the Church its religious and moral value. The Church does not attenuate the sacrament into an empty symbol, or into a sign of grace which obtains all its efficacy from subjective faith. On the contrary it is a real expression of our Lord's gracious will, a sign of Christ (*signum Christi*), and as such it already ensures the presence of His grace through itself, through its actual performance. That is a fundamental point of Catholic sacramental doctrine. "A sacrament is not fulfilled by the fact that one believes in it, but by the fact that it is performed." (*Sacramenta non implentur dum creduntur, sed dum fiunt.*) Thus through the sacraments the divine wins tangible reality and becomes a visible and present value. Therefore the Catholic has an immediate experience of the divine, an experience as immediate and objective as is the child's experience of the love of its mother. In the Sacrifice of the Mass we are not merely reminded of the Sacrifice of the Cross in a symbolical form. On the contrary the Sacrifice of Calvary, as a great supra-temporal reality, enters into the immediate present. Space and time are abolished. The same Jesus is here present who died on the Cross. The whole congregation unites itself with His holy sacrificial will, and through Jesus present before it consecrates itself to the heavenly Father as a living oblation. So Holy Mass is a tremendously real experience, the experience of the reality of Golgotha. And a stream of sorrow and repentance, of love and devotion, of heroism and the spirit of sacrifice, flows out from the altar and passes through the praying congregation. These are not mere words. From this re-presentation of the Sacrifice of the Cross thousands of Catholics daily draw strength and joy, so that they may face the sacrifices, small or great, of their everyday life. And it was in the shadow of the altar that the Catholic · saints—those examples of heroic devotion to Christ and to His brethren—grew to maturity. The Protestant theologian, Niebergall, draws attention to this high value of Holy Mass. "We cannot," he writes, "set too high a value on the Roman Mass as a spiritual power in the religious life." [1]   And Heiler laments in vigorous terms that the Reformation was not able, while renewing the common worship, of God, "to enkindle that intimate and fervent life of prayer which is excited by the Catholic service of Mass." "I have observed," he says, "the life of prayer in both communions, long and carefully and with complete impartiality, and I have again and again received the impression that—apart from certain limited sects and minor bodies—there is more and more inward prayer in

[1] *Praktische Theologie,* 1919, p. 41.

Catholic than in Protestant worship.   When I reflect upon
my experience, I am continually reminded of Wellhausen's
characteristic saying that Protestant worship is at bottom
Catholic worship . . . with the heart taken out of it." [3]
The heart that Wellhausen and Heiler intend is the Catholic's experience of reality in the great Mystery, his assurance that in it the divine really and truly enters our world
of space and time and touches his soul.

The power of this real experience to purify, sanctify,
console and rejoice, is manifested particularly, apart from
the Mass, in Holy Communion and in Confession.   The
faithful Catholic does not merely hope that Jesus will come
to him.   He knows that He does.   He knows that Jesus
is there as really and truly as He was once present in the
Upper Room or by the Sea of Galilee.   This consciousness
of His presence evokes in the soul the whole scale of
religious sentiment from the deep humility of "Lord, I am
not worthy" (*Domine, non sum dignus*) to the happy intimacy of "Jesus, the only thought of Thee" (*Jesu dulcis
memoria*).   Holy Communion is a living intercourse with
Jesus truly present, and is therefore a perennial spring of
devotion to Jesus.   As Heiler rightly remarks, it is "the
culminating point of Catholic piety.   In it the Catholic life
of prayer attains that depth, fervour and strength which
only he knows who has himself experienced it." [4]   And
since Jesus is not present only in the moment of reception,
but so long as the "species," the visible, ocular signs of
His presence last, He also enkindles the religious and
moral life of the Catholic outside the liturgy proper, in
every church in which the most Holy Sacrament is
reserved.   It is not the friendly glimmer of the sanctuary
lamp which burns before the altar, nor the solemn figures
of the saints on the walls, nor the dim, religious light of
the building and its majestic silence, that radiate over a
Catholic church its charm of divine intimacy and devotion.
Those things may serve to protect and promote devotion;

[3] Heiler, *Das Wesen des Katholizismus*, 1920, p. 105.
[4] *Ibid.*, p. 110.

but the thing that enkindles it, is living faith in the presence of Jesus.   Here, before the tabernacle, the Catholic soul enacts its most sacred hours, here it drinks in life in its deepest, most divine quintessence, here all time is silent and eternity speaks.   Heiler's statement that Catholicism has a syncretic character, being overlaid with alien material, cannot be better rebutted than by his own words, in a previous book, about these eucharistic devotions in Catholic churches.   "He who observes," he writes, "in Catholic churches these men praying in contemplative absorption, must admit that God's spirit truly lives in this Church . . . and he who seeks for a parallel to this life in the Protestant churches, must recognize to his sorrow that they have nothing similar to show." [5]

The Catholic sacramental idea, the idea of a divine reality sacramentally presented, shows its power of moral renewal not only in Mass and the Holy Eucharist, but also and not least in Confession.   The Catholic knows that the priest does not hear confessions in his own right but as the representative of God, and that whatever he binds or looses on earth in the name of Jesus will be bound and loosed in heaven also, and this knowledge gives confession its deep seriousness, its absolute truthfulness and its bracing power.   In every good confession the holiest victories are won by the power of conscience, by love for purity and goodness, by desire of God and of peace of soul. Confession has given new courage and new confidence and a fresh start in life to millions of men.   No less a person than Goethe praises the profound wisdom of Catholic confession, and laments that he was prevented in his youth from settling his strange and religious scruples by recourse to it. [6]   Harnack does not hesitate to say that Protestantism was guilty of "culpaple folly" in "uprooting the whole tree of confession because some of its fruit had gone bad." [7]   Yet the "tree" is no good, if it be not a

[5] *Ibid.*, p. 110.
[6] *Dichtung und Wahrheit*, Pt. II, Bk. VII.
[7] *Reden und Aufsatze*, Vol. II, p. 256 (Geissen, 1906).

living tree. And it gets this life from the Catholic doctrine that the absolution imparted in the sacrament of Confession is no mere expression of a hope, but is a consoling
actuality.

But it is not only this realism of the Church's sacramental belief which makes Catholic sacramental practice so
fruitful. The Church plays an equally effective part in the
psychological tact and comprehension with which she conveys the sacraments to her children. She does that partly
by the positive requirement that all who would be accounted
members of her communion shall attend Mass on Sundays
and Holydays and so acquire for themselves the spirit of
love and sacrifice for their daily life, and further by
stipulating that every one who has come to the use of
reason shall renew his moral life at least once a year
by a good confession and at Easter receive the Body of
the Lord. By these positive stipulations she ensures that
all the faithful shall have at least a minimum of a
supernatural moral and religious life. But, still more
effectively than through these positive enactments, the
Church promotes sacramental piety by wisely embedding
the reception of the sacraments in the rhythm of everyday
life, in the course of a man's personal and social life and
its duties. Goethe says (*op. cit.* above) that "in moral and
religious matters—men do not like to do much impromptu."
The Church is aware of that fact and therefore she does
not wait until men come to the supernatural of their own
accord. On the contrary she sets it amid the activities of
human life, so that in and through these activities men
must at the same time perceive and take notice of the
supernatural. That is the meaning of the ecclesiastical
year and its solemnities. The whole history of redemption, beginning in Advent with the hopes of patriarchs and
prophets, and passing through the Crib and the Cross to the
alleluia of Easter and the mighty wind of Pentecost, is
interwoven with the course of the natural year. With the
revolution of the months and weeks and days there is a
change also in the preaching of the Church and in her lit-

urgy. New depths of the divine mystery are continually being disclosed, new visions of the love and grace of Christ. So the Catholic is being constantly summoned out of his everyday life and enriched with constantly new impressions, insights and powers. He is thus able in a living and progressive manner to get into touch with the Church and to maintain a sympathetic contact with her. In particular the Church's feast-days are popular feasts in the noblest sense of the word, a joyful thanksgiving and jubilation before the Most Holy Sacrament. Nor they alone, for every day is made to serve the Church's life and its mysteries—from the morning Angelus to the evening Ave bell. There is no day but bears some saint's name, no week-day that is not consecrated to some special devotion. Thursday is assigned to veneration of the Sacrament of the Altar, Friday to remembrance of the Passion of Christ, Saturday to veneration of the most pure Virgin. And every month too has its special religious character. May is the month of Mary, June the month of the Sacred Heart, July the month of the Precious Blood, October the month of the Rosary, November the month of the Holy Souls. And the personal life too, like the general course of the year, is seized and permeated in its inward rhythm by the mystical power of the sacraments. Every devout Catholic has his own special feast days on which he approaches the table of the Lord. There is no joy and no sorrow that enters his life which does not take him to the altar, from Nuptial Mass to Requiem. For all his personal interest, hopes and anxieties, there are triduums and novenas before the Blessed Sacrament. And in order that the rhythm of social life may be made harmonious by religious and sacramental concords, the Church approves innumerable confraternities and sodalities, confraternity altars and banners and feasts, in which religious effort aims at a specially intimate and lofty community expression. And to that extent it may be rightly said that Catholicism is the "religion of exalted moments." From out of the infinite abundance of its wealth it is constantly, as the hours pass, bringing new gems and new treasures to light, and these give a constantly new stimulus to the faithful and enrich them and do not suffer their interest to flag.   So Niebergall describes the Church as a "mistress of joy to her children."   The life and activity of the Church are irradiated with innocent joy, serene brightness, devout gladness.   The source of all this devout happiness is the Tabernacle, belief in the beneficent presence of the eternal Love.   All ecclesiastical art has originated in this devout gladness.   "Gothic architecture," said the Protestant Dean Lechler, "is at home only where the mass bell rings." And he justly adds: "Without the worship of Catholicism neither Raphael nor Fra Angelico, neither Hubert Van Eyck, nor the younger Holbein, nor yet Lorenzo Ghiberti, Veit Stoss and Peter Vischer, would have produced the marvellous achievements of their art and endowed the churches of God on earth with a wealth of sacred beauty which will remain a treasure for all time." [*]   I am not sure that this intimate connection of Christian art with the Holy Eucharist, of the cathedral with the Tabernacle, is generally recognised. Catholic churches, whether of ancient or modern times, with all their wealth of beauty, are eucharistic creations.   They have sprung from a living faith in the sacramental Presence of our Lord.   And where this faith has departed they lose their deepest meaning and are left without the idea which created and inspired them. They are beautiful but dead bodies without a soul.

Much more might be said to show how the Church, in her sacramental work for souls, embraces also the inanimate creation, consecrating the altar stone, consecrating also the church's bells.   We might speak of her Rogation Days whereon she blesses the produce of the fields, and tell how on Corpus Christ Day she carries the Blessed Sacrament out into the spring-time.   The whole of nature, the flowers of the field, the wax of the bee, the ears of corn, salt and incense, gold, precious stones and simple linen—

[*] K. Lechler, *Die Konfessionen in ihrem Verhaltnis zu Christus*, 1877 p. 161.

there is nothing which she does not bring into the service of the sacred Mystery, and bid them speak of It with their thousand tongues. Under her hands all nature becomes a "Lift up your hearts" (*Sursum corda*) and a "Bless ye the Lord" (*Benedicte Domino*). "Everywhere," says Niebergall, "she makes men see the Holy and she fills the whole environment of her adherents with its charm and radiance." And where the Church herself is not active, there her children are at work. With hands that are rude and humble, but with eyes shining with the light of faith, they erect their sacred images and crucifixes in fields and by mountain paths, and carry the light and consecration of the divine up to the soaring peak and down to the foaming torrent. Amid a Catholic folk and in a Catholic land— there statues of our Lady stand by the roadside, there the Angelus bell is heard, there men still greet one another with the words, "Praised be Jesus Christ."

. . . . . .

We have endeavoured to estimate in a few brief sentences the Church's sacramental and mystical action in the formation of the *homo sanctus,* the saint. We have seen that she is able both comprehensively and profoundly, with realistic force and with psychological insight, to bring the divine down to men, and amid the dust and turmoil of everyday life to make the All Holy visible amidst innumerable candles. Yet that is only one aspect of the Christian work of redemption. In the next chapter it shall be our business to explain how the Church, in accordance with the Catholic conception of justification, achieves the other half of her task. We shall have to show, that is, how the Church not only brings the divine down to men, but also draws man up to the divine.

CHAPTER XII

THE EDUCATIVE ACTION OF THE CHURCH

Sanctify them in truth; thy word is truth (Jn. xvii, 17).

ACCORDING to the Catholic conception of justification the redemptive function of the Church does not consist only in bringing God down to man, but also in raising man to God, i.e., in educating his moral will, by preaching and discipline, for Christ and His grace, and in establishing him ever more and more firmly in this grace. We have to consider, therefore, besides that pastoral activity of the Church which is sacramental and brings grace to men, her educative activity also, that is to say her earnest endeavour that "the tree planted by the running waters shall bring forth its fruit in due season and that its leaf shall not fall off" (Ps. i, 3).

Of primary importance for this educative task is the Church's claim to authority, to the special divine authority which she asserts in her preaching of the word of God. It is true that non-Catholic bodies also preach of Christ and His Kingdom, and we thank God that they do so. But the Catholic Church alone preaches like her divine Master, like one "having power" (Mt. vii, 29). By the unbroken series of her bishops she stands in a real, historical connexion with Christ and His apostles. She alone can truly say, Lo, here is Christ! here are the apostles! And the unimpaired unity of her faith and love guarantees that her objective connexion with Christ is a connexion of the spirit also, inspired by the Spirit of Pentecost. No mere human authority can have intruded itself here where Christ alone preaches. As the one group of our Lord's disciples extended through space and time, the Church and the Church alone can stand before men and claim for her preaching the authority which Jesus gave to His disciples in the words: "He that heareth you, heareth me; and he that despiseth you, despiseth me; and he that despiseth me, despiseth him that sent me" (Lk. x, 16). Therefore the Catholic hearkens to the Church's teaching with unfeigned respect and unlimited confidence. He does not pick and choose, or exercise private judgment, or withhold his assent, or take up an evasive attitude. For him the words Christ and the Church form one phrase and connote a single thing. So that the Church's preaching has an overwhelming power and an absolute validity. It sets a standard, and it is a law. But it is not a law that comes upon the Catholic as something external and alien to himself, to which he submits resignedly as he would to the ukase of an absolute monarch. Catholicism does not recognise any heteronomous morality of that sort, which submits itself to some alien law because and in so far as it is an alien law. The theologians are unanimous in deprecating that spiritual state wherein a man's moral activity is determined only by fear and compulsion. The Catholic recognises in the ordinary and extraordinary teaching of the Church the expression of God's will. He knows that the Church does not make the divine law of faith and morals, but only authoritatively attests it, its contents and its validity. The law is the requirement of God, nor is it as such an arbitrary dictate of the divine will—no important theologian, not even Duns Scotus, has ever understood the divine law in that way—but the revelation of the divine Wisdom, Sanctity and Goodness. Its positive ordinances represent the ideal of humanity as the eternal Wisdom and Love desire it to be realised, and the new man as God's design would have him. Of its essence, therefore, the law of God does not impose a burden on human nature, but is an enriching, fulfilling and perfecting of it. It is a life-giving truth and a life-giving law. And therefore the Catholic affirms it with his whole heart and by a free choice of his will makes it his own, so that it becomes his own law, an act of his moral freedom, a determination of his moral conscience. Thus Catholic morality may be described as neither heteronomous, nor autonomous, but theonomous, inasmuch as the Catholic conscience aligns itself with the objective laws of divine revelation. Yet the Catholic in his moral life has only one subjective law, and that is his conscience. So that if a divine ordinance be not plain and evident to his conscience, or if he be in a state of invincible error, then the Catholic is not bound by the objective law. He is bound by that which presents itself to his conscience as God's will, even though the judgment of his conscience be objectively false. In the last resort the decisive factor in all matters which concern his faith or morals or in any wise determine his religious attitude, is the pre-eminence of conscience. And it is the decisive factor even in the question whether a Catholic may ever be justified in refusing obedience to the Church. Let us treat this last question more fully, for it illustrates in a unique way the decisive importance which the Church assigns to conscience, and the relation of the subjective dictates of conscience to the objective ordinances of law.

Being conscious that she is the infallible teacher of revealed truth and the sole effective institute for salvation, the Church can never admit that Catholics are in the same condition as those who have not yet come to the faith, so that they can have just cause for regarding the faith which they have already received by the authoritative teaching of the Church as doubtful, and for withholding their assent until they have completed a scientific demonstration of the credibility and truth of their faith.[1]

Therefore, according to the Vatican Council, the spiritual relation of the Catholic to the great kingdom of supernatural reality and its problems is profoundly different from that of the non-Catholic. The Council lays it down that the divine evidences, to which the Church and the Church

[1] Vatican Council, Sess. III, cap. 3, canon 6.

only can appeal, are too many (*multa*) and too wonderful (*mira*), for a Catholic's faith to be disturbed by a serious and objective doubt. The Church's claim to the truth is so deeply set in the hard granite of historical facts and of logical consistency, and is so intimately bound up with the ultimate and profoundest requirements of conscience, with its reverence before that which is holy and divine, that it can stand fast and prevail over any possible enquiry, whether past, present or future. Moreover the Catholic cannot become the prey of any merely subjective doubt, resting upon false presuppositions or erroneous deductions, so long as he does not proudly and arrogantly exclude that light of grace which is refused to no man of good will.

This light will always be clear and strong enough to reveal the sources of any misunderstanding and to prevent him sinking into invincible error (*error invincibilis*). The Catholic is therefore generally protected from that radical attitude which deliberately detaches a man inwardly from the professed faith of Catholic Christianity and, revelling in a purely negative criticism, embarks upon research about Christ and the Church as though neither existed. On the other hand the Church does not compel the Catholic to shut his eyes to the religious problems which arise, nor does she even permit him to do so. The Vatican Council condemns blind faith, and stipulates with the apostle (*cf.* Rom. xii, 1) that the obedience of our faith should be in accordance with reason (*obsequium rationi consentaneum*). So that the Catholic is morally bound to give himself such an account of the faith that is in him as is required by his education and by his circumstances. It may happen, in a time harassed as ours is by problems of knowledge and of bibilcal criticism, that his studies will lead him to profound conflict of soul. He must wrestle with God until He bless him, and there is no help for him save in grace alone.

But when a man deliberately excludes the influence of grace and consciously abandons himself to the dangers of self-sufficient and isolated thinking, then he may very well, in pursuing an eccentric subjectivism, lose his clear appreciation of the essential and decisive points in the testimonies which the Church adduces for herself. He may go continually more and more astray with regard to Church authority, and in the end reach a point at which he sees himself compelled· in moral sincerity to leave the Church. But it is especially here, in this extremest conflict between authority and conscience, that we realise again the intense earnestness with which the Church guards the rights of conscience, even of an erroneous conscience. It can scarcely be doubted that in most cases of lapse from the Church, the ultimate causes lie not in the intellectual, but in the ethical sphere. If a man have little respect for authority and considerable self-confidence, he withdraws his work and his research from the influence of the Church's life and from her blessing, in particular from the influence of the grace of faith, and so his tentative doubts and scruples harden into invincible errors. But it is important to note that Catholic theologians teach plainly and unanimously that the sometime Catholic is bound to follow his new attitude of mind, so soon as it has become a genuine and invincible conviction of conscience. Even though the judgment of his conscience be objectively false and even though it be not in its genesis ethically irreproachable, yet he is bound to follow conscience and conscience alone. Moreover, Catholic theologians are coming more and more to the view that it is certainly compatible with the Vatican Council's pronouncement, which has been quoted, to hold that "an apostasy free from moral fault is possible in exceptional cases, as for instance where a man's faith has to meet almost insuperable difficulties on account of a wholly defective religious education, or to encounter influences overpoweringly hostile to it." * In this connection Father

* B. Poschmann, *Grundlagen und Geisteshaltung der katholischen Frommigkeit*, 1925, p. 94. Among the best recent contributions to the solution of this problem is Father Pribilla's exposition of "Catholic Authority and Modern Freedom of Thought" (*Katholisches und modernes Denken*, 1924). Pribilla draws attention (*Stimmen der Zeit*, 1923, p. 265, note 1) to the fact that the distinguished controversialist, Cardinal Bellar-

Pribilla justly quotes the words of St. Paul: "Judge not before the time, until the Lord come" (1 Cor. iv, 5).

In the light of this fact it is an unfair and untenable charge—which does not become more tenable by constant repetition—to say that the Church enslaves conscience by requiring an unqualified obedience in matters of faith and by claiming divine authority. As the authorised preacher of the truth, the Church will never cease to give her authoritative witness to it and to oblige all consciences to accept it. Yet she does not seek to overpower conscience, but to convince it. She seeks internal, not merely external assent. And when a man cannot give this internal assent, she leaves his conscience to the mercy of God and sets him free. That is not fanaticism or severity, but a service to truth and sincerity. For the Church cannot and may not endure that there should be some among her members who are Catholics only in name. She requires that all such men should draw the logical consequence from their new state of conscience and leave the Church. And in this she protects the sincerity of their consciences as much as she guards the sincerity of her own being. The Church does no injury to free-thinking laymen or theologians when she excludes them from communion with her children. On the contrary such people do an injury to the Church if they remain in her communion when they have lost her faith.

In conclusion we say that the Church's careful consideration of the rights of conscience is by no means incompatible with her resolute assertion of her divinely established authority. On the contrary the first is pre-supposed by the second. The law of the Church is intended to operate no other wise than in and through conscience, and from conscience it gets its penetrating force and comprehensive influence. The Church does not supplicate or discuss

mine, solemnly emphasised the believer's moral autonomy. *"Cum dicimus conscientiam esse superiorem omnibus humanis judiciis, nihil aliud dicere volumus, quam eum, qui sibi bene conscius est, non debere metuere, ne a Deo damnetur, etiamsi omnes homines, qui cor non vident, secus forte de ejus rebus gestis judicent"* (De Rom. Pont. IV, 20).

terms with conscience; she makes a direct demand upon it, and requires that it surrender itself to the word of God as proclaimed by her.   Her word is power, and men need this strong word of divine power.   They cannot live long by a purely philosophical morality, which is constructed by themselves' and owes nothing to authority.   Such morality is like "the perfume that remains in an empty bottle." The Church's principle of authority, in its powerful forward sweep, has a stimulating power which arouses conscience and forces it to scale the heights.   When the Church speaks to conscience, there can be no subjectivism or antinomianism, no doubt or scepticism.   Hence the simplicity, solidity, strength and sureness of aim of the Catholic rule of life.   And hence also the comprehensive character of the Church's educative influence.   The radiance of her authoritative teaching penetrates to and illuminates those profound depths to which no ray of purely philosophical knowledge can reach.   By the categorical imperative of her preaching the Church has won infinitely more souls to a better life than all the moralists together, whether of pre-Christian or post-Christian times, who "could not convert so much as the street in which they lived" (Voltaire).

The educative power of the Church lies secondly in the special emphasis laid in her preaching on the other world and on the supernatural, i.e. on the eschatological element. "We have not here a lasting city, but we seek one that is to come" (Hebr. xiii, 14).   No truth of the faith is so deeply impressed upon the Catholic as the declaration at the beginning of the catechism: "God made me to know Him, love Him and serve Him in this world, and to be happy with Him for ever in the next."   That is the Catholic's deepest reality, the reality of the eternal God.   In respect of that reality every other natural or intellectual fact is secondary and subordinate.   Certainly he regards such natural things as real and as valuable, but he does not rest in them as in his last end.   He regards them somewhat as a ship in which he is for the moment travelling, and which he knows that he must presently leave. He acts in the spirit of that saying of our Lord which is inscribed on a gateway in Northern India: "This world is but a bridge; pass over it, build not thy dwelling here." His soul tends continually forwards and upwards. Every day the liturgy of the Mass summons him: *Sursum corda!* And every day he answers: *Habemus ad Diminum.*

Hence the Catholic outlook on life has these two characteristics. In the first place it is easy and light-hearted in its attitude towards the troubles of everyday life, and has a serene detachment. Our Lord's saying concerning the lilies of the field, which labour not neither do they spin, and yet are arrayed in greater beauty than Solomon in all his glory, is deeply imprinted on the Catholic mind. And indeed Catholicism has for that very reason been charged with being culturally retrograde. If it be meant by this that the genuine Catholic does not regard culture as the supreme and ultimate value, or as an end in itself, then the charge is a true one. For the Catholic believes too firmly and really in the heaven of the next world, to be able to believe in a heaven on earth. There have even been Catholics—it is true—and there will always be such, who have lived so completely for the eternal hope, that they have despised and spurned the earthly and natural, and have forgotten the divine injunction to cultivate the earth. That was and is an exaggeration of the Catholic ideal. We have already shown how the Church fought the Gnostic sects of the early centuries and of the Middle Ages, defended natural and bodily values and asserted man's right to the goods and joys of life. The Catholic ideal teaches us not to destroy nature but to transfigure it. It is an ideal which embraces both nature and supernature, both this world and the next, for both nature and supernature belong to the life of the Catholic. If he disowns either of these, he is a heretic; whereas the true Catholic is one who sets them in their right relation to each other. Every natural thing, every natural passion, including the sexual impulse, is a gift of God and therefore good. But it is a

THE EDUCATIVE ACTION OF THE CHURCH 201

transitory good, a good that points beyond itself, a secondary and subordinate good. It does not acquire eternal value until its is affirmed in God. So the true Catholic loves the earthly good, but does not love it like a hungry slave who would eat himself to death on it, but rather like the wandering minstrel from whom the gift elicits a glad song of gratitude to the giver. Wherever Catholicism is a living force, the poisonous plant of materialism cannot grow. Moreover the exclusive service of this world, devotion to work for work's sake, to gain for gain's sake, and all arid utilitarianism are alien to the Catholic spirit. According to Max Weber and Tröltsch the native soil of capitalism is Calvinism, and it was born in Puritan England and Scotland. Every unprejudiced social psychologist who compares the manifestations of the popular soul in Catholic Bavaria or the Catholic Rhineland with those say of Saxony or Thuringia will recognise a characteristic difference in temper and outlook. The life of this world seems to the Catholic too unimportant for him to take it very seriously. He is really serious only in regard to God and His Kingdom. So he has kept a certain serenity, and a certain child-like indifference. And it is mainly from this child-like quality that he gets his feeling for and understanding of serene and unstudied art, and especially popular art. Along with this child-like character he has humility of spirit and is reverent towards holiness and excellence. The Catholic has no sort of passion for autonomy and self-glorification. From this point of view, as well as from others, Kant's "moral autonomy" is a product of Protestantism. And the Catholic has not lost his interest in life or his faculty of admiration, and therefore he is still able to believe and to pray. Joyful trust in God, child-like simplicity, humility: these are the elements of the Catholic character. There is no need to point out how closely this spirit corresponds with the temper which our Lord requires for His Kingdom.

The second characteristic quality of Catholicism, arising out of the Church's proclamation of the next world and forcible emphasis on man's supernatural end, is its ascetical trend. The Catholic attitude towards the supernatural, with its conviction that earthly things have only a limited value, leads to that *"tantum quantum"* principle which has received its exact and classical expression in the Exercises of St. Ignatius Loyola. According to this principle, earthly things are to be used only so far as they are serviceable for the attainment of the supreme and ultimate end; and they are to be renounced in so far as they withdraw one from God and become ends in themselves. When any earthly good threatens to become an end in itself, then our Lord's words hold: "If thy eye scandalize thee, pluck it out!" "He that doth not take up his cross and follow me, is not worthy of me." In this way renunciation and patient endurance become part of the life of the Catholic. Yet they are not to be regarded as other than ministering forces, subservient to the love of God and our neighbour; for love must be our supreme directive force. The new life of Christianity is founded on the precept "Love God with thy whole heart and thy neighbour as thyself." The purpose of renunciation and asceticism—which is the methodical practice of renunciation—is to set the soul free for the exercise of this love. They are not meant to destroy man's sensitive impulses and passions, but to control them, so that they may be directed convergently towards the one great goal, the formation of the new man of a whole-hearted and unselfish love, and may not, like untamed natural forces, break their banks and produce ruin and destruction. The purpose of asceticism is love and love alone. When it is treated as an end in itself, when men renounce for renunciation's sake, when they fast, take the discipline, and practise celibacy for the sake of these things, when the spirit of rivalry and competition enters in, then their asceticism is no longer Catholic, but Gnostic and pagan in character. The practice of asceticism, the deliberate methodical exercise of self-control, makes our souls free and strong, so that, as St. Paul requires of them, they exercise and practise "charity from a pure heart, and a good conscience, and an unfeigned faith" (1 Tim. i, 5). For us men, bound as we are to the body and burdened from our birth with the effects of original sin and of the passions of our ancestors, asceticism is an indispensable necessity, so that we may not only hear the Word of God but do it. It is a fundamental element in our Lord's teaching and must therefore occupy a principle place in the Church's educative effort. All the ordinances of the Church, and in particular the law of fasting, have for their end the training of the faithful in self-control. The Church's priests endeavour systematically in sermons and instructions, but especially in confession, to remove all weeds and evil growths from the souls of her children, so that they may grow more and more like to Christ. And to these normal pastoral methods the Church adds such extraordinary ones as retreats and public missions. Who can estimate the blessings and the beneficial effect of the countless public missions held by Franciscans and Capuchins, Jesuits and Redemptorists, in town and village and for every stratum of society. Such missions are a rich source of well-being, not only for the religious and moral life of our people, but for their national life also. And a retreat, for which a man goes to some retreat-house and there in retirement and under the guidance of an experienced director orders his interior life and makes God supreme in it: such a retreat is a school of the soul. It is a means whereby a man may refresh and recreate his soul, become spiritually sound and strong, and re-discover himself in God. Karl Ludwig Schleich, late Professor of Surgery in Berlin, has some remarkable words about the "Spiritual Exercises" of St. Ignatius of Loyola. "I am profoundly convinced," he writes, "and can therefore say it quite confidently, that with these exercises and these rules in his hand a man might reform all our asylums, and prevent at least two-thirds of their inmates from ever entering them." *

Celibacy and monachism are to be understood in the light of the fundamental purpose of asceticism, namely,

* K. Schleich, *Vom Schaltwerk der Gedanken*, 1917, p. 143 ff.

the methodical training of the will. When a Catholic priest vows perpetual chastity, and when a monk binds himself solemnly to the observance of the "evangelical counsels," i.e. poverty, chastity and obedience, neither in the case of the priest nor of the monk is it a mere matter of voluntary renunciation, as though renunciation of itself had a moral value. They esteem the moral goodness of marriage too frankly and too completely for that. They regard marriage as a great and holy thing, as a sacrament, as being indissoluble and founded upon the faithful love of Jesus for His Church. The Catholic priest should be secure beyond all others from the suspicion of despising marriage, for he confesses and preaches the sacramental dignity of marriage as a tenet of the Church's faith. Why then does he renounce it for himself? And why does the monk go further and renounce gold and riches, and that great good of being his own lord and master? St. Thomas [4] gives us the decisive reason. It is that they may be free for the things of God. And long before St. Thomas, St. Paul had said as much: "He that is without a wife is solicitous for the things that belong to the Lord, how he may please God. But he that is with a wife is solicitous for the things of the world, how he may please his wife" (1 Cor. vii, 32-33). The Catholic priest and the religious are by their vocation devoted to the things of God. It is their business to establish and propagate God's Kingdom, not only in themselves, but also in others, in the world. This task is so sublime, so sacred and delicate, so difficult, responsible and sacrificial, that it demands and engages the best of a man's being and precludes family life. A man cannot be a good apostle and the father of a family at one and the same time. Our Lord Himself was unmarried, and He spoke the noteworthy words about those who have voluntarily become eunuchs. The apostles left everything and followed Jesus. Although they were when called, with the exception of St. John and St. Paul, married men, yet after they had undertaken the apostolate they no longer

[4] *Summa Theol., Secunda Secundae,* Q. CLII, Art. 5.

lived as married men, but as servants of Christ, as men, in St. Paul's words, who "had made themselves free as to all, to become the slaves of all" (1 Cor. ix, 19). Consequently celibacy derives its meaning, its power and its serious purpose from the apostolate, from resolute self-surrender to Christ and His Kingdom. The love and care which a married man gives to the restricted circle of his family, are given by the priest and monk to their Lord and Master, and to the thousands of souls entrusted to them by the Lord, to the sick, to children and to sinners. So the priest's personality becomes richer and deeper, the more he sacrifices himself and gives himself to others. What he loses in spiritual values by his renunciation of family life, he gets back in richer abundance by his life of prayer and by his loving pastoral activity. The Church encompasses the priest's life with many safeguards, and sanctifies it by the obligation of the daily Office and by the frequent celebration of Holy Mass, so that the ideal priest —there must always be occasional hirelings—cannot help but be a pattern to his flock. The Gospel of the Kingdom of God, of the supernatural and other-worldly, of the precious pearl for which one should give up everything, is personified in him, in a form that is manifest and inspiring. The Catholic does not receive from his priest nothing but pious and benevolent words, nor does he love him merely for his noble character. He also expects from and finds in him the uncompromising spirit of the Gospel and a literal belief that the "kingdom of heaven suffereth violence." Hence the reverence which Catholics show towards their priests. F. Nietzsche observes that "Luther allowed priests to marry. But three quarters of the reverence of which mankind . . . is capable, rests upon the belief that a man who is exceptional in this respect will be exceptional in others also." [*] And Schopenhauer goes so far as to say that "Protestantism, by eliminating asceticism and its central belief in the meritoriousness of celibacy, practically rejected the very core of Christianity, and in

[*] *Fräkliche Wissenschaft*, 1887, p. 295.

that respect Protestantism must be regarded as a falling away from Christianity." *

That which holds of the Catholic priesthood in general, holds in a special way of Catholic monachism. It is the literal following of our Lord's teaching concerning the pearl of great price and the treasure hidden in the field, and in particular of His counsel, "If thou wilt be perfect, go sell what thou hast and give to the poor. . . . And come, follow me!" (Mt. xix, 21). Our Lord's gospel in all its spiritual power, stimulating force and immense austerity, is objectivised in the religious life. That life implies no new morality, nor is it regulated by any new ideal of perfection, other than that which is common to all Christians. The religious is not able to do anything higher than imitate in his own life the example of Jesus, than exercise a perfect love of God and of his neighbour. And that ideal is the common ideal of all men. But this single ideal can be striven for in infinitely various ways, according to a man's education and vocation in life, according to his personal gifts and aptitudes, and according to the special opportunities and guidance which come to him. Now of all possible ways of following Jesus, that way is the most magnanimous and courageous, if we regard the matter objectively, which entails a resolute renunciation of all those values and goods which are able to allure man's senses and to hamper his freedom in seeking God. Therefore the religious life is objectively the best way and the surest way to realise the Christian ideal. But in saying this we by no means imply that it is also the best way subjectively, that is to say the best way for all men. For men are too differently made, and external circumstances are too various, to allow of any one way of life being equally good and profitable for all. According to the wise designs of God's Providence the great majority of men are so made that the subjectively best way to perfection for them is to live and work in the world. Yet it remains true that,

* *Die Welt als Wille und Vorstellung*, ed. Grisebach, Vol. II, p. 736. Eng. tr., *The World as Will and Idea* (London, 1883-6), Vol. III, p. 447-8.

regarded in its objective nature and in abstraction from all particular circumstances, the religious life is the strongest and purest expression of the high aspirations which pulsate through the Body of Christ.

It is, however, only a way to perfection, and not perfection itself. The evangelical counsels, as St. Thomas explains, are "certain instruments for the attainment of perfection." [7] They are nothing but specially suitable means for maintaining and deepening that unselfish, holy love, which St. Paul celebrates in his First Epistle to the Corinthians (Chap. xiii), and which constitutes the essence of holiness and of the Christian character. If this love be not present and alive, then the religious life is being violated in its profoundest meaning. St. Paul's words would then apply: "If I should distribute all my goods to feed the poor . . . and have not charity, it profiteth me nothing" (1 Cor. xiii, 3). Monasteries are meant to be homes of love, shrines of the Holy Spirit, schools of the following of Christ. All their asceticism, all their vows and rules, aim only at the one thing necessary and seek to form the man of the new love, the man whose life is wholly love of God and his neighbour.

In saying that, we have described the ideal for which Holy Church works in her educative activity. That ideal is the man of perfect love, the man who has put away from him all self-seeking and who enlarges his little, narrow heart until it becomes a sacred temple of God in which the fire of sacrifice burns, the man who every days fulfils the words of St. Paul: "I most gladly will spend and be spent myself for your souls" (2 Cor. xii, 15). It would be a pleasant task to describe the noble fruit produced by the Church's action in all the saintly figures of her history. How exceedingly various are the ways by which they followed Christ, and how manifold their forms of saintliness! By the side of the saintly hermit and the ascetic of the desert stands the social saint, the saint of the great city and of the industrial classes. By the side of the foreign mis-

[7] Op. cit., Q. CLXXXIV, Art. 3.

sionary stands the saint who gave his life to cripples, or idiots, or to the criminals condemned to the galleys. By the side of the saint who is arrayed in robe of penance and rough girdle, stands the saint of the salon, the refined and saintly man of the world. By the side of the saint of strict enclosure and constant silence stands the joyous friar, who calls the swallow his sister and the moon his brother. By the side of the saint of divine learning stands the saint who despised all knowledge save of Christ. By the side of the contemplative mystic, the world-conquering apostle. By the side of the saint who does penance in filth and rags, and values ignominy beyond all things else, stands the saint robed in imperial purple and crowned with the glory of the tiara. By the side of the saint who fights and is slain for his faith, stands the saint who suffers and dies for it. By the side of the innocent saint stands the penitent. By the side of the saint of child-like meekness, the saint who must wrestle with God until He bless Him.

How infinitely various are all these saintly figures! Each one is marked with the stamp of his own time, some very plainly so. There are many, indeed, with whom we can no longer establish any genuinely sympathetic contact. For there is but One who is ever modern, never out of date, One only who belongs to all time. Yet however much the saints may be marked with the stamp of their time, and however imperfectly they may represent the perfection of Christ, there is but one spirit that animates them all and makes them all dear to us, and it is the spirit of Jesus, the spirit of His great and holy love. Their lives were lived according to the word, "The charity of Christ presseth us."

And around all these outstanding saintly forms, in whom God's power and grace have won their most beautiful triumphs, shine the thousands of lesser lights, the countless little flames that have caught fire at the Heart of Jesus— from the little child that dies in the fatherly arms of God to the old man who has barely escaped the dangers of life and sorrowfully prays, "Lord, be merciful to me a sinner!"

O world! a sea of love and light sweeps round you. O world, so poor and cold! Thou art rich, thou art fair . . . O Holy Church!

CHAPTER XIII

CATHOLICISM IN ITS ACTUALITY

Needs must scandals come (Luke xvii, 1).

IN the previous chapters we have been busy with the question, What is Catholicism? We have described and insisted on the fundamental conception that the Church is the Body of Christ and God's Kingdom on earth, and by means of this fundamental conception we have illustrated her dogma, worship, constitution and community life; we have shown that she is distinctively both popular and universal; we have explained her claim to be the sole source of salvation; and finally we have described the particular means she employs in saving men. We have striven to set forth the essential and permanent, that which lies outside the changes of time, and therefore to discover and expound the idea of Catholicism in the clearest possible way and apart from the conditions of space and time. In this last chapter we shall answer the question, How is this idea realised in actual fact? From ideal Catholicism we pass to actual Catholicism, and we ask how is the one related to the other, and how does actual Catholicism fulfil the divine idea.

That there is no perfect equation between the ideal and the real, that actual Catholicism lags considerably behind its idea, that it has never yet appeared in history as a complete and perfect thing, but always as a thing in process of development and laborious growth: such is the testimony of ecclesiastical and social history, and it is unnecessary to establish these points in detail. The primitive Church was never at any time a Church "without spot or wrinkle" as St. Paul puts it.   One need only read his epistles and the epistles of St. James and St. John, and for a later period to consult Hermas, Irenæus and Tertullian, to find that the early Church for all its brilliant light had grievously dark shadows also.   And the same is true in general of the Church throughout the centuries.   As long as Catholicism lasts, it will feel the need for reform, for a more perfect assimilation of its actuality to the ideal which illumines its path.   Bishop Keppler declared that "the trend to reform is native to the being of the Church.   It is sufficient to recall the magnificent reforming work of her numerous founders of religious orders and of so many popes.   And the same trend to reform is still active." [1] But the existence of such a trend implies a need for reform, and implies the belief that the ideal has not yet achieved realisation.   Consequently there is no need to waste words in showing that ideal Catholicism is not yet realised and has never so far been realised in history.   Our business to-day is rather to explain why it is that the ideal cannot be realised in this world.   We wish in the first place to trace the causes of the great tragedy of this continual conflict between the ideal and the real, and secondly to expound the Catholic solution of these tragic conflicts.

The first and most obvious cause of these conflicts lies in the very nature of revelation as the incarnation of the Absolute.   "And the Word was made Flesh."   In revelation the divine is united to the human, the infinite to the finite, the ineffable and transcendent is clothed in visible forms and signs.   We bear our treasure in fragile vessels (2 Cor. iv, 7).   Two distinct factors here impinge on each other, factors which of their nature cannot be simply assimilated the one to the other, but can only achieve a relation of similarity, a relation of analogy.

Let us go into details.   We can grasp the actuality of

---

[1] *Über Wahre und falsche Reform*, 1903, p. 24.   Paul Wilhelm von Keppler (died, 1926), Bishop of Rottenburg, was a most influential and revered figure in Catholic Germany.   The earlier editions of this book were dedicated to him.

the absolute and infinite and incomprehensible, the essence and existence of God, only by means of conceptions borrowed from the world of our experience. No man has ever seen God. We have no immediate perception of the essence of God. Therefore we can know and describe God only by means of "alien species" (*per species alienas*), that is to say by means of concepts which originally denote created things, and which must first be purified of their creaturely imperfection and in their positive content infinitely intensified, before they can be used by us to represent the divine essence. So that no assertion that we make about God is an adequate or exhaustive assertion, but possesses only an analogous value. We can speak of God only by comparisons (Wisdom xiii, 5). We are therefore aware that all our conceptions of God's being lag infinitely behind the reality. All our names of God are but "shy gestures, which would gladly approach God nearer and yet can only greet him from afar." [1]

But even God's supernatural revelation, even all those truths which go beyond the data of nature and are directly taught us by divine revelation, especially through God's revelation in His Son, do not enter our consciousness in their original nature and in their self-evident force and immediacy, but are mediated through human conceptions and notions. The dogmas, in which these supernatural truths have been authoritatively formulated by the Church, denote the Absolute, but are not themselves the Absolute. The conceptual forms in which they are stated belong to specific periods of time, being borrowed mostly from Greek philosophy, and express the supernatural truths truly and aptly and in a form intelligible in every age, but by no means exhaustively or perfectly. "We see now as in a mirror, in a dark manner." Those words of St. Paul hold true of all supernatural knowledge.

So there lies over the whole of our supernatural knowledge, and over the life which is rooted in this knowledge, an air of insufficiency, of sorrowful resignation, a touch of

[1] P. Lippert, *Credo*, Vol. I, 1916, p. 62.

melancholy, such as Nietzsche discerned in Greek sculpture. We walk not in the sun, but in semi-darkness. It is true that our faith gives us the strongest certainty that the world of the supernatural is no mere dream, but absolutely genuine reality, the reality of God and His eternal life. And therefore our goal is clear, and the way is clear. But we see this sublime reality only through a veil and from afar, like a mountain wrapped in clouds. Of course that fact gives our life of faith its nobility of spirit and its moral character. Were divine truth to come to us unveiled, then faith would not bring any separation of souls and would not discriminate the noble, pure and unselfish man from the calculating, self-seeking egoist. The Kingdom of God would be so obvious that it would be a mere matter for argumentation and cold reasoning, and would not call forth magnanimous souls who show the purity of their love for the ideal and for duty by the very fact that they remain faithful even in the darkness of night and amid the raging tempest. Yet, on the other hand, the semi-darkness and the permanently enigmatical character of the truths of our faith may sometimes lame our glad initiative and entangle us in conflict and trouble, so that our faith is not always a quickening grace and blessed gift of God, but also a hard and difficult task, a wrestling with God that occupies our whole life and calls upon our best powers.

We have seen that the Divine, the Absolute, can in the nature of the case be conveyed to us mortal men only in inadequate human conceptions and notions. And in the second place those instruments, by whom our faith is conveyed to us, are men, that is to say intelligences conditioned by space and time, restricted by the limitations of their age and of their individuality. Above all they are *true now* conditioned by the limitations of their age. Every period of time has its special character, its "spirit," i.e. a characteristic way, conditioned by its special circumstances, of seeing, feeling, judging and acting. The eternal light of revelation is differently reflected in the prism of each age, with different angles of refraction. The supernatural reality is not manifested in naked truth, as it is in itself, but enters into the particular age and therefore in a form determined by that age. In this way it becomes an enkindling and fruitful and present force; but at the same time it loses in the process something of the austerity and majesty of its supernatural being. It suffers a sort of "emptying" (κένωσις), it despoils itself, and takes the form of a slave, as the Divine Word despoiled Himself when He became man. And supernatural truth may sometimes be so far "emptied," and so much modified by time and circumstance, that the eternal is scarcely visible any more through the veils of time and we are puzzled and distressed. The faithful Catholic is distressed by the "servile" forms which the Divine took in certain periods of the Middle Ages. He is distressed, to-day more than ever, by the medieval Inquisition and by the auto-da-fé. However much he knows that these contrivances are explained by the boundless zeal with which the medieval man, in his utterly objective attitude, willed to protect the stern reality and sublime dignity of supernatural truth; and however much he appreciates the intimate inter-connexion of Church and state in the medieval period: yet he cannot but grieve that zeal for objective values in religion and society should have sometimes weakened men's understanding of personal values, especially of the rights and dignity of conscience, albeit erroneous. He cannot but grieve that pure logic restricted the power of psychological sympathy, so that men sometimes were blind to several of the most luminous teachings of the Gospel, as for instance to the teaching that the Kingdom of God is not of this world and is not a kingdom of the sword, that a man should forgive his offending brother seventy times seven times, and that fire should not be invoked from heaven upon unbelieving cities. And the Catholic is grieved also by the witch trials and their numerous victims. However much he may be aware that this delusion must be regarded, not as a Catholic and religious phenomenon, but as one belonging rather to social history, and that many hundreds of witches were persecuted and put to death in Protestant countries also, and that the first enlightened men to have the courage to range themselves with the Calvinist doctor, Johannes Weyer, and to fight in the sixteenth and seventeenth centuries against the general delusion, such men as Loos, Tanner, Laymann and Spee, were Catholics and mostly Jesuits; yet he grieves very deeply for the "Witch Hammer" [3] and for the Bull *Summis desiderantes* (1484) of Pope Innocent VIII, which although it had, as is clear from the context, no *ex cathedra* and official authority, yet "incontestably helped to further the witch delusion." [4] The Catholic is appalled at this abasement of the Divine, and sorrowfully recognises that even the holders of the highest and most exalted office on earth can be children of their age and slaves of its conceptions, and that the Holy Spirit in governing the Church does not guard every act of the pope and every papal pronouncement from error and delusion, but is infallibly operative only when the pope speaks *ex cathedra*, i.e. when basing himself on the sources of the faith and in the fulness of his power as Head of the Church and successor of St. Peter, he pronounces a decision in matters of faith or morals which embraces and binds the whole Church.

Therefore the men through whom God's revelation is mediated on earth are by the law of their being conditioned by the limitations of their age. And they are conditioned also by the limitations of their individuality. Their particular temperament, mentality, and character are bound to colour, and do colour, the manner in which they dispense the truth and grace of Christ. And these influences will operate also in their hearers, that is to say in the "learning Church" as well as in the "teaching

[3] *Malleus Maleficarum*, a book written by two Dominican inquisitors, Henry Kramer and James Sprenger, and published at Cologne in 1489, which became the standard text-book of witchcraft in Germany. An English translation, sumptuously printed, has just been published (London, 1928).

[4] A. Ehrhard, *Der Katholizismus und das 20 Jahrhundert*, 1902, p 168.

Church." So it may happen, and it must happen, that pastor and flock, bishop, priest, and layman are not always worthy vessels of the Divine, and that the infinitely holy is sometimes warped and distorted in passing through them. Wherever you have men, you are bound to have a restricted outlook and narrowness of judgment. For talent is rare, and genius comes only when God calls it. Eminent popes, bishops of great spiritual force, theologians of genius, priests of extraordinary graces and devout layfolk: these must be, not the rule, but the exception. God raises them up only at special times, when He needs them for His Church. We may and should pray for them, but we cannot reckon on their coming. And so as a rule it is the ordinary and average man who bears God's truth and grace through the world. The Church has from God the guarantee that she will not fall into error regarding faith or morals; but she has no guarantee whatever that every act and decision of ecclesiastical authority will be excellent and perfect. Mediocrity and even defects are possible. "The weak and the little hath God chosen that He may confound the strong." It is true that the power of God is manifested all the more gloriously because of this weakness. But reflective Catholics must feel and be pained by the conflict which arises out of the contrast between the sublimity, depth and power of divine revelation and the weakness of the human, too-human factor. The same phenomenon is repeated in the history of the Church throughout the centuries which so tragically moulded the relation of our Lord to His disciples. They were unable in their small mirrors to receive all the rays of light which went forth from His divine Person and to transmute them without loss into living forces.

Still more palpable and painful does the conflict between the divine and human elements become when the instreaming life of grace and truth is checked by human passions, by sin and vice, when Christ as He is realised in human history is dragged through the dust of the street, through the commonplace and the trivial, and over masses of rubbish. That is the deepest tragedy, the very tragedy of the Divine, when It is dispensed by unworthy hands and received by unworthy lips. An immoral laity, bad priests, bishops and popes—these are open, festering, never-healing wounds of the Body of the mystical Christ. This is what saddens the earnest Catholic and inspires his sorrowful lamentation, when he sees these wounds and is unable to help. "The Church," says Cardinal Newman, "is ever ailing, and lingers on in weakness, 'always bearing about in the body the dying of the Lord Jesus, that the life also of Jesus might be made manifest in her body.'" [5] It is an essential property of the Church to be so, because of her vocation to save men. Nowhere else does evil become so visible, because nowhere else is it so keenly fought. "She can never work out of the sphere of evil." [6] As her Master came not for the whole, but for the sick, so the Church in this world will always have her sick, will always have sores in her members, great and small.

To sum up: the first series of tragic conflicts arises out of the nature of Christianity as a supernatural and revealed religion. When the Absolute expresses itself in time, when the Divine takes human form, it cannot but be that human imperfection should come into inward conflict with divine perfection. In this respect Schopenhauer, and before him Hegel, and later Hartmann have judged correctly. The entrance of the Divine into time necessarily implies its abasement, its "self-emptying." Those philosophers erred only in this that they attributed God's entrance into time, not to a free and loving act of the personal God, but to a necessity of God's being. And so they went on to conclude that creation was the Fall of God.

The second source of these conflicts lies, not in the nature of supernatural revelation in general, but in the nature of Catholicism in particular, in that which constitutes the special character of Catholicism.

a. In the first place there is that conflict between authority

[5] *Via Media,* 1877, Vol. I, Lect. XIV, §19, pp. 354, 355.
[6] Möhler, *Symbolism,* London, 1843, Vol. II, p. 29.

and human liberty which necessarily results from the Catholic doctrine of authority.   This conflict may be seen whenever the human ego runs up against alien, rigid and inexorable facts, against laws and ordinances which seem to crib and confine the free movement of the mind.   This is especially the case, therefore, in the region of theology, in the science of our faith.   Supernatural revelation is not human wisdom, but the Word of God.   Its new truth does not originate in humanity as its primal source, not even in the depths of human sub-consciousness, but is essentially given from above.   Therefore it can be communicated to men only by the way of authority, by that living series of bishops who are descended from the apostles and conjoined to them in a spiritual unity through the sacrament of the imposition of hands, and especially by the successor of St. Peter.   Church authority is a necessary correlative of supernatural revelation.   So that Church authority is the one pole of the Catholic life of faith.   The Catholic does not get his final decision regarding the truths of revelation from philologists and historians, but from the primary witnesses and depositaries of this truth, from the messianic authority of the Word, Christ, perpetuated through the centuries in pope and bishops.   Consequently the Catholic is in his faith inwardly bound to obey the authoritative teaching of his Church, which is the echo of the preaching of Jesus.   On the other hand the Church prohibits all blind faith and merely external conformity. The affirmation accorded to the Church's teaching must be a convinced and inward affirmation, and so an affirmation of the free moral personality, and an affirmation which rests, in proportion to a man's degree of education, upon personal insight into the grounds of faith and into its historical and philosophical presuppositions. And since this personal insight cannot be attained by a scholar without severely scientific method, therefore the Church cannot possibly be an enemy to sober criticism, least of all to the so-called "historico-critical" method. Even the much-attacked anti-modernist encyclical of Pope

Pius X (*Pascendi*) and the anti-modernist oath, do not forbid this method, but rather presuppose it. What they forbid is simply this, that men should make the affirmation of supernatural faith dependent exclusively on the results of this method, thereby subjecting it wholly to philologers and historians, and to profane science. Our faith does not rest upon dead documents, but upon the living witness of that stream of tradition which has brought its doctrines down from Christ through the apostles and the apostolical succession of bishops to the present day. Christianity is not a religion of dead documents and fragmentary records, but a life in the Holy Spirit preserved from generation to generation by the apostolical succession of commissioned preachers. The historico-critical method, if it would not lose itself in extravagant and unlimited criticism, must adjust itself to this life which pulsates through the heritage of revealed truth. That was what the papal encyclical meant when it declared—in words that have been so much misunderstood—that holy Scripture and the Fathers are not to be interpreted "merely by the principles of science" (*non solis scientiae principiis*). The surging life of the Christian present flows over the dead records of primitive documents, or rather, these documents are themselves nothing but that life grown stiff and numb, nothing but a deposit of that holy and supernatural life which still enfolds us in the present. Therefore those documents can be fully deciphered and yield their true revealed sense only in the light of this life. So the Church does not quarrel with the historico-critical method, or dispute the right and duty of scientific research. What she does is to guard against the abuse of these things, to prevent the neglect of that living element in Christianity wherein these methods should find their final norm and standard. By means of this life of hers, by means of the clear daylight of her revealed knowledge, she is ever throwing new light upon the problems of the lower and higher criticism, upon the problems of scriptural and patristic theology. And when she believes that central thoughts

of the Christian revelation are menaced, then by means
of her Congregations—not in the name of science, but in
the name of her faith—she utters her prohibition against
such teaching.

And here is the point where Church authority and the
individual's right to give himself an account of the faith
that is in him, may come into conflict. It is possible that
the teaching authority of the Church, as in the case of
Galileo, may in the name of the faith forbid a scientific
opinion which is only in apparent contradiction with fixed
dogmatic truth, and which becomes later on an irrefutable
certainty. Of course the Catholic knows that the decisions
of these Congregations, even though confirmed by the pope
himself in the ordinary form (*in forma communi*), may be
and have been erroneous. And he knows that the true
inward assent which they require can therefore not be an
unqualified assent, but only a qualified one. For such
decisions, although they claim an eminent degree of consideration as emanating from the pope's teaching power, yet
appertain for all that to an earthly and fallible authority.
For the same reason the faithful Catholic knows that he is
by no means forbidden to reckon with the possibility of
error in such decisions, and that he is permitted to prepare
the way by more thorough study for a final solution of
the question. He knows also that the Church, when such
a decisive solution has been reached, has withdrawn her
veto, so that that veto did not tend to the suppression of
truth, but rather to its thorough demonstration, and in
any case safeguarded her theology from hasty and insuffi-
ciently-supported hypotheses. Theology is the science of
life, and its propositions influence life directly. The teaching authority of the Church, as being appointed by God
to guard the supernatural life of the faithful, cannot and
may not stand quietly by and let the congregation of the
faithful be disturbed by revolutionary assertions which are
devoid of a sound scientific basis, and which for the most
part bear within them the seeds of decay before they have
rightly got into the world. All this the Catholic knows.

In theory therefore there is a balance established between the official teaching authority and theological freedom of movement. But in the practical activity of research, where the questions dealt with are not such that an exact solution, an unobjectionable, exhaustive proof can be submitted to the Church's teaching authority, but rather problems which of their nature do not lend themselves to solution by a severely exact method, but ultimately only by intuition and by a comprehensive grasp of all the data, then conflicts are possible. In such a case the scholar suffers from the conflict of his ideals, when the service of truth seems to be at variance with his loyalty to the Church. It is a sacred suffering, yet a very real one. He is nailed to the "cross of his ideals," and no man can take him down from this cross.

Furthermore the special character of Catholicism gives rise to a conflict between the claims of personality and those of the community. The Church is primarily a community, it is that unity of redemption-needing mankind which is established in the person of the Incarnate God. But she is at the very same time a community of persons. The Church shows herself to be the living Body of Christ only in so far as she realises herself in living persons. Both these things, therefore, both community and personality, are of the substance of the Church, and neither can subsist without the other. From out of the community of faith and of love the personality draws its new life. And the new-born personality in its turn gives the community the best that it has, the awakening and enkindling power of its faith and of its love, and thereby gives the community fruitfulness and growth. But a community implies a common life, and therefore there must be a definite norm for the community, a creed and a law. And the individual must willingly accept this norm, in dogma, morals, law and worship. Here is the point where conflict is possible. Individualities are too rich and too variously made— being each a unique historical creation, each the result of a separate and special word of God—to be able to adapt

themselves always and everywhere, full and without friction, to the organism of the community. There are bound
to be interior difficulties and obstacles, and the process calls
for self-sacrifice and devoted self-denying love. And the
richer a personality is, the more does it suffer from the
community, especially from that average level of life and
its requirements which go necessarily with a common
organisation. It is true that the community richly repays
whatever the personality sacrifices to it. The community
exercises an educative force, for it compels the individual
to love and sacrifice, to humility and simplicity. The community deepens our personalities, for it enlarges them by
all that goodness which we show to our brethren. And
—its highest excellence—the community is the Body of
Christ, the fundamental source of all the truth and grace
of Jesus. But however precious the community is, there
remain sacrifice, and self-denial, and self-subordination and
—suffering with the members of Christ. For "if any
member suffer, all the members suffer with it."

Connected with this, is that third and last series of conflicts which arises from the nature of Catholicism. We
shall refer to it only briefly. It is the conflict between
living piety and Church authority, between the enthusiasm of Pentecost and the rigidity of Church law. This
conflict is vividly represented in the life of St. Francis of
Assisi. Both these factors are necessary for the life of the
Church. The Spirit of Pentecost must always and will
always awaken new life. Ever and anon it will touch the
depths of the Church's soul and set free mighty impulses
and stirring movements. But so that these movements
may not come to nothing, but may be permanently fruitful, they must be guided by Church authority by means
of rules and laws, fixed ordinances and regulations. So
personal piety requires that the Church regulate it, and
define it and give it strict form, if it is not to ebb uselessly
away. But on the other hand the form needs the flow of
life and experience if it is not little by little to become
rigid and crusted over. It needs it the more, the older and

more venerable it is. In the right co-ordination of these two factors lies the secret of the Church's vigorous life. When this co-operation is not maintained, or not sufficiently maintained, then "the Spirit groaneth." And there is no pain that a Catholic may endure so profound and penetrating, yet so sacred and pure, as this is. The letters of St. Catharine of Siena illustrate it, as does also the life of St. Clement Maria Hofbauer. Well may the Catholic soul exclaim with Peter Lippert: "O Catholic Church, thou angel of the Lord, thou Raphael sent to guide us in our pilgrimage, mayest thou ever find the strength to walk with such mighty strides that thou thyself mayest be able to shatter the forms that have grown stiff and antiquated. Catholic Church, angel of the Lord, mayest thou ever find strength so to stir thy wings as to raise a mighty wind and blow away the dust of centuries." [1]

We have spoken of the conflicts which arise from the nature of revelation and from the nature of Catholicism. What solution do Catholics find for these conflicts?

They solve them in the light of eschatology, in the light of the fact, that according to our Lord's promises, the perfection of the Church is yet to be, that the Church of glory will not appear until the end of time, and that therefore it is according to the economy of salvation that the Church of the present should remain unfinished, incomplete and imperfect until the Coming of the Son of Man. This incompleteness is therefore not something forced upon us for the first time by the cold logic of facts. On the contrary our Lord Himself from the beginning left us in no doubt about it. From the beginning He described the Kingdom of Heaven as a net that contains bad fish as well as good, as a field that contains cockle as well as wheat. When He warned His disciples against coveting the "first places" in His Kingdom He indicated the possibility of jealousy and strife among the leaders of the Church (Newman). When He delineates the steward who began to "strike the men-servants and maid-servants, and to eat

[1] *Das Wesen des katholischen Menschen*, 1923, p. 54.

and to drink and be drunk," we think involuntarily of
those stewards of the Kingdom of God, to whom as successors of St. Peter were committed the Keys of the Kingdom, and who so grievously abused their sacred office.
As Cardinal Newman says, our Lord expressly warns us
not to expect the Church of this world to be without spot
or wrinkle. And His disciples give us that same warning.
In particular it is a favourite thought of St. Paul's that the
Church of the present, albeit pervaded by Christ, bears
the marks not of His glory but of His suffering, manifests
his "dying" (νέκρωσις, 2 Cor. iv, 10) and His wounds
(Gal. vi, 17); that the sufferings of Christ "abound" in
His members (2 Cor. i, 5), so that one must speak of a
"fellowship of His sufferings" (Phil. iii, 10). Therefore
suffering in all its forms is an essential trait of the Church
of this world. As St. Augustine says of the present state
of the Church: "It is still night" (adhuc nox est). And
again: "The Church stands in darkness, in this time of her
pilgrimage, and must lament under many miseries." [8]

But on the other hand—and this is the second principle
whereby the conflict is solved—if Christ plainly prophesies
sin and distress, weakness and imperfection for the earthly
Church, He promises quite as definitely that the gates of
hell will not prevail against her and that His spirit will
abide with us unto the end of the world. The Church is a
leaven which works slowly, and yet will in uninterrupted
process leaven the whole resisting mass of humanity. So
the Catholic cannot fear, even when the Church at times
seems to sink into a state of torpor, or even of lingering
death. History has shown over and over again that bad
periods are followed by happy recoveries, recoveries so
glorious that the time of stagnation seems to be a sort of
transitional stage, preparatory to the wondrous thing that
is to be, a kind of winter sleep wherein the powers are
collected, before the awakening of spring.

That which is true of the life of the Church in general,

[8] *Obscura videtur ecclesia in tempore peregrinationis suae, inter multas
iniquitates gemens*, Ep. LV, 6, 10.

is true in particular of her preaching of the truth. The Spirit of Truth, the Comforter, abides with the Church for ever, and He will constantly bring truth to light and truth in its complete fulness, in all its heights and depths. Though many of the depths of truth and many of its heights may have been obscured for centuries, yet a day comes when the beam of the Holy Spirit pierces the darkness and discloses the truth to the faithful. The history of the fortunes of Aristotelianism in the Church is an instructive illustration of this fact. Catholic theologians are using in our own day, for the philosophical statement of Catholic doctrine, essentially that same Aristotelian philosophy which eminent Fathers of the Church called the "source of all heresies," in particular of Nestorianism and Monophysit-ism, and which, when it found its way into scholastic circles in the thirteenth century, was several times forbidden by ecclesiastical authority to be used in the public lectures of the University of Paris, chiefly on account of its misinterpretation in Latin Averroism. Thoughts are like living organisms. They need not only their special soil, but also their due time, so that they may strike root and develop. And the Church has abundance of times. She does not reckon in decades, but in centuries and millennia. So she can wait until thoughts have in the light of her teaching become perfectly clear and pure, until what is genuine, true and permanent in them is recognised and disengaged from what is spurious, false and transitory. The Church believes in the development of the supernatural knowledge of the truth. She teaches a progress of faith, and that not merely in a subjective, but also in an objective sense. The Vatican Council expressly defined the dogma that not only the individual believer, but also the Church herself can and should penetrate ever more perfectly and more profoundly into the depths of revealed truth.[*] And so the Catholic scholar has the glad assurance that no seed of truth is vainly sown in the field of the Church. The spirit of truth will bring every seed to maturity, when its

[*] Sess. III, cap. 4.

time is come. And therefore the faithful Catholic scholar
can never lose faith in his Church, since his confidence in
the complete triumph of truth in the Church is unlimited
and unshakable. Though he be not understood by his
own age, yet he is never solitary. His thought, provided
it be based on truth, will be taken into the life-stream of
the Church and clarified in those pure waters, so that it
may in some future time, in this stream and through it,
become the fertilising water of life for many souls.

If we ask in conclusion for the ultimate and deepest
reason why the "Church below" (*ecclesia deorsum*) as St.
Augustine calls it [10] shall never in this world attain the
spotlessness and beauty of the "Church above" (*ecclesia
sursum*), and why we may never do more than look forward hopefully to the Church of glory, we are seeking to
know the mind of God Himself, and to search into the
depths of His counsel. "Who hath known the mind of the
Lord? Or who hath been His counsellor?" (Rom. xi, 34).
We are face to face with a mystery which we shall never
completely comprehend. We may only suppose this much
about it, that the fundamental forces of God's revealed
action, His Holiness, Justice and Goodness, will prevail
in this mystery also.

Wherever we encounter the God of revelation, we do
not find Him to be the characterless God of some feeble
pastoral play, but a God of holiness and justice, a God
who requires vigorous action and moral decision, the ath-
lete's struggle for the crown and perseverance in the race
until the prize be won. The new order of grace does not
displace the old order of moral responsibility before God.
And that is true not only of the members of the Church,
but also of the Church as such. The Church too is subject to the great law that the Kingdom of Heaven suffereth
violence. It is true that as the supra-personal unity of
redeemed mankind, a unity based upon the God-man, the
Church has her own essential nature, her own law and
her own life. And the Holy Spirit will abide always with

[10] *Enarr.* in *Ps.* CXXXVII, 4.

her, so that she may remain true to her God-given nature. But on the other hand it is equally true that the nature of the Church must be expressed through the faithful, and not without them. The Body of Christ must maintain and perfect itself in its members and through them. Therefore the Church is not only a gift to the faithful, but also a task for them. They have to prepare and foster that good earthly kingdom in which the seed of the Kingdom of Heaven may take root and flourish. In other words, the life of the Church, the development of her faith and her love, the progress of doctrine, morals, worship and law, stand in an immediate relation to the faithful and loving personal life of the members of the Body of Christ. God rewards the merit or punishes the demerit of the faithful by the rise and fall of the earthly Church. We may therefore truly say with St. Paul (Eph. ii, 21, 22) that the Church founded by Christ is at the same time co-built by the faithful. St. Augustine says profoundly: "The temple of God is still a-building" and "The house (i.e. the Church) is now being constructed." [11] God willed a Church which in her ripening and perfecting should be the fruit of the true grace-inspired life of the faithful, of their prayer and love, of their fidelity, penitence and devotion, and therefore He did not found her from the beginning as a thing complete and perfect, but as an imperfect thing, which leaves room for and calls for a continual activity of construction, and in whose inward history His Holiness and Justice continually triumph.

And God permits so much weakness and wretchedness in the earthly Church just because He is good. One may even venture the paradox that the mystical Christ has taken so much weakness upon Himself for our sakes and for our welfare. For how might we, who are "prone to evil from our youth," who are constantly stumbling, constantly struggling, and never spotless, not even in our fairest virtue—how might we love and trust a Church, which

[11] *Adhuc aedificatur templum Dei* (Sermo CLXIII, 3). *Modo enim fabricatur domus (Enarr,* in *Ps.* XXIX, 2, 6).

displayed holiness not as a chaste hope, but as a radiant achievement? Her very beauty would be a stumbling block to us. Her glory would not allure and gladden us, but accuse and condemn us. How could she, the rich and glorious, be our mother, the mother of poor and wretched mortals? No, we need a redemptress mother, one who, however celestial she be in the deepest recesses of her being, never turns coldly away from her children, when their soiled fingers touch her, and when folly and wickedness rend her marriage robe. We need a poor mother, for we ourselves are poor.

And we need this same mother that we may be rich, rich in humility, love and devotion. How could we endure it, if the earthly Church were without spot or wrinkle, if all members of the Body of Christ could regard themselves as without error and without fault? God would no longer inspire us with awe as the Only Holy. All humility and inwardness, all poverty of spirit, all love and delicate feeling would be destroyed, and their place taken by a loathsome Puritanism and a loveless fanaticism. Such was ever the fate of those sectaries who have regarded themselves as already pure and holy, here and now, in the full sense of those words, from the ancient Montanists and Donatists to the Cathari of the Middle Ages and to heretics of our own day. And, even if we did not fall into this spiritual pride, we should perhaps incur the danger of deifying the Church itself, of worshipping the merely human, a Peter, or a Paul, or an Apollo. So God's Goodness and Mercy are manifested even in the imperfections of our Church. Through her weakness "we are healed."

Therefore we love our Church in spite of, nay just because of, her poor outward appearance. The Catholic affirms the Church just as it is. For in its actual form the Church is to him the revelation of the divine Holiness, Justice and Goodness. The Catholic does not desire some ideal Church, a Church of the philosopher or the poet. Though his mother be travel-stained with long journeying, though her steps be sometimes halting and weary, and though her countenance to be furrowed with care and trouble—yet, she is his mother. In her heart burns the ancient love. Out of her eyes shines the ancient faith. From her hands flow ever the ancient blessings. What would heaven be without God? What would the earth be without this Church? I believe in One Holy Catholic and Apostolic Church.

INDEX

THE Index is mainly a subject index, but includes references to authors cited in the text or notes. Scriptural quota-
tions are not indexed. The index numbers cover the entire
page, notes as well as text.

modern man, his intellectual and moral needs, 7 ff.

modernism, 24, 136-137, 156-157, 218-220

Moehler, J. A., 15, 40, 49, 217

monachism, 203-207

morality of the Church, Christocentric, 17 ff.; its ideals and methods, 193 ff.

Mystical Body of Christ, St. Paul's description of the Church, 14-15; implies a mystical oneness of Christ and the Church celebrated especially by St. Augustine, 15; a relation which is expressed in her every activity, 16-24, and especially in her sacraments, 24-28; essentially an organism and a community, 31 ff.; born with the Incarnation, 35-36; the true organ of the redemption, 36; its differentiation of functions, 36-38; its constitution, 38-41; its spirit the spirit of love and brotherly equality, 41-45; its structural organs and its members, 97-98; the activity of its members in the Communion of Saints, 98 ff.; the relations of its earthly members to the saints, showing closest solidarity in mutual sympathy and aid, 114 ff.; relations of earthly members with one another, 124 ff.; its prayer a prayer of all for all, 128-129; a fellowship in the faith, 129-138, and in love, which is its lifeblood, 138-139; dislocated by heresy, but not seriously nor permanently, 150-151; necessarily unique and exclusive, 159 ff.; the visible body and the invisible soul, 170-175; ailments and wounds of, 139, 213 ff.; must perfect itself in its members, 227. See also Church, Kingdom of God.

Newman, Card., 150, 151, 158, 217, 223, 224

Niebergall, 186, 191

Nietzsche, 205, 213

Orders, Sacrament of Holy, 18, 126 ff., 185

Origen, 15, 24

Original sin, 33, 34, 153

Orthodox Church, attached to passive tradition and in danger of petrifaction, 151; has maintained apostolic succession and valid orders, 165, 167; sanctity of some of its members, 167

Other-worldliness, a mark of Catholicism, 78-80, 199-201, 223 ff.

papacy, Macaulay's testimony to, 6-7; see Pope

Pascal, 4

Pastor Angelicus, 95

Paul, St., his conception of the Church, 14-15; his testimony to the pre-eminence of St. Peter, 83-84, 86-92; his universalism, 145; teaches that the purpose of the Church is the sanctification of men, 176; his attitude towards celibacy, 204-205; the Church of the present manifests the suffering, and not the glory of Christ, 224; and cited *passim*

Penance, sacrament of, 18, 185, 188-189

Pentecost, the experience of and its effect on the apostles, 51 ff.; see also Holy Spirit

per Christum Dominum nostrum, 17; see also Mystical Body of Christ

personality, its relation to the community, 221-222; see also Authority, Conscience, Piety

Peter, St., his confession of faith, 49, 51, 56, 86 ff.; his pre-eminence among the apostles, 82-85; unsatisfactory explanations of this pre-eminence, 85-86; true explanation to be found in the positive act of our Lord, 86-92; his Catholicism, 145; see also Pope

piety, Catholic piety completely Christo-centric, especially in its sacramentalism, 17-20, 24-28, 184-189; expressed in a community worship, 128, 129, yet individual and infinitely various, 145-150, 207-209; embraces whole life of the Catholic, 153-156, 189-192; causes a specifically Catholic temper, 200-201; resists formalism and is a source of rejuvenation for the Church, 132-133, 222-224; non-Catholic piety, 166-170

Printed in the United States
139090LV00005B/140/A